WILDERNESS
JOURNALS
OF
EVERETT
RUESS

MW00617282

WILDERNESS JOURNALS OF EVERETT RUESS

Edited and with an introduction by
W. L. Rusho

GIBBS·SMITH
PUBLISHER

SALT LAKE CITY

First Edition
02 01 00 99 98   5 4 3 2 1

Copyright © 1998 by Gibbs Smith, Publisher
All rights reserved. No part of this book may be
reproduced by any means whatsoever, either
mechanical or electronic or digital, without written
permission from the publisher.

Published by
Gibbs Smith, Publisher
P.O. Box 667
Layton, Utah 84041
Visit our Web site: www.gibbs-smith.com

Design and production by J. Scott Knudsen,
Park City, Utah

Printed and bound in the U.S.A.

Library of Congress Cataloging-in-Publication Data
Ruess, Everett, b. 1914.
The wilderness journals of Everett Ruess / edited and
with an introduction by W.L. Rusho.
p. cm.
ISBN 0-87905-863-3
1. Ruess, Everett, b. 1914—Diaries. 2. Poets,
American—20th century—Diaries. 3. Explorers—
Southwest, New—Diaries. 4. Wilderness areas—
California. 5. Wilderness areas—Arizona.
I. Rusho, W. L., 1928– . II. Title.
PS3535.U26Z474 1998
818'.5203
[B]—dc21   98-17502
                                    CIP

Contents

BLOCK PRINT MADE BY EVERETT FROM VIEW IN
THE SIERRAS, 1933.

FOREWORD

In 1980 I learned of Everett Ruess in a conversation with Edward Abbey in Moab, Utah. I had read the line or two that Ed wrote about Ruess in *Desert Solitaire,* and I visited with Ed about Everett. He viewed Everett as a kindred spirit and urged me to try to find more about him. After some detective work, I located Everett's brother, who entrusted me with Everett's letters, other writings, and artwork. We both hoped that a new book would be the result. This was now 1982. I worked with the material for two years in my spare time, then asked my good friend W. L. "Bud" Rusho to help organize a book. Bud and I worked together, and the book *Everett Ruess: A Vagabond for Beauty,* published in 1983, was the result. The book has seen several printings and has had a great effect in expanding awareness of Everett's writings, artwork, and his story to thousands of people around the world.

Over the years we have received letters from scores of people expressing their admiration for Everett and what he stood for. I've lived with Everett now for eighteen years, and I love the same country he loved, both in California and Utah. I often think of him when I see the Escalante Canyon country or the Navajo Reservation, and when I'm in San Francisco, on the Monterey coast, or in the Sierras. Sometimes I imagine him visiting with Edward Weston, Maynard Dixon, Navajo traders, and the people of southern Utah in the 1930s. I've reflected about why his story grows in popularity with each passing year.

Everett Ruess was truly a remarkable person. He was naive, brave, idealistic, adventurous, talented, and ambitious. He was gone before he reached his mid-twenties. The mystery of his disappearance adds a

7

poignant element to his story. But the overriding importance of Everett that will keep his reputation growing, in my opinion, is that in his writings is the first expression of what I see as a modern point of view regarding the red-rock-canyon desert of southern Utah and northern Arizona. He articulated first and best that this land's importance is its spiritual and aesthetic richness. He also saw the Monterey coast and the Sierras the same way; he probably knew that others such as Muir and Weston had already charted this vision of these lands. But in the red-rock desert Everett was the pioneer. Although he disappeared at a very young age, Everett's writings have made his place in history.

GIBBS M. SMITH
PUBLISHER

INTRODUCTION

In late 1934, when Everett Ruess was but twenty years old, the young artist, quixotic visionary, and budding writer mysteriously disappeared in the red-rock-canyon labyrinth south of Escalante, Utah. Since then, who he was, what he had done to merit so much attention, why he was bent on plunging into the remote and isolated region, and particularly, his ultimate fate, have puzzled a number of researchers, authors, and outdoors people.

In their Los Angeles home, Everett's parents, Christopher and Stella Ruess, were the first to inquire into their son's disappearance. After finding no conclusive evidence, they sought to present their collection of Everett's letters, poems, essays, and journals to the world. A man named Hugh Lacy, perhaps a family friend, was either employed or persuaded to act as editor for this collection, which was entitled "Youth Is For Adventure." Although never published, it formed the basis for the 1939 publication, in *Desert Magazine,* of a number of Everett's letters, and for the subsequent 1940 book *On Desert Trails with Everett Ruess.*

What these publications did reveal was an Everett Ruess slowly growing in maturity, but quickly perfecting his ability to articulate his own subjective reactions to the natural world. The writings also revealed a soul in torment, a young man driven to the margins of society, yet almost pathetically desirous of human companionship. To say that he was unusual would be an understatement; so different was he that he has been analyzed and reanalyzed, through his letters, by many different writers. In his book *Mormon Country,* Wallace Stegner gave these thoughts about Everett:

What Everett Ruess was after was beauty, and he conceived beauty in pretty romantic terms. We might be inclined to laugh at the extravagance of his beauty-worship if there were not something almost magnificent in his single-minded dedication to it. Esthetics as a parlor affectation is ludicrous and sometimes a little obscene; as a way of life it sometimes attains dignity. If we laugh at Everett Ruess we shall have to laugh at John Muir, because there was little difference between them except age.[1]

Yet the question naturally arises, what kind of a person leaves his family and friends to wander alone, save for burros or pack horses, into the high mountain regions of California, or into the scenic deserts of the Four Corners region? To answer this question, we must first examine Everett's background.

Stella and Christopher Ruess were compassionate, intelligent, and well educated. Yet they had fundamentally different interests. Christopher, employed as a probation officer, was essentially businesslike, concerned with material well-being but also with philosophical questions of morality. Stella, on the other hand, was a trained artist, who taught drawing, produced block prints, composed poetry, and was active in art and writing clubs.

Everett, born 28 March 1914 in Los Angeles, was the younger of two boys and probably received the bulk of his mother's attention. Stella directed Everett into the world of art, emphasizing her own areas of proficiency—lyric prose, poetry, block printing, and sketching. Although older brother Waldo was the more practical, he shared the mentorship of young Everett with their parents.

During Everett's childhood years, the family lived in Brookline, Massachusetts, then in Valpariso, Indiana, finally returning to Los Angeles, where Everett attended Hollywood High School. From the time he was twelve, Everett kept an occasional journal, recording his experiences, writing essays and poems. While he took enough art classes to learn fundamentals, he never became an accomplished artist. What he did excel in was subjective nature writing, that is, describing in detail his own reactions to the phenomena of nature.

The Ruess family considered itself to be a cohesive unit that gave each of its members individual strength. On one occasion, under

---

1. Wallace Stegner, *Mormon Country*, reprint, (New York: Bonanza Books, 1942), 321.

Stella's leadership, they published a collection of poems, essays, and block prints under the heading *Ruess Quartette,* with a family seal featuring a sundial with the words "Glorify the Hour." Their unity provided a shield for each to craft his or her own individuality, regardless of worldly persuasions to conformity. With his family's moral and financial support, Everett could venture forth into the unforgiving wilderness, trusting to adventure and using his family for his basic—and always approving—audience for his letter-essays and artwork. Of course, he also wrote to friends but was often disappointed in their seemingly fickle loyalty to him.

Everett's letters have been collected in the book *Everett Ruess: A Vagabond For Beauty,* which I edited in 1983. In these letters, Everett amply displays his gift for nature-writing, but one should not conclude that they clearly display his personality or his deepest thoughts. No young man wants to confide everything to his parents, or even to his friends.

A comparison of the journals to his letters reveals that Everett carefully crafted his letters as lyrical essays, whereas his journals took the place of companions, a place where he could enter his joys, complaints and details of day-to-day events, and especially his observations of nature. Quite probably, Everett composed his letters slowly, perhaps even preparing a first draft before the final version. He even sketched or painted individual letterheads, as if he wanted the recipients to save them as works of art—which many of them did.

Many young men and women dream of casting off their family anchor ropes and venturing forth into some adventure of their choosing, yet few accomplish it for any length of time. Even fewer perform such adventures alone, without companionship to share the hardships as well as the joys. Yet Everett, only sixteen years old, did just that. During the summer of 1930, with the blessing of his family, he set out, hitchhiking, for Carmel, where he camped out by the Pacific Ocean. After only two days, he boldly ventured to the door of famous photographer Edward Weston and made friends with him. During the years ahead, Everett repeatedly displayed this aggressive friendship trait, especially to artists and photographers, but also to cowboys, Navajos, Indian traders, and tourists. He was sometimes rebuffed—Navajos were shocked—but generally his positive air of friendship was reciprocated.

From the coast he traveled to Yosemite National Park, where he hiked with a fifty-pound pack along trails to lakes and mountain peaks.

He vowed, however, that on his next sojourn, he would have a burro to carry his gear and supplies. At the end of the summer he returned home to complete his senior year of high school.

Graduating early, Everett departed Los Angeles in February 1931 for Kayenta, Arizona. After purchasing a burro from a Navajo, he wandered alone throughout Monument Valley as far as the San Juan River, then south to Canyon de Chelly, the Hopi mesas, San Francisco Peaks, and the Grand Canyon. He traveled north to Zion National Park, where he contacted poison ivy and fell desperately ill for several days, then returned to the Grand Canyon. With winter approaching, he moved south to the warmer clime in the desert mountains east of Phoenix. Finally, in December 1931, having been gone from home for ten months, he returned to Los Angeles.

In March 1932, Everett was off, again to southern Arizona, but this time he was accompanied by two companions: his friends Bill Jacobs and Clark (whose last name remains unknown). For perhaps a few weeks, this threesome had a fine time touring areas near Theodore Roosevelt Dam in the Superstition Mountains. Yet only two letters even mention their travels together.

What split Everett from his two companions remains a mystery, yet it must have been bitter, particularly between Everett and Clark. Everett's letter of 20 April 1932 does not mention his friends. On Friday, 13 May 1932, Everett began his journal, which follows below. Apparently, that was about the date when he left the other two boys and set off on his own. You will note that he made some caustic comments about Bill and Clark.

During all his travels, Everett may have suffered from an immune deficiency, then known as pernicious anemia. His journal entry for 21 July 1932 contains these words:

> Physically I feel weak. I would not be surprised to learn that pernicious anemia had set in again. A slight bruise has taken three weeks to heal. My injured toe will pain me for weeks to come. Diet more trouble.

Again on 16 June 1933, from the Sierras, he wrote to his family:

> . . . health and complexion have greatly improved, and every once in a while I feel quite ecstatic, but I slip out of such moods quite easily.

Apparently he had been diagnosed with the malady in the past, probably by a family doctor. Reportedly, he had little energy while in high school, attending only half days.[2]

Pernicious anemia, also called tired blood, is now known as vitamin B-12 deficiency and can be easily remedied by regular injections of B-12. Vitamin B-12 was unknown in the 1930s; it was not isolated until 1948. Victims of the anemia are lethargic, have stomach pains, and are often depressed with thoughts of impending doom. Since he was still young, Everett probably went through bouts of symptoms, having both good days and bad days.

Another author has studied medical journals on anemia and has learned that vitamin B-12 deficiency affects people primarily over the age of fifty and of northern European or African descent. Everett, therefore, could have been suffering from folic acid deficiency anemia, caused by lack of green leafy vegetables in the diet. The two anemias, he says, look very similar, requiring careful diagnostic tests to distinguish between them.[3] Yet, whatever the illness, it was real, and it probably was a factor in Everett's death.

A note about the journals: Everett probably kept journals for 1930 and 1931, but, if so, they have never been produced by the Ruess family. He undoubtedly kept a journal in 1934, but the disappearance of that journal, like Everett himself, remains a mystery. What we do have are the journals for 1932, when he traveled from central Arizona, northeast to the Four Corners area, including Canyon de Chelly and Mesa Verde National Park, and for 1933, when he visited Sequoia, Kings Canyon, and Yosemite National Parks.

After Everett's disappearance, the Ruess family read through the 1932 and 1933 pencil-written journals and, in some cases, actually erased sentences that might prove embarrassing to them or to other people. Then one of them, probably Stella, transcribed the journals, performing additional editing in the process, apparent in a comparison of her typescript with photocopies of the original journals. Whenever Everett criticized other people, mentioned his cigarette smoking, his butchering venison, his agnostic beliefs, or his occasional beatings of his

---

2. Verbal information from movie producer Diane Orr, 16 December 1997.

3. Gary James Bergera, "The Murderous Pain of Living—Thoughts on the Death of Everett Ruess" (unpublished ms, 1998).

dog, horses, or burros, she simply omitted the offending phrases. She eliminated all stories of his killing rattlesnakes, a sport that Everett thoroughly enjoyed. In places she cleaned up Everett's grammar, or left out comments she deemed unnecessary.

This editor has therefore disregarded the Stella transcript version and has provided Everett's actual written words, transcribed as accurately as possible, from photocopies—all of them unedited except, of course, for the erasures. That some of his words may seem to be mundane, offensive to others, or that they imply that Everett was something other than an ideal environmentalist just shows that, in many ways, he was a typical young man of the 1930s—not of the 1990s—and that he should be judged accordingly.

As these two journals conclude, we find Everett heading for San Francisco, hoping to immerse himself in civilized culture and intelligent conversation. It was to be a pivotal time in his life, affecting his painting, his writing, his emotions, and particularly his outlook for his own future. Fully optimistic, he plunged into the Bohemian life, living in a cheap room but visiting museums and the seashore, attending the opera, and meeting as many interesting people as possible. He apparently kept no journal for this period, so we have only an occasional letter to describe his actions or impressions. With his usual lack of restraint, he introduced himself to Ansel Adams. He left a number of his block prints on consignment with the Paul Elder Gallery, but he never mentions selling any. He also called on painter Maynard Dixon and Dixon's wife, photographer Dorothea Lange. Dixon gave Everett a couple of lessons in painting, while Lange took Everett's portrait and gave him a tour of the city in her automobile. Everett even attended a meeting of the local Communist party. For a while, at least, he seemed to be very popular. Then suddenly it all ceased—probably over a girl.

The girl was Frances—Frances who, we don't know. Yet letters to Frances do exist and they imply a newly found love, or at least infatuation. What Frances said or wrote to him is not recorded. We know only that he returned to his home in Los Angeles in March 1934 and, vowing never to return to the congestion of a large city, was anxiously planning to return to the deserts of northern Arizona. Defeated in human love, he resolved to retreat to his other love, a love that would not reject him—Nature.

It is significant that when Everett was around other people—

at home, in San Francisco in 1933–34, or during the winter of 1931–32 (when he toured the Superstition Mountains east of Phoenix with two other boys), he kept no journal. His journal-keeping, and, of course, his essay-type letters, were his outlets while he was alone. Yet he occasionally mentioned how much better it would be to have a congenial companion. And every time he encountered a tourist, a ranger, a hunter, or a fisher, he rushed over to strike up an acquaintance.

Most people have always believed that Everett was a loner who did not enjoy being with people. He was, of course, highly particular about the character, personality, and intelligence of those he called friends. But he was anything but a loner. In fact, as these journals reveal, he was very lonely, always seeking out new friendships—but always being disappointed.

Some have questioned Everett's sexual orientation, based on the phrasing in some of his letters. Yet, save for the May 1932 emotionally bitter separation from his two boyhood friends in Arizona, nothing in his journals would even hint at a homosexual tendency.

Everett's disappearance and probable death in the rugged canyon region south of Escalante, Utah, during the winter of 1934–35 has always been a subject of conjecture and debate. If he kept a journal for 1934, which is almost certain, it has never been found, nor have his camp equipment, paint kit, or supplies. Perhaps one of the searchers in 1935 found Everett's belongings and kept them for his own. Perhaps, less probably, Everett hid his gear so that no one would ever know that he had committed suicide. Certainly he was despondent over the value of life, which is evident in his letters, but between the lines and with these journals as background, one can sense that he was more disappointed over the lack of a warm, understanding companion and his despair over ever finding one.[4]

If he was sometimes lonely in these two summers of travel, he also encountered many disparate individuals—cowboys, Navajos, park rangers, tourists, old school chums, and religious zealots—as well as many others. And on the way he had several adventures, some of them almost life-threatening. Yet he always seemed to emerge from both minor and major tragedies with good cheer and with a hopeful outlook

---

4. For an earlier view and a fuller discussion of Everett's disappearance, see W. L. Rusho, *Everett Ruess: A Vagabond for Beauty* (Salt Lake City: Gibbs Smith, Publisher [A Peregrine Smith Book], 1983).

for the future.

In his journals, Everett occasionally showed touches of humor, such as when he commented about his burro, Grandma: "Grandma, it is now beyond doubt, will be a mother before long. Poor ignorant creature, she had no knowledge of contraceptives!"

National Parks, Indian lands, cities and highways of the American West have changed greatly in the many years since Everett passed their way. Thus in these journals we get a glimpse not only at another side of this complex, emotional, and probably very likable young man, but also on a different age, before high-tech travel and computers and before vast summer crowds regularly spilled into scenic attractions such as Yosemite Valley.

In our search for Everett Ruess, we follow what is but a faint sinuous trail, branching into cul-de-sacs that contain no answers yet offer clues for endless conjecture. In the sixty-plus years that have elapsed, we have at least narrowed our focus, not only on his disappearance but also on his personality and the inner turmoil he endured. That he was one of the most emotional writers ever to describe the red-rock-canyon country or the high Sierras is unquestionable, at least in his letters. Everett's journals, however, provide another side of this complex individual, a window into the personality of this thoughtful, intriguing young man of the 1930s who often wrote quite lyrically of his wanderings through desert and mountain lands of the American West.

EVERETT
RUESS
JOURNALS

BLOCK PRINT OF MORO ROCK, SEQUOIA
NATIONAL PARK, BY EVERETT RUESS, 1933.

1932

A R I Z O N A

After spending the winter months of 1931–32 in Los Angeles, Everett, together with two friends, Bill Jacobs and Clark (last name unknown), journeyed to Roosevelt, Arizona, in the Superstition Mountains northeast of Phoenix. For the next two months the boys traipsed in all directions, exploring their rugged surroundings. Only two short but cheerful Everett letters, one dated 30 March 1932 and one dated 20 April 1932, remain from this period. The camaraderie disintegrated on 13 May, when, in a bitter but unexplained separation, Everett left the others to go his own way through northeast Arizona into New Mexico and Colorado.

MAY 13, FRIDAY

At four o'clock Bert Henderson drove in with Bob McShane. Bert brought my kodak, but not my mail. Mrs. Frazier and Ben were gone, and the old man Thad did not know who Evert at the cliff dweller was.[1] Bob had a cup of coffee and drove off. Bert ate breakfast and went back to bed after telling us about the beautiful girl he met at the dance at Pumpkin center. Ruby Jay stayed with Bob Ruth. Howard asked his dad and Charlie if they wanted to trade Pacer for my young bronco. Charlie said he gave no damn. Howard and I wrangled the horses.

A buyer was coming to look at the yearlings in a few hours, as the three brothers saddled up in a hurry. I led out Pacer and Howard gave

---

1. As a nom de plume or simply a novelty, Everett was signing his letters "Evert Rulan" in 1931 and early 1932.

me an old lariat that was broken in six or seven places. Before I could thank them for anything they were gone.

I put on my canteen and kodak, led Pacer to the gate, then rode bareback to Wilson's. Bill came out to meet me and asked me why I hadn't kept Curly with me. I told him and he said Curly killed 3 of W's chickens. Ray was there. Clark said he wanted to see how I looked on Pacer when he was galloping, and he shot a pistol, but Pacer didn't buck me off. Then he rode him and Ray did. Clark found a lump on Pacer's back.

There was a nasty scene with Wilson. I gave him a dollar and a half and told him it was all I had. He took it and said he expected me to send him 3 dollars as soon as I got it.

I asked Bill what he intended to do and he said he was leaving everything to Clark. I don't think much of a person who would leave anything up to Clark.

Clark insisted on giving me half a dollar of Bill's money. Bill has two pots he is going to pay for as soon as he gets money.

Wilson's dog knocked a plate out of Bill's hand, and Wilson squelched Bill and told him it was all his fault. Bill cringed with disgusting obsequies. Thank god I'm not as selfish and ingratiating as those two I've known.

Clark asked if I had anything I'd give him—as if he hadn't squeezed me dry already. Then he went in the house and Bill said goodbye while Wilson wished me better luck. Clark flung a parting shot about a $3.40 obligation. I shook the dust of the place off my feet.

At Casuse's house, Luther Jackson tightened the cinch for me. I forgot to thank him, and the thought of my ingratitude troubled me for hours. I still remember vividly the time Aaron made me a wooden sword in New York. When he had finished he said, What do you say? I thought of Excalibur and wondered if he meant some magic word. Paul told me to say, Thank you, after a short silence. I said I knew that all the time. Aaron said he'd never do anything more for me.

It was soon quite hot. We followed the canal to the ford. I slipped, and tying an end of the rawhide to Curley's collar, led my two into the current of Salt River. The water came up to my thighs, and the stream was so swift in the center that I could hardly hold Curly against it.

Soon it was terrifically hot. My shoulders ached and burned. My racking cough kept up. The water in the canteen was hot as fire.

I reached a farmhouse just before my strength would have left me. An old man was irrigating. His wife looked like a witch, with snaky gray locks and hooked nose. They thought nothing of the distance I had come, and gave me nothing but water. I sat in the shade, then flopped to the ground. There were lumps on Pacer's back. After three hours or so I set off again. They said it was four miles to Pocket Canyon. The country changed quickly. Junipers replaced the sahuaros. Brown sand replaced the red rocks. The asbestos mine was right above. Soon it was dark and we had not reached the canyon. Pacer would not hurry. A canyon with red fissures and twisted junipers looked weird by moonlight, with Four Peaks silhouetted beyond.[2]

I found a camping place, unpacked and watered Pacer, and set some rice to boiling. I thought of Bill & Clark below and wondered if they pitied me as I pitied them

MAY 14, SATURDAY

Woke in the cool, saw Pacer's red shape, and slept more.

Made good rice cakes. Read poetry, especially Fletcher's "Green Symphony" and Walt Whitman.

Man came by and talked. He is caretaker at the asbestos mine which has been closed for three years. Been here with his family since last October. Used to drive the ambulance in Globe.

I rode up to the mine and looked down on the valley. High on a lonely cliff edge. Read old magazines in the shacks. Steep trail as I led Pacer down and let him eat lupines on the way. Stopped and talked to Loeffler and his wife for a few hours. They told me about parched corn and jerky, and garlic in beans. They gave me a pencil and some lard, and I went down to camp.

Hobbled Pacer and tied the lariat to his hobble. Cooked supper. Biscuits slow to rise. Put gravy on them and had cocoa. Was reading about Hans Castrop of Magic Mountains when I remembered Pacer. Had fed Curly but only half myself. Dashed frantically in all directions for half an hour, then found his trail back up the road. Half a mile along was the rope, broken again. Soon sighted Pacer and he galloped off ahead. Prayed to God and cussed him. Dark, but half moon. Shouted to car but he went around it. Another car stopped and the

---

2. Everett was evidently east, or upstream, from Theodore Roosevelt Dam, about twenty-five miles northwest of Globe, Arizona.

driver had Pacer by the neck but I didn't have the rope ready, and Pacer got off over the hill. Driver must have thot me stupid. Ran and ran. Pacer kept slowing and looking back. Finally got a loop over his head. Both drenched with sweat. Tied both ends of the rawhide on his neck and rode him back. Ranger mistook me for another man and we talked. Pacer's back was sharp but I rode him all the way back. Reminded me of the helpless feeling when Pegasus got away from me near Oljeto, and when I ran Pericles down near Red Butte, and again at Big Meadow Creek near Zion. Curly had eaten all my supper. I called him and beat him severely. Fried spuds and wrote. Thot of fluent, blistering swearing.

I must have a rope. Shud have a forefoot chain too to keep him from running. Grain to make him come in. Food for Curly. Something for myself. [2 lines erased]

Tomorrow on toward Pleasant Valley, Pueblo Canyon, and the Mogollon rim. There is poison ivy here and I fear I have it already.

MAY 15, SUNDAY

Slept late. Curly wasn't in camp.[3] Called and called as I left. Thot I heard barking, but he didn't come and I didn't search. I thot he would trail me but he didn't. Stopped at a store. Kindly old man. Much talk. He sold me a good rope for 50 cents. Lard, flour, milk and candy for 45 cents. No signs of Curly. Probably when he finds me gone he'll go back to Wilson's, kill more chickens, and J. C. will write to my parents. I wish he were shot. His distemper is still bad. He doesn't know enough to get out of the road. He kills chickens and steals food. I can't afford to feed him. Curly might drown in the river, but its unlikely.

The pack sack slid back and skinned Pacer's back. Camped under pines by a creek. Cooked squaw bread and read Magic Mountain, then continued when it was cool.

Passed Aztec Lodge and started uptrail to Petersons' ranch. White fir, Douglas fir, spruce and yellow pine. Steep trail, Waterfalls. Pink cliffs above. Pacer climbed splendidly. Reached Petersons at sunset. He is Dutch. No chance to earn grub or grain. They did not ask me to eat. No feed up ahead. 8,000 feet. No good campsites. Sulphur and cream.

---

3. Considering the beating Everett gave Curly the day before, it's no wonder the dog left in the night.

MAY 16

Mr. Peterson told me of a trail to Pueblo Canyon by way of Cherry Creek, and I decided to take it. I chased Pacer around and around the pasture, but he would not be caught. Peterson tied one of his to the gate and let the other in the pasture, but Pacer would not go to them. Finally he led his horses up and down and into the corral, and I drove my beast behind them. It seems I've traded one outlaw for another. After a late start we climbed for two miles, then started down the east side of the mountain. I lost the trail, I believe, but found another very rough one. Twice I stopped to repack. The trail was blazed part of the way. There was fine grass on the east side, but no water. I stopped and read and ate the handful of raisins that remained.

We came to a fence and found a gate, but I had to march up and down until I found a trail leading off. It was a precipitous descent, and I had to pull Pacer, because he insisted on nibbling each tuft of grass. We came out on a barren plateau and I had to reconnoiter until I found another trail leading to the shelf below. Between two rocks a rattlesnake was coiled, and he did not rattle. I was small and black with amber bands. I mashed him with a rock, stepped on his head when he started away, flung him back on a level spot by his tail, and crushed him. I had no pocket knife, but I cut off his rattle with my fingernails.[4]

Cherry Creek was spread out invitingly below. Green trees bordered the sandy bank, and a barn was set out in an emerald field, with scarlet ocotillo blossoms. We stumbled and scrambled along, reaching the water at dusk. I thought I would try the ranch before heading up canyon, and I asked at the gate if there was any chance to earn a couple of meals and grain for my horse. Expected to be turned down but was not.

I led Pacer thru the gate and unpacked, discovering that the saddle blankets had slipped out. Supper was excellent—tender steak, biscuits, lettuce, milk, Dutch cheese and good cookies. My host was Walter, a true comedian, who called everyone a "button," and was jolly about everything. There was also an old cowman turned prospector who was "laying over" for two or three days. He has three horses and a dog. After milking the cow and washing dishes, we played pitch.

---

4. Everett frequently killed rattlesnakes on his desert travels, but such action at the time was considered appropriate and even desirable. Environmentally conscious people today know that snakes, including rattlers, fill valuable niches in the ecosystem and should not be harmed.

May 17, Tuesday

I slept on springs. Up early. Good breakfast. I climbed up the mountain backtracking until I found the saddle blankets. I helped Walter work on the trail. Then the roadmaking crew came, the prospector helped, and we all picked and shoveled and chopped the hillside. Then the caterpillar came down, dragging a plow behind it. In spite of the steepness, it did not fall over. I followed behind, throwing out boulders and picking. It was fiercely hot, but I kept it up until lunchtime. The grader turned over and rolled down the hillside.

Dinner was fine. How cruel that gustatory delights should be so transient! I talked with the prospector while we washed clothes and dishes. I didn't want to start digging again. Not much more work was done, however. After strengthening the steering rod of the grader and replacing it, we sat and talked until the roadmen went home. We hung up jerky and sat in the moonlight.

Gnats, but no poison ivy.

May 18

After eating, the prospector and I wrangled horses. They were at the far end of the pasture. He made me a come-on to lead Pacer by. He has fine, big horses, two pack and one to ride. He told me about the price of grain and shoes. I'm sorry I ever listened to Bill and Clark and decided to switch from burros to horses. [1 line erased] Walter opined that Pacer would soon give out on me or run away from me, and advised me to trade for a burro. He convinced me that my kyaks were too heavy and put all my stuff in sacks. Gave me jerky. The prospector went one way and I the other, leaving my kyaks behind.

I wet my feet fording the creek. I saw Rus Ellisson [?] in his garden and he told me to ask his father about the cliff dwellings. It was a hot two miles to old Pearl's. There was no trail to the house. I shouted, and whistled, but tho the dogs barked, no one answered. I started to pick my way up the cliff-side near the cabin, and came upon a rattlesnake right away. I killed him, and old Pearl heard me throwing rocks, and came.

I put Pacer in the pasture after unloading under an oak. The old man showed me his garden and gave me some vegetables. I felt too weary to climb the cliff dwellings, so followed the old man about working in the gardens and making fence. I was so weak I could hardly listen to what he said. The gate was left open, and Pacer and his horse came out into the garden. Pacer would have escaped in another minute, but I drove him back in time.

We were nearly driven crazy by the gnats and mosquitoes. Pearl aired his views about cattle banks, gods, cow men, etc. He told me the story of his battle with Wilson for his land, which he won. Wilson is president of the Old Dominion bank which failed. He was in the Tonto feud. Gov. Hunt is his brother in law. His son has spent all his money. He wouldn't trade his mule for my horse.

Supper of sourdough bread with jerky gravy, and preserved elderberries, eggs and coffee.

He talked till I could hardly sit up. I slept in the tent on a cot. The sky was very cloudy.

MAY 19

Up late. Caught the horses and made a messy job of packing. Pearl thot I was a fool to discard the kyaks. How I wish I had two good burros, one to ride and one to pack. Alas poor Cynthia! Burro shoes cost a fourth as much as horse shoes. Burros eat scraps, keep fat on anything, learn not to run off, and get there. The only advantage a horse has is speed, and everyone tells me Pacer will knuckle under. Hendersons should have been honest with me. I told them time and again that I wanted an animal that would not give out, and they assured me Pacer wouldn't.

Pearl went with me a few miles, searching for cows. I took a picture of him on his horse leading mine across Cherry Creek. The sweat streamed off me. Pearl showed me a campsite with grass and water, between Pueblo Canyon and Devil's Chasm. Pink cliffs again. Pearl showed me how to tie a horse, how to approach him and how to place the saddle blankets. He said he thot I'd never get to Colorado.

I'm in a bad position. No dog. An old broken down horse. [2 lines erased] I may not be able to trade Pacer for a burro. I will die if he does give out on me. I can't afford to feed and shoe him. I may not have any money to buy a burro, and I may not be able to find any burros for sale. Clark has my burro pack saddle.

Pearl went on looking for his cows. I unpacked and staked Pacer out. After chewing some jerky, I went around the cliff to Rockslide Canyon and scrambled up to a dwelling. It looked insignificant—two story, one door and one window. But it was excellently built. The lower room went far back. So did the upper. There was another above it that went even further back, turned out and opened out on the other side of the cliff. I had to go out the way I came in as the other opening was high in the sheer cliff. There was tricky work in the rim rock. I found another small ruin, and a spring. I went around a few more turns, scratching myself painfully and hurting my feet, but saw no more ruins. There was a grand old sycamore in the canyon below me. Pines climbing along the steep side canyons. I went back, watered Pacer and staked him out again, then read the Brothers Karamazov. I spilled the rice. There were no raisins with it anyhow. Filled the canteens at the spring, tied Pacer close by, set the beans on, and read about Father Zossima. Clark was very sniffy about Brothers Karamazov.

Killed a scorpion in the gunny pack sack. Gnats and mosquitoes. Alone again. The crazy man is in solitude again. Pearl told me to look for rubies in the ant hills of the Navajo reservation. Pacer munched fox-tails. The full moon, round and yellow, in the chalky blue sky over distant mesas. No Curly to pet. No [word missing] to hold [8 lines erased]

MAY 20, FRIDAY

Slept until the sun made my bed uncomfortable. Ate and read and lazed. Tied Pacer to a tree in some grass. Repaired the pack sack, put in the sketch case, poetry, camera and canteen, and slung it to my shoulders. Made a chin band for my hat, put on my gloves, and clawed thru the brush to the edge of Pueblo Canyon. It was very steep. I had to remove my gloves to have full use of my hands. Scrambled down to the level of the sycamores and willows, then slid down the trunk of a huge sycamore to the water. Thru rocks and brush to a grassy ledge, which I followed up the ridge. Then I climbed two more ledges and wormed my way through manzanita and dwarf oak till I came to the fourth ledge, which I followed up the canyon. At one point it nearly receded into the sheer cliff, but I edged by. Then I came upon the cliff dwellings.

They were strung along for a quarter of a mile, all right against the cliff, and few of them extending more than one room beyond it. I was disappointed they were not more picturesque. Douglas Cummings was here, had sawn the beams, and placed the age of the ruins at 500 years.[5]

5. Everett was confused. The father of dendochronology, or tree ring dating, was Dr. A. E. Douglass, who might have visited these ruins. Also, these ruins may have been examined by Byron Cummings, archaeologist at the University of Arizona.

Some rooms were large and the beams were a foot thick, but not a roof was intact. I came to a dripping spring, but there was no pool below it, and not much water coming down. Around the next bend, however, was a clear, cool pool, and gladly I drank. The rest of the dwellings did not cling so slavishly to the cliff, but they were all crumbled. There was nothing around the next bend, but I saw the waterfall and heard the water thundering over the cliff. I don't think these dwellings are the ones meant by the 70 room dwelling in Pueblo Canyon but I was unwilling to push thru more brush. I was scratched sufficiently as it was. I took one photograph. There was nothing to paint. I read some poetry, gathered an armful of grass by the spring and stowed it in my pack for Pacer, and started back. I crossed at a different place. The trees at the bottom of the canyon are deliciously, refreshingly green. I took a bath but decided it was too cold to swim. Soon I was sweating on the upgrade. I watched a pale green lizard catch and eat a cricket.

Very glad I was to be back in camp. I boiled the beans again and ate while I read about Alyoshus Dmitri, Grushenka, Katerina, Ivan, Smerdyakov, Ilusha, Kolya, and Trifon Bonsiovitch. I watched the sun fade from the distant brown hills, thot wild thots, and went to bed.

MAY 21

I should have made an early start, but as I had been denied loafing the last few days, I slept late and read until the sun was quite hot.

The trail was vague and disappeared altogether frequently. We went up and down some extremely steep places. After crossing a couple of fences, we went down to the creek, and followed it for a mile or so. It was very rough, and its a wonder Pacer didn't break his neck on slippery rocks. Finally we came to an impasse. I had to lead Pacer back until we found a side canyon with a gate. There were deer tracks, horse tracks, cow tracks, and shoe tracks in the sand.

There was no trail up the side canyon, and Pacer had a good chance to show what was in him. We went almost straight up, crashing thru brush all the way. Pacer did wonderfully well. Finally rediscovering the trail, we followed across a few more canyons, and stopped at a cattle trap beside a stream. There was no grass, but the saddle blankets had slipped out. I read and chewed jerky, then repacked. I vacillated for some time trying to decide which side of a fence the trail was on, but at length I crossed it and went down to the creek once more. It was much wider here, and I followed it without difficulty, but again it closed down and I did not know where to go. I caught two turtles and saw an oriole. I decided to leave the creek, and went through a gate up a side canyon. Half a dozen calves with their mothers stampeded. There was no real trail. The sun had set, but I pushed on until another fence blocked the way, and I still did not know where the trail was.

There was no grass, but Pacer nibbled oak leaves, and I gave him some grain. I boiled rice and ate it without raisins or brown sugar. I had cocoa too. After eating, I lay back to rest a moment, and could hardly get up again. I had intended to write, but it was all I could do to spread out my bed and crawl in. Pines were between me and the stars. The night was cold.

MAY 22, SUNDAY

I made rice cakes from what rice remained, and had the last half a dozen of Clark's pound of prunes. After a long walk, I found the trail, came back and broke pack. The sacks made loading a slow process. I shall endeavor to procure some light kyaks. I noticed burro tracks, and after a few hours I reached a cabin and clearing, but no one was there. The barn had collapsed and everything was in disrepair. Half a dozen dilapidated burro saddles were stacked in the shed. I found a good cinch.

Again I had trouble finding the trail. After a few hours, I heard bells, and along came half a dozen horses and a cowboy leading four pretty pack mules. He could not stop long but said his boss owned burros and would be along soon. They were moving into the old cabin to prepare for a roundup. I stopped by a spring near grass and waited, but he did not show up. I ate a tremendous quantity of jerky and finished the Brothers Karamazov. It fell flat toward the end, and I didn't like Dostoievsky's chatty way of speaking, but it was a real book.

It was late, but I did not want to stop there. I lost the trail once more, but then it was plain. I saw three sleek burros, two brown and one black, with white noses and obstinate heads. Soon we were on a vast grassy shoulder with only a few small canyons. Long shadows spread out before me. Junipers dotted the ridges. I saw a large bluebird.

Camp was made under a spreading juniper with good grass all

27

around. It was quite a pull to the creek and back for water. Elboroni and onion soup, with cocoa. The sage has disappeared.

Pacer's bell tinkles and a coyote howls. [9 lines erased] A few bars of music consoled me. I shall never forget hearing the ninth symphony.

[2 lines erased]

I often wish people meant something to one another, and one could find people to one's taste.

MAY 23

Rather a late start. I left the bell on Pacer's neck. Came to a ranch inhabited by a friendly old couple. The men had been blown up in a mine and were rather disabled. They said it was nine more miles to Young.[6] I walked and walked but could not seem to get there. Finally I came to another ranch where I inquired about Young and burros. Just before reaching Pleasant valley, I saw three scrawny, runty burros in a field. At the post office were two fine letters from father, five dollars from Edith May, and ten from home. I cashed ten dollars and went to find Hoggy Jones who owned burros. He was not home, but I waited and talked to his brother in law. A young man rode up and stopped to talk. He was six feet three, rather handsome, with chaps and an old black sombrero. His name was Homer Joy. He said he would catch two burros for me and trade for my horse. He rode off and I followed more slowly, stopping to buy some provisions at the store.

I came to the ranch of a Mr. Baker, at dusk, and there I had supper and spread my bed on a cot. Mrs. Baker was very nice. She is Hazelwood's sister. I showed them my pictures (including some new ones received in the morning's mail, which I'd shown to Homer). The fare was simple, but there was butter, cream and jam. I showed them my pictures. Some neighbors, the Spurlocks, came over to talk and borrow a windlass.

MAY 24

After breakfast I went out to drive Pacer in. He was a mile away, by himself. I drove him almost back, with two black horses, but he ran around me until I despaired of catching him. I saddled a big black horse and drove him into the corral.

---

6. Young, Arizona, is a small village on Cherry Creek about ten miles south of the Mogollon Rim. It is surrounded by Tonto National Forest.

A sheepherder with five good pack burros was driving a flock down the road. I came to the ranch of Ed Joy, Homer's father. Homer was gone, looking for burros. Ed told me all sorts of tales of old days in Texas. I kept thinking we would have lunch, but it seemed to be three o'clock, and no dinner. It turned out to be only twelve, and Ed gave me a honeycomb to chew while the beans boiled some more. We had corn bread and gravy, bacon, buttermilk, and beans.

Then more tales of Indians, scalpings, horse thieves, gunfights, etc. Ed told me of a time when he was driving cattle and had to go four days without water, until it rained on the flat rock. He would catch dew on a handkerchief and wring it out into a cup.

Homer came in, but he hadn't been able to catch any burros. He said he knew a chap, Bently or so, who would trade two burros for a horse. He said they were poor, had been used for plowing and packing. Since there seemed no alternative, I agreed when he offered to make the trade for me.

I went to the spring with Ed and brought back a couple of pails of water. There is no running water and the spring is some distance from the house.

John Joy stayed at the ranch. His wife and baby were here. Two grandsons, Winston and Edward, were cutting capers. There is a Dutch oven in the yard into which the dishwater is poured for the chickens and pigs to drink. There are two pigs. The boys scratched them. The baby was afraid of the hen and the pigs.

We sat by the fireplace for a while, but I turned in early. It became bitterly cold. The moon stared at me and I buried myself in the cover.

MAY 25

The sun was shining when I crawled out, but it was still quite cold. After breakfast I carried water and chopped wood. Ed showed me a bee tree.

Then I tried to drive Pacer in. Wink and Ed were riding the big white jenny and they helped me. Pacer was by himself at the end of the section. We drove him nearly to the corral when he started to run around again. Homer and John rode up to cut him off, then the hound began chasing Pacer, baying at his heels and he ran like a thing possessed. Homer set off at full tilt on his sandy gray horse. They streaked across the pasture, but suddenly the gray horse stumbled on a rock and turned over. Homer jumped but was badly bruised. When I came up he was sitting in the shade holding his knees. John went off to catch the gray horse. Homer had cuts on both sides of his head. His hand was all bloody and his hips and legs were skinned. John brought back the horse. It had stepped on the bridle rein and broken it off short. They caught my horse and John took him over to trade him.

The women doctored Homer. Ed told tales of falls that killed and maimed, and of men dragged thru cactus and gravel that had their scalps scraped off onto their foreheads. John's wife nursed the baby.

Dinner was very good. There was peach pie and cake. John did not come until late afternoon. The burros were quite small. I had considerable difficulty making Pacer's saddle fit the little burro. I patched an old pack saddle, cinched it on the smaller burro, and used my coat for padding. I wrote a letter home, and asked old Mrs. Joy to take my picture as I started off. I tied the pack burro to the riding saddle. The moment I climbed on, my little burro whirled around, the pack burro ran ahead and under a tree, and I was dismounted without more ado. Mrs. Joy didn't take the picture. Next time I got underway. There were several gates to open. I decided to name my burros Peggy and Wendy.

After a couple of miles I came to the Spurlock ranch, where I unpacked, watered the garden and chopped wood for my supper.

Mrs. Spurlock's mother, Mrs. Hall, fumbled about. She wore a long gray dress of corduroy. White hair and peaceful face. She couldn't find her food, and started to sit in the chair I was sitting in. I made my bed up in the attic on a cot with quilts. The two men, brothers, discussed plans for the barn they are building.

MAY 26

Young Roderick and I went out in the cold to wrangle the horses. After breakfast I ran my burros in. Mrs. Spurlock gave me a quilt to use for padding. Rod found a couple of light boxes and I sawed and nailed until I made them into kyaks. They are not at all strong, but they are light, and not as bothersome as the sacks. I lost the clapper from the bell coming into Young, so I found a nut that would make a clatter. Off we went. I had to whack Wendy before she would cross the creek. There were three gates to open. I passed some deserted ranch houses a couple of miles out, and remembered that I left my jacket at Spurlocks. I unloaded Peggy and started to ride Wendy back, but the saddle slipped and I tied her and ran on. Both burros are immature.

I arrived in time for dinner. Pickles and peach pie.

Packed again and started on for the X ranch, but couldn't find the way. Wandered back and forth till a rider put me straight, but then I couldn't find the trail he spoke of. Peggy pulled back all the time. Pacer's saddle does not fit her. It spreads the pack out too far. We went south, east, west and north. I was sure I was lost, but I reached the ranch in plenty of time to split wood for supper. Ransom Spurlock, whom I met at Bakers, lives here. Rice, ham, and gingerbread for supper.

MAY 27

Ransom said he would trade me a mule pack saddle and a McClelland for mine. There was no rigging on the mule saddle so we got some rivets and scraps of leather, and he made a couple of cinches out of cord rope. I made a breast strap and a couple of crude stirrups. When the saddle was mostly rigged, he went off to irrigate the field, but told me to stay that night.

I made a sort of breast strap, and a couple of stirrups. Then I labored mightily at the woodpile until lunchtime. I carried a dozen buckets of water to the peach trees and then we set up the windlass over the wall by the house. Charlie Wright, the rider I met yesterday, came along and helped. Ransom went to the field again while Charlie and I went to the swimming hole. I watered the peach trees again, and we sorted beans awhile. Chuck and he knew of a good big burro that didn't belong to anyone, and said he'd catch it for me to take the place of little Wendy. However, Ransom said it surely belonged to some sheepman.

Honey and applesauce for supper.

MAY 28

Started late. Peggy held back all the time and pulled Wendy's saddle off once. After two fences, the trail was plain. It led up to the Mogollon Rim, following a high ridge nearly all the way. The trail was blazed plainly. We came to a flock of sheep and Wendy seemed to delight in lunging thru the flock. The camp of the sheep men was a mile farther. There were several burros hobbled out, and three horses as well. I drove the donkeys up the steep part of the trail, then stopped for some crackers and jerky. Wendy lost one of the stirrup boards. The saddle felt uncomfortable at first, but I soon became accustomed to it. I shall try to get some good stirrups. I should have chaps in this brushy country. When I get a couple of rings I'll fix a better hackamore. I wish I had some light canvas panniers or kyaks that were bigger than mine are.

I was expecting to reach the **W** ranch by dusk. It is 20 miles from the **X̄**. I came to a road, and a sign, 6 miles to **W** in later afternoon. Peggy had been dragging along and Wendy finally tired of pulling her carrying me too, lay down. I drove them along then. I passed another sheep outfit. The burros touched noses. I came to a sign that said **W** was three miles back, while Holbrook was 72 ahead, and 13 ranch, seven. It was late, but I pushed on for two or three miles, until dark. There was no water, and little grass. Since the bell was lost I tied the burros.

Soon I had a blaze, and made some squaw bread, which I ate with peanut butter bought at Briggs store at Young. I chewed jerky and parched corn for the first time. It was rather good.

I fed the burros some corn, heaped up the fire, and crawled under cover.

May 29, Sunday

I lay in bed when I knew I should get up, but finally I did arise, hobble the burros, eat the rest of the graham crackers, and pack up. It was a superior feeling to be mounted on Wendy, surveying the world from my lofty position of ease, with Peggy carrying all the food and equipment I needed, so that I was independent of everyone.

The water was all gone. The country changed completely in half a mile or so. There was plenty of good grass, and the glittering green of the aspens showed against the gloomy green of the pines. I expected to go to the 13 ranch, but a road to the left led to Lake No. 1, 2½ miles west, so I took it. It seemed we would never arrive.

Lake No. 1 is mostly covered with rushes and swamp grass which ripples and sways in the wind, while the swallows glide swerving and dipping over the strips of water.

I camped under fine tall pines at the water's edge. It was hard to get clear water. There was fine grass for the donkeys. I boiled some rice and raisins, eating two pans full while I read, "The Magic Mountain."

Then a family from Holbrook stopped for their picnic lunch, and invited me to join them. It was a tasty meal.

I spent half an hour or so map gazing, marking the places I have been to. A piercing blast blew constantly. I read more of the book. It is very depressing, about a young German who visits his cousin at a tuberculosis sanitarium in the Alps, and finds that he too has the disease. What with the wind, it lowered my spirits considerably. I wish I had a companion, some one who was interested in me. I would like to be influenced, taken in hand by some one, but I don't think there is anyone in the world who knows enough to be able to advise me. I can't find my ideal anywhere. So I am rather afraid of myself. Obscurantism. Brot the burros in at dark, tied Wendy, hobbled Peggy, gave them some bread and scratched and stroked them. Too bad Wendy is not bigger. I'd hate to trade her for a bigger burro, because the two are such a fine pair. They even scratch each others necks. I gathered a big pile of wood, ate rice cakes with peaches and cream, then tried to chloroform my brain with reading, jerky, and dried peaches. I burnt the corn I meant to parch.

MAY 30, MONDAY

Back to the road and northward I guided the caravan. Half a dozen cars passed, and one tourist stopped and took my picture for me. Every once in a while Peggy would hang back and stop the procession. I don't like the names Peggy and Wendy for them. Cynthia was a perfect name for a burro. I thot of others—Scylla, Circe, Vivien, Gretchen, Dolores, Susie, Diana, but they didn't seem to fit.

I stopped for late lunch at a large corral with several subdivisions. There was no grass outside—the sheep had eaten it all, but inside it grew a foot high. There was some alfalfa in a trough too, and Peggy ate it voraciously. I read poetry.

When we started again, I tried to see if Peggy would follow without being pulled, but she would not. I couldn't drive her either. I braided a quirt as I rode. The highway led along a ridge with the forest sloping off each side. Wendy got tired and I walked and drove them for a couple of miles. The mail carrier stopped and gave me some water. The forest seems endless.

I stopped in an open place with fine grass, hobbled Wendy and tied Peggy to an old stump. There is only five pounds of food left. I didn't know what to cook, but finally made oatmeal and had it with peanut butter and brown sugar. I read further, about Hans Castorp.

The night was serenely beautiful, with the firelight sending shafts of golden brown up the wrinkled trunks of two tall pines, with misty blue trees circling around me, stars gleaming softly thru their boughs.

MAY 31, TUESDAY

I woke in the night and found that Wendy was gone. A new moon was low in the pines. I put on my sneakers and went up the road with my flashlight. I could see no tracks leading back. A bell tinkled, but tho I went in every direction I could not find where it was.

At prima luce I stirred .myself, expecting a despairful search, but Wendy was close by.

Again I had oatmeal. We started off fairly well, but soon Peggy began perplexing me. She would hang back, dragging Wendy, then run along side at a trot, all the time gasping, coughing and grunting. I could not see anything wrong with her, but it soon became impossible to lead her, as she kept twisting around me and nearly shook her pack off.

I drove the burros for a while, but Peggy kept galloping, nearly jarring her pack off, so I led them. The small canteen fell off. I went back for it. I thot I must be lost. There were no signs, and I could not find Heber. We left the forest of yellow pines and oaks for the juniper belt, with a few pines. Country like southern Utah. Finally I came in sight of Heber.[7] but Peggy grunted and lay down in the soft dust, nearly breaking the kyaks. She would not budge until I took off the top. I put the load on Wendy, feeling sickish, and unpacked again beside the store. No burros are owned here. The storekeeper said the burros were thin, but there was no telling whether Peggy was shamming or honestly worn out. He advised me to pack Wendy. I bought some groceries, and the storekeeper found me one strong kyak and a Union kerosene box which I converted into a kyak. I filled the canteens, climbed astride Peggy and went on, after watering the burros at a tank.

I seemed much higher and more comfortable on Peggy, but she would not hurry. We went a mile and a half, then Wendy started to lie down. Peggy jerked forward and prevented her, and I turned off into a swale and stopped under a pine, but Wendy lay down there. It is a question of what to do. The groceries and water were thirty or forty pounds more, and the kyaks perhaps five or ten, but even so it is nothing like the load Pegasaus and Pericles[8] used to carry. Fortunately

---

7. Heber, Arizona, on State Highway 260, was settled by Mormons in the late 1800s.

8. Two burros used by Everett during his 1931 travels.

the McClelland is fitted so that it can be used as a pack saddle in a pinch. Must I give up riding? It is 47 miles to Holbrook, with only one waterhole on the way, at Zeniff, 20 miles off. I'll not be able to carry much feed for the burros. I'll have to carry water. Wendy leads well, does not pull back, but she is the smaller. I think I shall pack both this afternoon.

I fried some cheese and peanut butter sandwiches and three eggs and ate a can of peaches, then read Magic Mountain, concerning biology. The burros are eating grass after resting in the shade. I don't like to disturb them—they need to feed up.

When Peggy flopped I felt quite queasy. Felt that the trip was foredoomed to failure, that I'd be overcome with melancholy if I visited the places I've seen before. Afraid to go home because that would be an admission of failure & I'd be ashamed to face Bill and Clark. [2 lines erased] If only Sam would write to me about New York. I can't believe that he has left me in the lurch. I felt distinctly different from other people; already I've drifted too far away from other people. I want to be different anyhow, I can't help being different, but I get no joy from it, and all common joys are forbidden me.

Peggy and Wendy are both skinned up. They were very poor to begin with. Wendy has a curly tail, and Peggy's is trimmed so. Peggy is the difficult, willful, guileful one.

I put the bed and canteens on Wendy and the rest on Peggy. We did not get very far before dark. Peggy began switching her tail and gasping, but did not collapse. I don't know what could be wrong with her. I camped under a pinyon on the edge of a grassy flat. I used sage to start my fire.

Supper consisted of macaroni with cheese and eggs. I fed the burros an ear of corn, hobbled Wendy and tied a chiseled stone to Peg's rope.

The kyak the storekeeper gave me was used to ship a little pig in. I take keen pleasure in possessions like kyaks, and pack saddles. I shall carve cliff dweller designs on the sides of the kyaks. I enjoy owning a burro too—it is such a droll creature. Wendy looked weird coming up in the firelight to get her corn, with her immense white face, solemn eyes, and long ears.

I did not read, but sat by the fire awhile.

June 1, Wednesday

Fried the leftover macaroni, packed Peggy, and rode off. I came to a cattle trap without a gate beside it, but I went back a short distance and got thru. Then I came to another such place with no gate in sight. I did not intend to go back or around, so I let the fence down. Soon Peggy began gasping, running ahead, and holding back. The ground was very soft and I was afraid she'd lie down, so I dismounted and drove the burros. We went along at a good clip.

I turned west from the highway and stopped at the Despain ranch. First I thot it was Duquesne, then DeSpane, but it is Despain. The grandmother was very cordial, and I was welcome to have meals without earning them. Two young men, Stanley and Bob, were there, having stayed on for a year. Also Claude Despain, his wife and four children. His wife is plump, rosy checked, with hair drawn back in a knot. Claude looks quite rakish, somewhat like Frederick March playing the role of Mr. Hyde. He has a two week's beard, a blue coat, and a villainous black sombrero, thick lips and blue eyes.

There was no work I could do, so I sawed my kerosene box into the shape of a kyak.

I let the boys ride the burros for a while. Then I made a bridle. They found me two old bells, one quite large, the other small. Boy, a son of Lin Despain of Holbrook said he thought Peggy was going to have a colt. He said he'd trade his little jack for her. That would explain why Peggy groans so much, but it is uncertain.

The food was rather good. Besides biscuits and beans (Mexican strawberries) there was rice pudding, pickles, honey, ham, milk, and corn.

After supper, Bob, who is red-headed, played the guitar and sang. I showed my photographs.

I slept in an adobe house with Stanley and Bob.

June 2

I did not wake up with the others, but breakfast is late here.

Yesterday I soaked some cowhide, and today, I cut it in strips and nailed it in the edges of the kyaks, with Boy's help.

I talked with Grandma Despain. She goes out on a trapline every winter, riding in. She spent her girlhood on the reservation, near the Little Colorado and Tuba City. Discussions of food.

I read the newspaper, then watched a day old calf, and ground corn to feed the burros. Felt weak. I carried water and covered tomato plants with cans. There was a sun dog in the morning, presaging rain.

The Despains are Mormons and say grace.

Earl, the baby, rode on Charlotte's back. Bob sang, You may change a fool, but a doggone mule is a mule until he dies. Stanley speaks brokenly, yet his speech pleases me somehow.

I shelled some popcorn to take along.

JUNE 3

Early up. Boy's burro trade won't go through. One can't do business with children. I had the heaviest load on Wendy.

Stopped to talk to two men digging a hole for a drain pipe. Decent chaps. Had a good talk. On to Zenith, which I reached at half past twelve.[9] Claude and Bob had beaten me there. I had lunch at Guy Despains. Some strange names here—Zelma, Sheila, Rilla.

On again to the highway, down a long lane. It started to rain. I was wanting to stop at the last ranch house, but the man was gone, and the women wouldn't act without him. Some cowboys who'd seen me down the road drove up a bunch of horses and corralled them. They had a white mule, low and long.

The shower passed. I filled the canteens with muddy water at the last tank. We trundled for a mile or so while the clouds scudded by overhead. It looked like rain when I camped, but the sky soon cleared to the edges.

Wendy was very tired and lay down right away. I made rice pudding and read, Magic Mountain. The book is becoming more interesting.

I petted the burros awhile. They were worn out. Again I am in the desert—the desert that I know—red sand, cedars, great spaces, distant mesas, and behind, the blue of the Mogollons.

The fire flamed straight up, and for awhile, I was almost able to be happy in the present, rather than in anticipation.

JUNE 4, SATURDAY

It rained in the night. I had gone a half mile down the road when a motorist stopped to talk. His name was Tom Reed. He asked me why I wouldn't stop at his ranch a few days or as long as I liked, and rest up. It was a few miles back, but the sky was unfriendly, and he was so generous

---

9. Zeniff was a small settlement southwest of Holbrook. It is now shown on maps as "abandoned."

that I decided to accept the invitation. He drove on to Holbrook. He had heard of me at $\overline{X}$.

It hailed and rained a little. I followed a fence past a pond to the ranch. His wife, Olive, three children, and Bill Clarke, a nephew, were there. We unloaded the burros at the barn and put them in a small pasture.

It rained hard for a short time. After lunch I helped Bill, who is fifteen or so, to rake up the yard, which was full of trash. We made piles of the rubbish, then shoveled all the chips, glass and Prince Albert cans into a trailer which we dragged off to the dump.

Tom came back at dark. Bill and I rode out and drove in the cows to be milked. There were several dogies.

I slept in a large bed with Bill.

JUNE 5, SUNDAY

We cleared up some more trash and burnt it. Rance and Georgia Spurlock came over to discuss a cow deal. There was a good dinner.

JUNE 6

Tom went to Holbrook. Bill caught a horse that hadn't been used in a long time and rode it. We galloped about and drove the cows and burros in. Tom brought my mail—two letters written weeks ago. Mother wrote that Bill's mother drove out to take him home. What a fuss about him. I suppose Bill and Clark went because they certainly couldn't do anything in this country.

I told Tom I thot I'd go on in the morning, but he told me that if I'd stay he was satisfied he could get me a much better outfit—a pack mule and saddle horse.

He told me of the killing at $\overline{X}$. There were three brothers. They saw one of their mules running off with a rope. Two of them slipped out with their guns and were shot down, but the other accounted for several Indians.

We washed all the dirty clothes, mine included. The washing machine is run by a gasoline motor.

JUNE 7, TUESDAY

We wrangled the horses and I rode Ginger while Bill rode the filly with cropped mane. We rode several miles to the rim where the rocks were cracked and split, leaving chasms thirty feet deep. I killed a baby rattlesnake. A bat flew out of one hole. Then we rode to the House Rock, a huge balanced rock with a hawk's nest on top. I killed another rattlesnake by stepping on it.

The Spurlocks were here again when we returned in midafternoon. We set out some onions in the garden. I enjoyed driving the burros to water. They galloped at a great pace. They put their ears forward and scuttled along very comically, with their bells clattering noisily.

JUNE 8, WEDNESDAY

I went with Tom to the ranch of Jess Pierce who has mules. Only one was broken, and he was too valuable. Jess is hard bitten. He used to employ ten cowpunchers, but now he hires no one, and is in debt. He has lost money for two years, and is bitter against the forest service. We helped him start his car, and passing thru a dozen gates, went to Turley's dude ranch in the pines. Turley had no broken mules on hand, but he said there was a stray buckskin mule which had been there for five years, and he'd help me catch it. Tom says he'll find a horse for me.

I went out to drive the burros to water at dusk, riding a big black that hadn't been used for a while. He made the burros run like rabbits and then passed them. I swung him around with difficulty and as we approached the burros, he stopped at a ditch and bucked hard. I was quite surprised, but reached down for the saddle horn right away. After several jumps, however, it seemed to slip through my fingers, my feet lifted out of the stirrups, and with a rather pleasant flying sensation, I sailed up in the air and nose-dived into the ditch, seeing black and blue as I toppled over on my side. My lip was cut and my moustache was bloody, and my arm all full of burrs when I got up. I went over to the black but he ran off to the other end of the fence. I caught him and drove the burros to water without further mishap.

JUNE 9, THURSDAY

Tom and Olive prepared to camp on the mountain, while Bill's mother came to care for the kids. I mounted Ginger and set off for Turley's. Ginger's 15 or 16 and Tom told me not to lope him. I stopped once at the Jackson ranch for water and came to Turley's about one o'clock. After lunch, young Lavon Turley on his bay, King, went with me to catch the mule. First we chased some horses to water. I nearly lost

Lavon in the pine forest. He told me how his knees had been dislocated five times in basketball games. He is only nineteen, but twice my size, hefty, and well-set. We made a half circle, then, as Ginger was tired, Lavon told me to wait for him down road while he ranged off in the woods. He did not meet me until the sun was low. King was all lathered with sweat. Lavon said the mule jumped out of a wire corral on two occasions, left the herd, and went through three fences, cutting himself in the process. Barr Turley told me he thot the mule was too wild to use, and offered me an old white horse. I wasn't enthused but decided to accept.

JUNE 10

Early up. Went to a nearby ranch with Lavon to bring back some borrowed saddles. I stayed for lunch and talked with a couple of dudes. Turleys have 60 or 70 saddles, but they did not have any that were old enough for me to buy. Lavon showed me the camp quarter and I took a shower at the swimming pool.

The Turleys are Mormons. We talked about religion. Barr told me how Jess Pierce had tried to cheat the forest service by driving cattle around and back of the ranger trying to count the herd. Mr. Turley seems a weak character. There are two huge silos and the odor of stacked corn in there.

The white horse is in a very large pasture. I rode within sight of the fence, saw several horses, not mine. Near Bushman's tank were more horses of all colors. The white is 15 or more [and] has a $\triangle$L and $\vee$ brand, and is supposed to run with a bay colt. I cruised up and down the draws until sunset, looking at 60 horses or more. I came within ten yards of a hawk, perched on a juniper. A coyote crossed in front of me.

I reached the ranch as the last glow was leaving the sky.

Tom wasn't back. After the third meal of beans today, I had to sleep with Bobby, Billy's brother. I was nearly eaten alive by some kind of insect, and then I had horrible cramps. In the middle of the night I went barefoot out to the barn and got in my bed roll.

JUNE 11

I was sick almost all day and ate no lunch. I decided never to eat beans again. I can't seem to digest them. I tried several remedies. Billy fed his sense of self importance by reminiscing.

In the afternoon we rode over to Bushman's and looked vainly for the horse. At the ranch I met the notorious Hot Cakes, blustery horse breaker, whom Tom had found ragged and hungry on the streets of Holbrook a few years back. He tries to seem tough, but he was pretty decent after I talked to him awhile. He said he was pretty sure he could get me a good horse or two for $10 at the camp he was in. He is working for Jess Pierce, driving wild horses to the reservation to trade them for blankets, also breaks them as he goes and tries to catch more.

JUNE 12, SUNDAY

Harold went with me to Bushman's tank to get my gray. He rode the black horse and I rode the filly. They both bucked a little. We found my horse running with the bay colt, corralled him and led him back. He is a sorry looking steed with a bony back and all the ribs showing.

Dellmer and Arlow Hunt had come over with Van Bushman and some others. We drove in the horses, caught a black and a bay, broncos, and turned the others out. Harold had said he would ride them.

They blindfolded the black to get a saddle on him and Harold climbed on. The horse bucked hard and went around and around in circles. Every little while he would pitch again. Finally Harold went overboard. I took his picture just as he fell. Soon he got back on but was thrown again. Tom ragged him considerably and Harold came back at him—said he didn't see why he should break horses for nothing. Then Van Bushman got on. I thought the horse would be tired but he showed plenty of life. Van rode but held to the saddle horn all the time. It caught in his shirt and tore it to shreds.

Then they caught the bay. It fought the rope and dragged thru the gate once. When it was blindfolded it broke loose again and broke a gate square in two. Tom rode his big black horse, Nig, with a pine tree brand and snubbed the bay until Harold could get on. It took one big leap, pitched hard, then fell down near the chute post, hurting Harold. He picked himself up, but refused to ride any more unless he was paid. Tom offered him five dollars if he would qualify, but that was too much to expect. Dellmer and Arlow, both huge fellows, would not try. Two more old fellows came up, and after a while, Van said he would ride. He wanted to use his saddle so they tried to take Harold's off. The bay broke loose again and crashed right up on the trough where he was sitting. Tom jumped over the fence in a hurry.

Van rode him, tho he pulled leather all the time. He nearly was brushed off on the fence pickets, but kept his seat. After a while, Tom snubbed the horse and Van got off. Dellmer gave him the dollar he'd promised if Van rode him. The black was a three year old and the bay a two year old. They put up good shows.

Hot Cakes was naturally nettled at the turn things took and especially when Tom refused him the job of breaking him and offered Van five dollars to break the black. It was late in the day when the crowd dispersed. Harold and I had intended to visit his camp that morning and inquire about horses, but now it was too late for me to go. He said he'd bring a horse tomorrow if he could.

June 13, Monday

In the middle of the night, Harold came into the barn where I was sleeping and startled me, then went out again. Toward morning I saw that he was sleeping beside me, wrapped in a couple of saddle blankets. I gave him my coat for a pillow.

We were up with the dawn. While we waited for breakfast two men, Willis Pennington and Gene, a mechanic from Holbrook, came in. Their car had stalled on the highway, they'd slept in a gunny sack and had come for assistance.

After breakfast, Willis said he would ride the bay. He took his time, saddled it himself, and mounted alone. At first it seemed the bay would not buck, but he did, scraped Willis on the fence, and finally dumped him. Willis got on twice again, however, and was not thrown.

Tom fixed their car and I rode into Holbrook with them. Willis said he could sell me a good horse for ten. They said they'd meet me in the Pastime Pool Room at 3 o'clock. I bought a pair of overall trousers at Penney's. My Levi's were all worn out. Then I had a malted milk at the drug store and bought a good pocket knife. I cashed two money orders at the bank, so now I have the ten for the horse. The town didn't seem very interesting.

I waited and watched until after five, then I grew weary of watching pool and passing tourists. An immense colored chef passed by riding on twenty sacks of flour on the back of a truck.

I walked across the Little Colorado and a mile or so beyond, while the sun blazed fiercely. Then I stopped in the shade of a hillock, ate almonds and read Tom's newspaper, the Snowflake Herald. A little before dusk, they finally came in another car. Willis said he knew every tank and waterhole from Salt River to the San Juan. They sang cowboy ballads and yodeled. They went back to Holbrook after supper.

JUNE 14, TUESDAY

Every morning we bring in the calves and pen them up till night after they are fed. Every night we bring in the cows and pen them up until the morning's milking has been done. One calf, only a few days old, can't suck. He has no roof to his mouth. First we tried to feed him with a spoon. He couldn't drink, the milk went out his nostrils. Now we siphon from a quart bottle.

Yesterday Tom started to dig a cellar. Today we went at it in real earnest and dug a hole six feet deep, ten long, and eight wide. It was finished by noon. I dug the most. Hot Cakes dug only a few shovels full. He decided to move on. My white horse came to water by himself. Harold roped him and loped after the others. The old plug showed some speed. Harold chased them all over the pasture. Washed clothes again.

After dinner we hitched on the trailer and drove over to the sawmill beyond Turley's. The mill has not been running and most of the lumber is several years old, warped and full of knots. At the first steep hill we had to get out and push. When we came back, Harold had pulled out. We all felt sorry for him. He has no place to go except to Pearce's, and he hasn't so much as a change of clothes. Tom and Olive went to water the garden. Hot Cakes has an inferiority complex, I think, and he talks big in order to hide it. No one knows what kind of parents he had, or what he did before he came to Arizona. Bill and I ate dozens of crackers with apricots.

JUNE 15, WEDNESDAY

Bill and I drove over to Fred Bacchus' and I mailed a letter and some films. Then we went to Prince's for nails. We built a roof for the cellar and started digging the entrance way. This was hard work. We dragged out the dirt in a wagon and threw it on the roof. At noon we had a long rest and plenty of laughter. Fred Bacchus and his tribe came over to see what we were doing. Dorothy ran in the house as soon as she saw little Fred Bacchus, changed her dress and powdered her face until she looked as if she had fallen into the flour barrel.

In the evening we dehorned and castrated ten calves. Bill sat on their sides and held the front leg back while I pulled one hind leg out straight and set my foot in the crook of the other. Tom performed the surgery and poured sheep dip on the cuts. We saved the marbles and had them for breakfast. I put one of the bags on my saddle horn. Olive made some unsuccessful doughnuts and some cookies. She makes very good cake.

June 16, Thursday

We went to the sawmill for more lumber and got a heavy load. Harry Turley had an old horse he would sell for six dollars, but I didn't think I wanted him. He is as skinny as a rail, and twelve years old. He is tenderfooted and his back is scarred by a pack saddle. He hasn't finished shedding yet. He was used for driving horses to the reservation last fall, and as soon as he got back, the snows set in. He wintered out, but fared very badly. I wanted to see what Pennington could offer, but Tom thot this horse good enough for me.

Harry got me in a corner and began to extol the horse. He said that he paid $40 for him two years ago, that he'd never part with him if he weren't going away. That when he was fat I could sell him to a cow camp for 75 dollars or trade him for two young ones because he was so gentle and well reined and good for wrangling horses. I thought that was a bit thick, but I finally bought him.

Little Ross Hunt had come with us. He said he wouldn't give two hoots for the powder to blow my horse to hell. I rode him a mile or two, then Tom caught up and we tied him behind the trailer. He led perfectly. After several miles he went on the wrong side of a cedar, and the cotton rope parted. Then Ross, who had been itching to ride him all the time, climbed on and loped him several miles. He didn't even blow or work up a sweat. I don't see how Ross could ride him without losing all the hide on his posterior. I couldn't. We made the fifteen mile trip in about two hours. Ross changed his mind completely about my horse.

I put my old saddle on him. It is very stiff and the leather is folded. My horse has only one brand, 7V. He is a bay with black legs and a short black mane with a white spot the size of a dollar on his forehead. I rode out after the horses. They were very hard to drive. They all went in separate directions and would not budge until I was on their tails. I can see my white for a long distance. He has a circle dot brand on his cheek. All his brands are on the left side, but the 7V is on the right

44

side. I showed my horse to water, then rode Ginger after the cows. We milked by moonlight. After supper we discussed the rodeo at Holbrook, next week. We started work on the stairway to the cellar.

JUNE 17, FRIDAY

We caught old Felix, a two year old steer, put a surcingle on him and Bill tried to ride him. He was dumped right away. I got three pictures of him being spilled. Then it was my turn and I got a fearful jolt on my spine. I got on him again and went overboard under his hoofs and skinned my elbows. Bill got dumped once more, then we turned Felix loose. Tom drove off to Holbrook.

We sat and lazed but finally began digging just before Tom returned with Willis.

The children rode the burros.

JUNE 18, SATURDAY

We built a shack today. I sawed almost all the lumber, because Billy couldn't saw straight.

Willis said he and three or four other men were going up country as far as Ogden looking for good cow country to lease, and asked if I wanted to go. It will be a 45 day trip, and each man will have two pack and two saddle horses. Willis won't be sure about it until he sees the men at the rodeo next week.

We saw the dust of the herd being driven to Bushman's tank. Milking, with the children shouting "saugh" and "back a leg." The little calf does not struggle now when we feed him but he is very weak. I fed the porker. He saw me with the slop bucket and ran along at my heels to the trough.

JUNE 19, SUNDAY

A couple of the Hazelwoods came in and were followed by Oscar Reed and some others. Willis started to shoe my horses but only got one shoe on the bay before the herd came. It consisted of about sixty yearlings Tom is buying from Hazelwood. We corralled them and waited for the inspector, then we made a hot fire for the branding irons, drove half a dozen cows into the narrow end of the chute, put in a bar to hold them there, and began branding. Bill and I tended the irons while Willis and Tom put the rocking chair brand on them. It was hot work, but we were done by noon. Among others, Hot Cakes rode up in the afternoon, prepared to stay awhile.

Then we rode out to inspect brands on the rest of the herd of two hundred which Marshal Flake is buying. There were several brands.

Willis had driven to town, but Oscar said he would shoe my horses for me, so I wrangled my pair. They stay together like old friends now. Oscar is a small man, all muscle, with a turned up red rose. I like him the best of the bunch. Both horses were hard to shoe. We tied both hind legs to a rope around a post. Whitie was accustomed to this method, but not bay. The table was crowded. I had lunch with the chuck wagon.

JUNE 20, MONDAY

We corralled and helped brand two hundred cows for Marshal Flake. I roped five calves, one of them was too big for me to pull. Then I roped a few steers, finding them hard to turn loose.

In the afternoon we went out to find a bull. I rode Brownie, the biggest horse Tom owns. Hot Cakes tried to make him buck, but he wouldn't. Harold rode a black mare that was only partly broken. She bucked a little and wouldn't go or turn according to his desires. I saw the carcass of Old Blaze, mother of almost all of Tom's horses. Then the black mare knocked Harold off going under a tree. He lost his temper and jerked her head back and forth and hit her with a stick. He is surely contrary. He couldn't manage her so I tried to lead her, but Brownie kicked and the lead rope cut my leg. Harold wanted me to ride her while he led, but finally he made her go. Bill had a dogie in front of his saddle. Brownie stumbled once. He nearly jolts me off when he trots. I have to hold the horn. I am a head taller than the others when I ride him. Tom made a few sarcastic remarks to Harold in his lazy Texan drawl. The pond was all dried up. Old Nig had gotten loose and lain in the mudhole with his saddle. The saddle blanket weighed more than the saddle when it was wet and muddy.

Sunday I wrangled horses afoot and had to walk to the farthest corner of the section pasture near the road before I found them. They stampeded as far as the gate, then split into two groups. I tried to drive both at once, but one group, headed by Nig, bolted off and I had to go all the way back to the other end of the pasture. They bolted again but I headed them off and then Bill helped. The bay colt with the chain on his leg bolted into the trap and went thru a barb wire fence cutting his leg and breast badly.

Jim and Orville Hazelwood and Oscar stayed overnight. Hot Cakes got to talking about himself as usual, and Jim became sarcastic. Hot Cakes certainly talks too much. Whatever is discussed, he decides he is an authority on the subject. He is more to be pitied that ridiculed.

JUNE 21, TUESDAY

Oscar woke me early. Chopped wood, carried water and shaved. Oscar made the biscuits—much better than Olive's. Roy, the chuck wagon driver, came in with his silent young wife. Jim and Oscar rode off for Pleasant Valley. Jim had a gaudy black and orange shirt. Hot Cakes pulled out on his sorrel.

We loaded two of Tom's bulls on Orville's truck, then piled 2500 pounds of salt, some chuck and bedrolls in back of them. Banana pie for dinner.

I read a while, then we went to the garden, and Bill and I hoisted water from the well hole to some tanks to be emptied in the cistern. We sloshed about and had a good time. A shepherd drove up five burros to water and filled his casks. I tried to talk Basque with him. Tom told me that Joy's got three burros for Pacer and gave me only the two. That explains why they didn't want me to go with them to Bentley's. They probably kept the best burro.

Tom gave me a good haircut. I hurt Dorothy's finger, and amused the children.

JUNE 22, WEDNESDAY

Wash day. We brot another load of water. Tom went to Holbrook. It was a very large wash. I was almost exhausted from carrying clothes to and from the line. Bill and I rode out to the Morris section, driving two bulls. He rode Ginger and I rode Star. The bulls made deep rumbling bellows and lowered their heads and pawed dirt when they saw another bull. We raced over to the post office. The sky was completely overcast. Star simply could not keep up with old Ginger, but we went like the wind nevertheless. Ginger is a fine old horse—about sixteen. He pranced and held his head like the noblest battle charger there ever was. We talked politics and other silly things. I haven't met anyone to talk to since Bill and Clark. Yesterday I wrote them a good long letter, with any irrepressible superiority complex showing thru. Ciark says I antagonize everyone and whoever learns to know me finally becomes disgusted.

There may be some truth in that. I don't try to please people I don't respect. I wrote Cornel a good letter too. I liked one sentence. "Not that I think you have outgrown your tendency to bicker repetitiously with Laurence over questions not worth breaking silence to discuss."

Tom brought my mail and a box of rivets. There was a package full of books, but they were all family books, not books I had requested. A seamless sack and some socks. Also a letter from father. [3 lines erased]

JUNE 23, THURSDAY

Kicked off all the covers. Cloudy sky. We went to the sawmill for another load of lumber. We had to reload a few times. Didn't get back till noon. Old Carusoe, Tom's mule, was at the gate when we came to it and we let him thru. He galloped along beside us toward water.

Bill and Tom made a floor for the shack while I got my outfit together. I drove my horses in the corral. The bay came right to my rope, but Whitie ran out in the trap. I fixed my mule pack saddle that had been on Peggy so that it would fit my bay. It was almost dark before I finished. I transposed the breaching and the breast strap, riveted buckles on to straps and riveted four straps to the breaching and two to the breast strap. It was more work than it sounds like. I had only an ax and my hatchet to work with. Tom did not take any interest in my work. He never seems interested in anyone.

I will be glad when I am alone again. It is too much work for me to get along with other people. Yesterday I lay on the bed looking at the ceiling papered with ragged yellow newspapers. Trees and skies don't give the same futile feeling. Labor wouldn't cure me of my troubles—it would only exaggerate them.

This morning as we drove, I imagined I bought a big black sombrero, a gray shirt, and a black and yellow neckerchief, and rode in the parade with my packhorse, and won the prize, of course.

I arranged most of my belongings. There were six mice in one kyak and I killed three with my big spoon. Tom told me what a bear Willis was. Willis is now on parole for cheating a boy in Holbrook.

JUNE 24, FRIDAY

At dawn I packed my kyak. Breakfast was long in preparation. I shook a jar of cream for a quarter of an hour before it turned to butter. We had hot cakes for a send off. I wrangled the horses, packed and saddled mine, but then Tom decided to shoe Robin and took half an hour to do it. He finished flooring the shack so it was later than ten when we started. My horses were glad to go. We trotted gaily northward for the first few miles. At noon we tied our horses to the only tree in sight and lunched. The saddle blankets had slipped and one kyak rope had cut Bay's back. In the afternoon Bill kept leaving me behind and Whitie would not hasten. The bay kept going beside me and scraping my trousers with the kyaks. Tom came by and told Bill to hurry so he soon left me behind as he was riding Old Nig, an immense fat horse, and leading Robin.

I sang and whistled but before long I began to tire. It was fearfully hot and my white horse settled to a slow walk. Then clouds covered the sun, making red and purple shadows on the orange buttes. North was a long range of serrated ridge. The saddle became very hard and I hardly had the vitality to kick Whitie in the ribs. I stopped a few times to see if anything was wrong with Whitie. He has not been used for a year and I believe he is soft. I felt completely enervated and almost went to sleep in the saddle from sheer exhaustion.

Bill drove by on his way back. I reached town after sunset. Crossed the bridge over the Little Colorado and clacked thru town, past the hotel and pool hall and around the block without seeing Tom. I found him in the barber shop being shaved. He told me to see the Crosby's and I located the house. Young Virgil and his brother in law, Orville, were the only ones home. They were just riding in from a vain search for their two white jerseys.

Virgil fried an egg, fixed us a glass of milk and some bread. I helped pull his boots off. It was some task. They had not been worn for a long time. The rest of the family were at Bible reading class.

I unpacked at the barn. They let the fence down and I hobbled the horses in the pastures near the rodeo grounds.

JUNE 25, SATURDAY

I was up too early. Breakfast was very slow in preparation. [3 lines erased]

I cashed my ten dollar money order and bought a 12½ black Stetson for 9 dollars at a store that was closing out. Also a gray shirt and a black silk neckerchief. The streets were thronged with cowboys wearing gaudy shirts. Navajos came in by wagon loads. I noticed that many of their saddles were McClellands like the one I gave Tom. The squaws waddled up and down with papooses in their arms. I saw Billy, and Arlow & Dellmer Hunt. We sat in Tom's car and watched the passersby. One old fellow in a leather hat told Dellmer and Arlow of his hard luck and asked for a dime because he was hungry. He could hardly stand. They turned him coldly down. Men and boys and girls on horses and burros displayed themselves. The whole town was like a bunch of manikins, showing off. Those with ordinary clothes tried to show by their demeanor that they were of a superior sort. After the parade I bought some dried fruit, etc., and walked out to the rodeo grounds. I sat on a roof on the outside edge of the fence. I was joined by a boy from Winslow and we became pretty good friends. We watched calf roping, bull-dogging, steer-riding, wild cow milking, pony racing, and bronc riding. No one was thrown off a bronc, but no one stayed on a steer or a wild horse with surcingle. A clown performed tricks with his mules.

When it was over I hurried to the post office. There was a letter from mother with the films from Cherry Creek. Then I went back to see Tom but he was drunk. He was riding old Nig with an old friend riding behind him, each with a bottle in hand. [7 lines indecipherable]. Ed tore Tom's shirt and Tom tore Ed's. Ed tried to pull Tom off his horse and told him to get out. Tom led Nig in drunken circles and swore he would take Ed home. It ended by vows of friendship. Tom said Ed wouldn't be angry no matter what he did. He spoke to me a few times. He was ashamed to go home and face his wife. It was the first time in 18 years that he had been drunk.

A sandstorm blinded us for a while. I went off to Crosbys, got my ropes and nose bag and walked along under the rim looking for my cayuses. I found them with the rodeo horses and rode Whitie back. After watering them I turned them out once more.

I talked with Virgil. He is a pugilist but has appendicitis, and his girl made him promise to stop fighting anyway. He writes poetry of a sort. I showed him my stuff. His family certainly don't approve of what I am doing. They didn't invite me to eat, and won't let me do any chores.

JUNE 26, SUNDAY

Mr. Crosby invited me to Sunday breakfast, of hot cakes, eggs, and cereal without sugar. Barely was I through when he probed into my religious upbringing and beliefs. He easily made as nothing my arguments proving this world to be older than 6,000 years. I told him I didn't believe in Hell, that I had some faith in evolution. We had it back and forth pretty sharply, but he in his ignorance, was able to have faith. He insisted that if parts of the Bible were not literally true, then it must be all false, therefore it was all true. Science was leading me to the devil, he said, and he wished to save me. I had to agree with many of his false beliefs, because it would have been absolutely futile to reason with him. He believed, for instance, in the creation of the world in six days. He invited me to Sunday school. He shaved me, and we drove down. This particular house of the Lord is in the back of a dry cleaning store. I was introduced to Mr. Brown, the pastor, and his wife. Three daughters, the eldest rather pretty. This was the first time in many years that I'd been to Sunday school, but my old training hadn't been in vain. I had no difficulty finding the chapter of Paphnalions, or whatever. I read that beautiful passage in the book of Ruth, "Intreat me not to leave thee, or to return from following after thee, for whither thou goest, I will go, whither thou lodgest, I will lodge." I read the sermon on the mount.

The songs are of the revival sort. Mr. Crosby and Mr. Brown believe the world is about to end any moment; signs of the times coinciding with prophecies in the book of Revelation. There were not many present, not as many as had been in the jail last night. One of Mr. Brown's small daughters made specific prayers for various absent sisters, that they might not go to Hell for being at the rodeo instead of church. We sang songs about judgment day, dining with Jesus, and the Royal Telephone, as Telephone to glory, oh what joy divine. I can feel the current coming down the line. I can talk to Jesus on the royal telephone.

We all had to quote a line. I quoted, "I will lift up mine eyes unto the hills, whence cometh my help." On the whole, it was quite interesting, and Mr. Crosby must have thot I behaved quite well for an unbeliever. Sunday dinner was quite good. Mr. Crosby thot it worldly to attend a rodeo and I think it is a boring affair anyway so I climbed in an easy chair a few hours, then wrote a letter to Sam and posted it. The rodeo was just over. I left my hatchet and sunbonnet with Tom. He was drinking again, but not drunk, and took no notice of me.

At Bible study, we prayed for the little boy of one of the women. He had broken his elbow and she was in hysterics for fear it would be stiff. Also for a lady who had heard the singing and wanted us to pray for her husband who was so drunk she couldn't do anything with him. Mrs.

Brown and the mother of the boy went into hysterics and then rejoiced because he was cured. Mr. Brown explained that he was not a Holy Roller, had never rolled on the floor, but didn't believe in formal churches. He warned us against Christian Science, Universalism and Unitarianism. Then in his sweet, gentle voice he sang the Feast of Belshazzar. Discussed the need of prayer. If they had thrown aside restraint, I believe I'd have rolled on the floor and been momentarily converted too. Before I left, Rev. Brown gave me some tracts and the book of John to carry with me.

JUNE 27, MONDAY

We abandoned the highway for a narrow dirt road, and after a few miles I left it to go to a ranch. There was a pond bordered by tamarisks. The owner was cordial. I put the horses in the pasture and sat on the porch. The heat was intense. An Irish lady related to Gar Wood discoursed volubly on various topics. The Holbrook water tastes like brine, but this is soda water. I read a magazine and sipped lemonade. In midafternoon I rode out on Wendson's black horse to wrangle mine. My hat blew off twice and the mount didn't like strangers but didn't buck. Wendson made me a map and I started for Stiles ranch twelve miles off.

My nags did not trot. We crossed Leroux wash. After a few fences we were in the bad lands. I killed a small rattlesnake. A very pointed peak,[10] like a volcano, came on the horizon, then five buttes[11] were visible. I opened a gate and the whole fence fell over. I had to lift it up to close it. The sun was setting. I whacked old Whitie, and peered into the gloom, looking for a windmill or a house. I traveled until the stars were bright, then came on a hummock, gave my beasts a taste of corn, and made a fire of brushes. The lard was rancid and the potatoes were bad. I couldn't eat them. I chewed jerky, dried apples and peaches, perused my map, and slept.

JUNE 28, TUESDAY

I saw the cattle moving towards a cottonwood and followed them. As I came nearer, I thought I saw hogans under it, but they proved to be houses. I met Stiles riding out. I asked if I could earn a few meals while my horses rested. He wanted to know if I had grub and said he'd

---

10. This would probably have been Mitten Peak, about twenty miles north of Holbrook.
11. The Hennessy Buttes are located about five miles southeast of Mitten Peak.

return shortly. I talked with the boy who runs the engine to pump water for the cattle. We drew different brands on the sand. The house is well furnished. Navajo rugs on the floor, cowhide chair seats, modern accouterments, a handsome daughter, a young fellow with a black Stetson. I read magazines, ate lunch without Stiles invitation, and pondered—nice house, my picturesque surroundings, red & black buttes, but Stiles has an ugly face. He hospitably invited me to leave as soon as it was cool.

I made a sketch which failed miserably, then went after horses. My eyes are wretched. They have been paining me severely. I couldn't recognize my horses until I was upon them. It was late when I left, bound for a spring seven miles up Cottonwood wash. I ate the rest of the almonds bought at Holbrook. The sky darkened. Clouds closed down. I came to the highway and found a road leading off to the spring which is on bare ground in the wash. I had cocoa with the rest of my sugar. In the night some horses came up—their eyes glowed like coals when I flashed at them.

JUNE 29, WEDNESDAY

Just as I was about to cook breakfast, some Navvies drove up a herd of sheep which stepped all over my equipment. After they were all watered they herded them off and I crawled under a thorn bush to read. There were no trees—no escape from the blistering heat. I read till my eyes burned. The bitter water gave me a sore throat. At noon the Indians came back with a herd of horses and mules. After a time, a cloudbank came athwart the sun, and I decided to move to the next spring. Packing was tedious and the sun was low before I was underway. I climbed upon a plateau and urged the nags along. I can't think of good names for them. I was passing between two of Five Buttes when a car of Indians came along. I stopped and asked how to find the spring. At my suggestion the driver good-naturedly agreed to make a mark where I was to leave the road. Cedar trees now appeared on the slopes. As the dusk deepened I came to the marker—a branch thrust through an inverted paper bag with another bag on top. There was a cement trough with water running from a pipe. I disembarked under a pinyon at the edge of a gully. I nearly fell asleep waiting for the rice to cook. I had too large a mess.

JUNE 30, THURSDAY

An old Indian astride a burro, driving two mules and horses, stopped and couldn't talk English but pointed when I asked about horses. He told truly for they were in the direction indicated. The next Indians were not so nice tho. They were three boys on burros driving goats. I went up to the spring before they left.

For hours I lay half dead on the sand under the pinyon, feeling too weak to rise. My eyes burned when I read, and nothing seemed to give joy. Finally I drank a can of milk and summoned enough energy to rise and search for the horses, while a cloud lessened the heat. On the course of the search I wandered considerably, realizing something of the beauty of my surroundings. I cooked early supper—macaroni, onions, and cornmeal. It began to sprinkle and I covered things up and pulled the tarp over my face.

July 1, Friday

It had rained lightly and the sky was black. The old Indian again showed me my horses. I put the bridle I made yesterday on Whitie.

We trundled up the hill, I singing lustily. We passed an Indian encampment and crossed a bridge over a deep arroyo. Then it began to rain. I put on my poncho which covered my whole saddle. Trucks passed. The rain beat down steadily. I made a sketch and photographed a butte. The beauty of the wet desert was overpowering. I was not happy for there was no one with whom I could share it, but I thought how much better than to be in a school room with rain on the windows.

The first day out, I felt like a hero just because I had a Stetson but that feeling has worn off.

I met two men in a mule cart near Indian Wells. At the trading post, I bought sugar, milk, and oats. We circled a butte, magnificently colored with vermilion and black, and came to a spring. I saw two hogans and a corral. They were empty, so I stopped at the larger hogan and turned the horses out to grass. I climbed the hill and looked at the rainbow, the red hills, cedar capped, the distant mesas. I read and cooked and watched the fire.

July 2

Packing took intolerably long. Soon I left the mesas behind and entered a treeless, rolling prairie. An Indian on a Palomino rode beside me for a time. Clouds threw vast cool shadows intermittently. It grew hotter, and I searched for a place to stop, with grass and shade. A hogan was barred stoutly. The road forked three ways. I went the wrong way, traveled till the horses were snailing, then stopped at a locked hogan. I was reading when it began to rain. Frantically I uprooted the wires that held the lock and moved in. I read "Magic Mountain" for a couple of hours about philosophical confusion, and Hans lost in a snowstorm, and the death of Joachim.

Again I set out and a Navajo showed me the way. I helped him drive his sheep to Greasewood Springs[12] and I stopped with a young Indian at a stone house and windmill. The cliffs were glorious at sunset. There are many stone houses here and no white people. I had cornmeal bread made with goat's milk, coffee, and mutton. I slept on goat skins. It was bitterly cold.

July 3, Sunday

After breakfast, we rode over to a hogan. I rode back behind another Indian. The boy had invited me to stay with him all day, but changed his mind. The Indians are very loath to give information and I could learn nothing about the road ahead. It was already hot. I saw roads diverging to right and left but continued up the canyon of the Pueblo Colorado. I saw a huge cottonwood and wanted to stop but there was no grass and the tree was fenced. I went to a hogan to ask for water but the man was away and the squaw ran off. I met an old whiskers driving a mule wagon and offered him a dollar for his saddle blanket but he refused. There was no grass but I saw herds of beautiful horses. There was a strawberry roan with a white face and corn silk mane and tail.

At length I came to a field in which two men were cutting hay with scythes. They said there was water. I went to it and asked if I could put my horses in the hay field if I cut some. I put them in and swung a scythe for an hour or two until noon. It was a pleasure to cut down the tall plants with yellow and purple blossoms and hear the angry buzz of disturbed bumblebees.

I ate broiled mutton and naneskadi and drank coffee. Then I set out to learn some Navajo words. Toheh eh yah—tired. Chynn ya go—I want to eat. Tin nu ul tsuh—look out, woman. Ado beg zduh ut si seh ut t un ha day sha to—Don't be afraid, little girl, I'm going. Eh sheh he ye se kiss—thank you, my friend. Ha ah to—where is water? Nahokush— North. Shi dh ah dayshla—I come from way south. Other Indians came and watched. I asked my friend if he would give me a saddle blanket if

12. Greasewood is a small Navajo community on Pueblo Colorado Wash, which is normally dry.

I worked very hard for him the next day. He said yes. He said he'd be back at ten o'clock. He lived at Greasewood. I stacked hay, then drove the team and stamped it down. At last I finished stacking but less than half the field is cut. I had supper with four Indians and slept on goat skins on the floor.

July 4, Monday

After breakfast the men told me that my Indian was not coming back and that the bay was older than the white. It turned out that he had deceived me concerning the definitions of Navajo words, too. I read Magic mountain, lying between my kyaks with the tarp above. Buck Jones idled nearby awhile. In the afternoon his brother caught two horses and we rode to Sunrise Springs but the traders were gone to Ganado. I rode a buckskin one way and a black the other. Then I put my bed on a sorrel and rode up to the encampment. The men persisted in talking Navajo in my presence. I had several pieces of mutton.

July 5, Tuesday

Breakfast was late. Goat's milk, hot, with naneskadi and coffee. There was a sheep's head but it was cold with burnt skin still on it. The cowboy with black hat and spurs said he was going to Ganado with me. He actually came as far as Cornfields and stopped. There was no trading post here or I'd have bought something to eat. No white people showed themselves. There was a long row of cottonwoods which had seemed half a mile distant but took hours to reach. At first my bay horse felt frisky, trotting up ahead and jigging his pack, but when the Indian's horse dropped out, he lost enthusiasm. We left the valley of the Pueblo Colorado and climbed high up on the mesa south of it. After weary hours, it swung back to Ganado. At Hubbell's post,[13] one of the men were at home. The woman said there was nothing I could do to earn a meal. I ate some mulberries and asked her where to camp. She then gave me a can of peaches and some cookies and charged it to the kitchen. I stopped under a tree and rested. An Indian told me where

---

13. John Lorenzo Hubbell began trading in the Ganado area in the 1870s. He constructed the Hubbell Trading Post building beginning in 1883. His post soon became the most important center of trade on the Navajo Reservation and the center of an empire of secondary trading posts. Hubbell Sr. died in 1930. At the time of Everett's visit in 1932, the post was operated by Lorenzo Hubbell Jr. It was purchased by the National Park Service in 1967 and is now operated as an active/living National Historic Site.

there was a little grass and looked at my equipage. I admired his saddle blanket. He invited me to stay at his place and rest my horses while I hoed corn. He came by in an hour and I moved a mile down river. We hoed until dusk while I told him about myself and he encouraged me. His oldest daughter, Alice, is the most beautiful Navajo girl I have seen. He has a round faced son-in-law. Potatoes for supper. Afterwards I taught him English. He has a dictionary, but seems unwilling to use it. His name is John I. Curly. For twelve years he has been head man at Ganado. He showed me his name where he appeared as a witness in various controversies.

JULY 6, WEDNESDAY

Weary awakening. Breakfast, hoed corn and melons, tutored. Tomorrow John is going to Fort Wingate to attend a council. He has a book written by a girl student at Columbia. Said the author was his friend and he was probably going to show her to Natural Bridge.

Two small pieces of bacon for lunch. I drove the horses to water, went to fill the canteen, and when I came back, John's white horse had gone off. More tutoring, then his son-in-law, Sam Johnson, Alice's husband, came. John is leaving in the morning and Sam wanted me to help him cut hay at his place, seven miles downriver. John took a picture of us—Alice refused to be in it. He rode my bay, carried two blankets behind while I carried the sleeping bag. John had given me an old saddle blanket with a star design. Sam speaks no English.

His home is near Cornfield—two rooms, glass windows, stove, bed, mirror, and other traces of civilization. I have been observing more and more fully that the Navajo owes almost everything he has to the white man. His food is mutton, bread, and coffee. All these were brought by the white man. His clothes are borrowed. All he has left is his language, ceremonies, and a few customs. In spite of all the things he did not have before, he seems a pitiful creature to me. Yet he is always ready to laugh and sing. For supper we had nothing but cold naneskadi and coffee. It seems crazy that Sam should not speak English when everything in his house is English. He can't even read the printing on the boxes.

We hobbled the horses in some alfalfa and cut a little wheat for them. Sam does not offer things to me first. I slept outside on some sheepskins.

July 7, Thursday

Sam got up at dawn. He has some very gummy wood to chop. There is no pleasure in cutting it. We threw some wheat to the horses and each took a hoe. For hours we worked like horses, grubbing weeds in the cornfield. He should use a cultivator, but then, how should he pass the time? He can't read; he knows only how to eat and work and sleep and be idle. I was soon anxious to stop but Sam worked like a machine and I felt obliged to follow suit. At noon, a boy, Lefty Johnson, came and drove my horses to water. They are beautiful seen in the distance—the dazzling white and deep red on a green foreground with vermilion cliffs and cobalt sky beyond.

For lunch we finally had meat—roasted mutton. I ate faster than usual and finally learned to swallow instead of chewing, but even then, I could not eat more than half as fast as they did. Sam childishly showed me various commonplace articles. They talk about me in Navajo and I retaliate by speaking French.

After an all too brief rest, we went to work again and hoed a whole field. I brought the water bucket. When this field was done, I was ready to collapse but we had to cut hay, which I did. All the time I was observing how time passed and l'heure du depart drew near. Sam walked off without a word of explanation (to me), and did not come back. Lefty and I burned several piles of dry sage and came in. He was anxious for me to do all the work. I brought water, cut wood, and cut the meat. One thing I didn't do—that was to throw out Lefty's wash water. I led him by the arm to it, placed his fingers on it, and showed him the door.

At night he wanted to sleep with me, outside. He crawled under and snored irritatingly. Late at night, the sky darkened, wind whistled, and a light shower moistened the air. We moved inside.

July 8, Friday

I managed to waken but fell asleep again while Lefty was preparing breakfast. I had an ugly dream about him. Dizzy with weariness, I sat down to breakfast. I managed to do some work, but once I stopped to water my horses. There is a deep well with a leaky bucket.

Again I did my best to last out till noon and succeeded, but slowed at the end. I read a magazine and ate roast mutton. A Navvy came in, shook hands with me. Then he stood over me, pawing over my diary.

Like the other Navvys who kept trying on my hat, I think less and less of these people.

Sam came back and did repair work on a harrow. Lefty and I went to get a blanket full of hay for the plow horses, and on the way we saw a rattlesnake. I stepped on its head, though I hadn't boots, and cut off its head with my knife and collected the rattles—seven.

We sowed oats. Lefty made a motion like hoeing but I shook my head. I ran the harrow up and down. I was enjoying myself because it was cool, and late in the day, and in the morning I would be going. Another Indian came up and Lefty told about the rattlesnake. They said I would die, and looked at the snake. They ran like little girls when I waved it at them. I pitched hay for my horses and now we are waiting for supper. They always start the fire an hour before they cook. I won't be chopping any more wood, though. It showered lightly. I creased my hat and thought about the future. I don't know if I will go to Mesa Verde, but Ill go to Roundrock and Lukachukai. I want to get two good saddle blankets.

[15 lines, erased]

July 9, Saturday

Sam and Lefty ran off at dawn. A Navvy woke me and I helped him carry barb wire. Breakfast was very late. I saddled Whitie and tied the blankets behind. It was noon when I reached Curley's. He was gone with Gertrude Reichard who wrote the book of Navajo genealogy and customs. I finished Magic Mountain and mailed it off. Alice was grinding a flat stone and putting the gray powder in a bowl. The children burned cedar boughs and saved the ashes. Alice would not tell me what it was for, but later I learned that the ashes are used for baking powder.

I read the report of the Indian Survey, in which John Curley, Lee Bradley, Tom Pavata, Dr. Koentz, Dr. Rieke, and others I'd known testified. None of the Indians spoke intelligently. My eyes burned. I played with Harriet and Margaret. I ate supper of beans and bread alone. Some rain.

July 10, Sunday

I struck across country toward the road, but became embroiled in a series of fences and deep gullies which I finally got thru. I sang:
"Hahryroohyah, boom agay,

Hahryroohyah, hoosangow,
Hahryroohyah, to tave ut fruh tin."

It is the Hawaiian version of the song "Hallelujah, born again, give us a hand-out to save us from sin." I found it in a book of Frederick O'Brien's, rummaging in Edward Weston's home in Carmel.

Then I sang Hot Cake's favorite, "Strawberry Roan." Cornel's favorite, "Rolling to Rio."

I stopped for a drink at Lizard Springs. I had only a quart of water, as some Indian had broken the pump plunger at Ganado, and there was supposed to be a windmill on the road five miles north. I climbed down from the plateau through some badlands. The windmill was two or three miles off the road though it looked close. I kept ahead on the tree-less prairie. As I approached the further rim, I rode up to a lone tree, under which a dozen horses and mules were standing. I took a picture and they moved off as I moved under.

There was a hawk's nest in the tree top. I cooked some sweetbread and read the letters of Mendelsohn, Wagner, Liszt, and W.S. Story and Jules Breton. After it had cooled a little and the horses had grazed awhile, I grained them and went onward. The road followed the rim of Beautiful Valley. If I had known I'd have gone down in the valley. I kept on the road steadily. My water was quite gone. I had been misinformed about the distance to Behikutso Lake. I met a car and the occupants told me that it was five more miles to the lake. They had no water. Before long I left the road and "followed the gleam." There were gullies and ridges to cross. Finally I came to a dry lake. The alkali glittered like water. Close by was the lake. I looked prayerfully across the wide water while the horses drank. I was in another land. I could hear some horses on the other side splashing as I drank. I waded in and filled two can-teens, then led my horses toward the road. Grass and water are never found together in the sheep country. I saw a small snake wiggle away. The moon rose. I stopped on a grassy knoll. There was no firewood, only a few dry weeds. Fortunately I found the remains of a summer hogan and used them for firewood. Just as I was ready to eat, it began to rain. I covered camp in a hurry and when I was half through eating, the storm passed over. Thunder still muttered and the sounds of an African jungle accompanied it. Some bulls roared just like lions and a band of goats, frightened by the lightning, sounded like hyenas, in the distance. It was decidedly weird.

July 11, Monday

We struck off at a trot for the long line of toothpicks that were telephone poles on the rim of Beautiful Valley. From a high ridge I could see the grove of cottonwoods that was Chin Lee.[14] Elated by its nearness, I pushed impatiently onwards. I came to the windmill where I turned south for Polacca last year. Then I came around a hill and there was Chin Lee, its schools, houses and churches. I had a fifty cent lunch at the clubhouse, then met Mrs. Carruth who got my mail. There were good letters from Waldo, father, mother, and the grandparents. Bill wrote a very unsatisfying note. He said Clark left Wilson's and punched cattle—probably at Reevi's & had just come home & was irritated because I had not sold him the bronc for ten dollars. Waldo's letter was written June 14, sent to Flagstaff. There was 5 dollars and films. The camera was not fast enough for the bronc pictures. There were some good shots, however. I was grateful for Waldo's letter. He is a pretty good brother after all. Father sent a box of books. Waldo has had no money except for gas and an occasional haircut, but he was not bitter. He said he was sorry that Clark hadn't the guts.

Then with considerable trepidation I rode toward Dunaway's. Mrs. Dunaway had had nerves last year, and a few things I did set them on edge. I had promised Dick to send a painting, but I only sent Christmas cards. I was not sure I would be welcome.

I was delightfully surprised. Mrs. Dunaway was very hospitable. Jean is plump and healthy now, and Sport, the fox terrier pup that played with Curly, is full grown now. Mrs. Dunaway started talking right away, telling me about the Navajo primer she is writing & her visits to California.

Then Mrs. Wetherill[15] came in, with Grace Gilmore,[16] an authoress (Windsinger), and a nurse from Kayenta. Mrs. Wetherill is looking for Indians without accents to act in the picture of "Laughing Boy" they are making. She remembered me. Miss Gilmore was interesting. We had supper of rabbit meat, etc., then they drove to Ganado.

---

14. Shown as Chinle on present-day maps. It lies on Chinle Wash at the foot of Canyon de Chelly.

15. Louisa Wade Wetherill could speak Navajo and was a special friend to the Navajo people. Her husband, John, was a member of the Wetherill family who discovered the major cliff dwellings of Mesa Verde. John then moved into the Navajo country as a trader, first at Oljeto, then at Kayenta. In 1909, he was the first non-Indian to walk under Rainbow Bridge.

16. Frances Gillmor and Louisa Wade Wetherill coauthored the book *Trader to the Navajos: The Story of the Wetherills of Kayenta* (1934).

Later Dick, the windmill caretaker, came in and later, Mrs. Garcia, the trader. We had a good discussion about the Indians, banks, etc. Mrs. Dunaway told me her story of her divorce & remarriage, the problem of Jean, who is Catholic & intolerant of other religions. She was glad to get back from California, says she never intends to leave the reservation again. She thinks we are near the end of the world.

I slept in the tent.

July 12, Tuesday

After breakfast I went out to wrangle horses. I tracked them over the hill to a wash, then their tracks seemed to disappear completely, and I wandered for an hour before I found them again. The horses were a couple of miles out, starting down the road for home. I rode in. Whitie fought the bit, but I put it on him. There is no grass within a mile or so.

I ate doughnuts and wrote a 3500 word letter to Waldo, giving him plenty to consider. Mrs. Dunaway told me of the beauties of Lukachukai with lakes and pine forests and of the White House canyon nearby. I listened to local talk, then read a book about the Navajo country & a boy who started in New Mexico, had money, good horses and equipment but was the grossest sort of tenderfoot, stayed on the highways for several months, met a friend in Santa Fe, then together they went up the Frijoles to Mesa Verde and to the reservation. They were here several years ago when things were much wilder. There was hardly any trail to Rainbow Bridge—they picked their way very adventurously. They were always changing horses—trading one and paying 8 to 15 dollars to boot. They got to see the Indian dances and sand paintings, met all kinds of interesting people. Then I looked at pictures in Geographics, and read Cowboy songs. Couldn't find Strawberry Roan but learned Home on the Range.

God, how the wild calls to me. There can be no other life for me but that of the lone wilderness wanderer. I think I'll extend my leave another year. I'd get a couple of good horses and a good saddle. The wild has an irresistible fascination for me. After all, the lone trail is the best.[17]

---

17. The unknown typist (probably Stella Ruess), who originally copied the journals, rewrote this to read: "God, how the wild calls to me. There can be no other life for me but that of the lone wilderness wanderer. It has an irresistable fascination. The lone trail is the best for me." More lyrical perhaps, but not accurate.

July 13, Wednesday

[Most of the first page, 21 lines, has been erased]

I packed Whity and went over the hill to Canyon de Chelly[18] to their homeland. [3 lines missing] The wind whipped up the sand in smothering gusts. We made slow progress but I was drinking in the glory of the cleanly chiseled canyon walls. Contrary to my expectations, I found water flowing just a few miles above the mouth. I came thru a grassy meadow to three majestic cottonwoods in the center of the canyon and there I stopped. We had not come far but I liked the place. I had halted here last May with Pegasus, only then there was a fourth tree of which only a black stump remains. In a cleft in the canyons wall was an interesting cluster of ruins, and I remembered the interesting designs on the wall.

I put the horses in the meadow and visited the dwellings. There is a large kiva with the front wall fallen and several rooms contiguous to it. Further off are crumbled walls and bases. I copied the most interesting designs. Some are so high up that a ladder must have been used and the painter was in danger of falling over backwards.

I read some Arabian Nights Tales and ate peanuts.

A Navajo dug a waterhole for me and filled my canteen.

July 14, Thursday

The sun flooded the canyon with light and the trees threw long cool shadows on the clean sand. When all was in readiness for departure I climbed up to the dwelling and made a photograph. The sun disappeared.

Around the next bend was Canyon del Muerto, but I continued to follow the course of el Rio de Chelly. Three times the rope got under his tail and twice I had to let Whity loose. He cut up and would not let me approach until I dismounted. Whity pulled back so that I tied his rope to the saddle horn.

Soon I passed the White House ruin. There were not many Indians

---

18. Canyon de Chelly, declared a National Monument in 1931, is the most colorful and dramatic feature of the Navajo nation. In earlier days it was considered the "Gibraltar of Navajo land" because of its impregnable character. In 1863–64, Kit Carson and his U.S. Army soldiers marched through the canyon, destroying crops and rounding up 7,000 Navajos, who were then sent on the "Long Walk" to Bosque Redondo in eastern New Mexico. The Navajo Treaty of 1868 allowed the Navajos to return to their homeland.

and only a few sheep. I stopped under some cottonwoods below the rock window and made naneskadi while the horses munched rushes. An Indian boy and girl, evidently courting, stopped under the trees.

It seemed about to rain when I started again. I rode Whity. I came to the fork of Monument Canyon and Upper Canyon de Chelly, recognizing the spot where Pegasus had stuck in the quicksand. I saw my old campsite and remembered how I raised my cocoa to my lips and drank to the long, long dead whose bones are there above me, (in the dwellings). I remembered how I fondled Curly, then a small puppy, and sang to the moon and the rising night wind.

I had intended to explore Monument Canyon, but at the last moment I swerved and went around the tall monument up Canyon de Chelly.[19] I soon passed into unknown territory. There were beautiful groves of cottonwoods. Great cliffs stood out detached from the canyon walls. I drank at a dripping spring. The sky was black and a fine rain was falling. I was searching for a deserted hogan in a grove of cottonwoods. I found one, but it was ragged at the edges and there was no grass near it. I passed an Indian family and a herd of goats. The canyon narrowed. There was another family in a dense grove of cottonwoods, under a cliff dwelling which looked inaccessible. Soon the stream was bordered by pines, junipers, willows, and aspens.

I saw a collapsed sweat house. After the next turn I perceived that there would be no more settlements. It was drizzling and I decided to go back to the old deserted hogan. I had to drag Bay. It was raining when I reached it. An educated Navajo rode by as I unpacked, asking the usual questions. The hogan is not in bad shape. Daylight shows at the edges and I can't stand up except in the middle, but it is quite wide.

I hobbled the horses and the rain stopped. I set the rice to boiling and finished reading Sinbad the Sailor.

JULY 15, FRIDAY

It did not rain in the night. I brought back the horses and fixed rice cakes. I'm surely enjoying the books Father sent. There a dozen or more, all small. I read Rip Van Winkle, The Legend of Sleepy Hollow, The Phantom Bridegroom, The Third Royal Mendicant, The Fifty Best Poems of America, and Shaw's Socialism for Millionaires. Thus I passed the time, reading and munching, until afternoon. I sauntered out around

---

19. This would have been Spider Rock, an isolated monolith standing apart from the cliff walls.

the hill and saw a few crumbled rooms under the cliff edge. While I was examining them, it began to rain. I was dry there and waited till the showers passed. Then I wandered further up the side canyon, hoping to find some untouched ruins. Up the talus slope I clambered. It rained hard and I crouched under a rock, looking up at the silver sheets of water between me and the sun. Again I climbed, not expecting to find anything, but I finally saw two or three small ruins. With difficulty I climbed on a ledge and followed it till it shelved off and I was below the lower dwelling. For a long time I looked at the dwelling and shuddered. Once I made as if to climb up, but the rock crumbled. There was absolutely nothing to brace myself on. The cliff fell sheer away below. I might have climbed up the narrow crack of soft sandstone, but I knew I would be terrified at descending, with no place to put my foot and the rock crumbling in my hands. Fifty feet above it was a ledge with more dwellings, but there was no way to reach them from above or below. Doubtless the cliff has fallen away since they were built several centuries ago.

I continued along the top of the slope, just at the base of the cliff until I reached another dwelling. There were no walls standing. I scratched the ground but found only pottery and ashes. When I was at the head of the canyon I saw there were no more ruins and I began the tortuous descent. When I was half down I crossed to a notch on the other side and came down the next canyon. It seemed I would never reach level earth again. My legs were shaky. After a moment's rest on my bed in the hogan, I got to my feet again, for I could not rest without knowing where my horses were. I followed tracks until I found Whity a league downstream. I was startled to find him alone. It rained violently. I found Bay on the hill where he was this morning. There were cactus thorns in his mouth. The grass usually grows with cactus here.

I dried my clothes by the fire and boiled macaroni with a can of corn.

July 16, Saturday

For some reason the corn for supper and breakfast made me sick. I read thru The Looking Glass, The Story of Aristotle's Philosophy, and Emersons Essays. Also I read all my letters, burned some and tried to apply philosophy to myself. I couldn't seem to do it. In the afternoon I brot in the horses and saddling Whity, rode out in search of adventure

and a sketch. Bay was hobbled, but terrified at being left behind, he galloped precipitately after. Then it began to rain again as I went back and
read Emersons Essay on Self Reliance. He like many others I have read
is horrified at the atheist, or rather, he pities him. Personally I seem to
be an agnosticist. I don't see how an intelligent person can believe anything, even determinism. By nature I am steady and sincere. I can't
believe in a God just because other people do, and because they consider me good or wicked according as I believe or not. Prayer is foreign
to my nature. I could not seriously attend church and worship.

I saddled Bay, knowing perfectly well that Whity would not follow,
and wandered up stream till I came to an interesting view of red pinnacles and cottonwoods. I had just painted in the stormy sky and one red
shaft when the rain spattered down. When it slowed I finished the picture. It has some spontaneity, vivid color, and interesting form, but it is
rather careless and the colors are not right. It is spotted with raindrops.
I made it in a 12 by 18. I prefer the large sheets. Then I went farther up
and entered an interesting tributary canyon. There was a clear stream
with cat tails and rushes, towering pines, and steep sides. When it
became too rough for Bay, I tied him to a log in grass and wandered up,
but saw no dwellings. The sky darkened and vivid flares of white lightning flashed out while the canyon resounded with the echoing crash of
thunder. I urged my old cayuse, permitting him no nibbling as he went.
We were out of the rocks and on the level when the storm burst. Loud
peals of thunder reverberated on all sides. I passed the sheep and three
boy herders, their wet burros standing stolidly. With a grinding, grating
sound, a mass of rock slid down the cliffside. It was a luxury to cross
the flood swelled river without wetting my feet. For a short distance we
galloped grandly. I am far from becoming a centaur, however. I always
feel a thrill of delight when my horse trots up a hill. It is exquisite to feel
his shoulder muscles rippling under me, to press my knees into his side,
and feel myself lunging upwards without exertion.

July 17, Sunday

I slept very late, lolling at my ease. Then I read a few books, and
after lunch, I walked after the horses. I explored some cliff dwellings,
found my animals, and rode back.

The Indians have been very good, not molesting nor intruding in
the slightest. I took a picture of the two boys on the burros. Harry Price,

the father, came to chat. He speaks good English. One of his sons, who rides the burro, is crippled. Last year his horse fell on him in the water at the White House. Harry has a cornfield and orchard there. I showed him my pictures and told him of my travels, then he taught me some Navajo.

July 18, Monday

Again I slept late, finally visiting Harry. He showed me a cliff dwelling, "assaze bekin," where I would find arrowheads. It began to rain as I approached but I was soon under shelter of the cliff. I copied a curious design on the wall. The pictographs were very high up. The aboriginal artists must have been precariously perched when they made them. Navajos had used the dwelling for a sheep pen. I turned over a stone, poked the dirt, and found an arrowhead. It was white, complete, but not symmetrical. I scraped away the topsoil in a kiva and found a piece of sandal, much corn and rope, a headband woven of soapweed, and coated with pinyon pitch and some pumpkin crusts. The dust made me feel faint. An excavator needs a mask. I've no doubt much could be found with a shovel, but I did not persist. I went down and up the slope, coming up whenever it rained. I found four more arrowheads, one a good specimen. Then Harry came up and we chatted a while. I went down and bought a hind quarter of mutton from him for half a dollar.

All afternoon I sat in my hogan reading poetry and Emerson's Essays & Ibsen's "Ghosts." I felt futile. It seems after all that a solitary life is not good. I wish I could experience a great love. I find that I cannot consider working on in art. To be a great artist one must work incessantly, and I have not the vitality. Neither would any kind of daily labor seem tolerable to me. I am not inspired by the Navajos, who herd sheep all day long. More and more I feel that I don't belong in the world. I am losing contact with life. It seems useless to paint, when Nature is here, and I can't paint anyway. I want to be in the city again, but how shall I get there, and how return?

The river is greatly swollen by the rains. I did not go after the horses today. I cooked too much rice and ate too much. The skies are clear again.

I read poetry aloud, with my flashlight, for an hour or so. Somehow this raised my spirits greatly, sonorously chanting melancholy lines of

Poe, Whitman's Death Carol, the Man against the Sky, and Prufrock's love song. It was good to see the stars again.

JULY 19, TUESDAY

When the shadows of the red pinnacles were long and cold, I trotted out after the horses. I made an outline sketch of the shadowed cliffs. Whity would not let me walk up to him at first. Packing was tedious. I had to throw out a quart of rice, I had cooked so much. I gave both horses plenty of oats. Whity fought the bit and broke the bridle strap. I twisted his ear and choked him till I got it on him. No denying he has an ugly nature, not a mild gentle demeanor like Bay. I worked myself into a sweat packing up, then we were off. We had gone only a few turns when my eyes pained me intensely and I could hardly see. I felt drunken. I reeled and swayed in the saddle and felt decidedly out of my usual nature. For some time I could hardly see. I had intended to investigate a turn or two of Monument Canyon, but felt unequal to it and let Whity carry me downriver. A lonely burro brayed vociferously so that the whole canyon resounded. I answered feebly and he came trotting up, then went up Monument Canyon making the walls echo, or so I thot.

I drank at the spring, rode up hill and down gully, splashed thru the stream again and again. Two ravens croaked hoarsely at me. I noticed the various cliff dwellings. The place where the Indian girl in a long brown silk dress had rushed out after the horses. By the time I was near the White House I was fairly sane, but weak. I made two pictures of it. The canyon was almost deserted. At the corner, where Canyon del Muerto joined the main stream, I stopped under a maple tree and put the horses to grass.

I made sickly naneskadi with mutton tallow. As for a week or more in the afternoon, clouds came up. After a few hours rest, I loaded up once more. There was no running water in del Muerto. I soon lost sight of the main canyon. Del Muerto is much narrower and the walls are sheer. Cliff dwellings are in every cranny. I passed the places where Pegasus bogged down in the quicksand last year, and the camp under the maple tree, then the camp that leaned on the cliff. We crossed a meadow of reeds. There was an inviting spot on the opposite bank— young cottonwoods and a peach orchard. It was not dusk and I went by, but finally summoned a little resolve and turned back to it. The horses are fond of the reeds.

The cliff is beautifully sheer here, with horizontal stripes of pink, red, and black. I walked up and down till I found a small pool of clear water. While the sunlight glowed on the cliff tops, I broiled a piece of mutton and cooked some ground wheat mush brought from Heber. A young Navvy rode up singing "Ya ta hai," quoth I. Later an old bemoustached fellow walked up with a proprietary air. He had been watching me write.

July 20, Wednesday

When the first sunbeams glinted in the farther clifftop, I bestirred myself, made a meal of mutton and mush, assembled my possessions, and brought in my steeds. We traveled in cool shadow on the moist sand and entered a sunlit field. The rushes swished against my feet. I lifted up my voice in triumphant rejoicing, making the canyon echo with my song.

We passed a towered dwelling, with antelope and deer painted on the cliff in white, brown, and black. I persuaded a young Navajo to take my picture for a penny, but I think he blundered it. A young man unrolling a barb wire performed the same office with more ability, for the same price.

The walls were grandly sheer. I watched a squaw making yarn for a blanket she was weaving. I passed cornfields and haystacks, goats, horses, and bones of cattle. Everything was invested with a strange beauty to me. We trotted between shadows. At a hogan where I watched a long skirted squaw at the plow, several men were gathered, and one approached me. He was the brother of Philip Draper, the Indian of the last settlement where I was last May. He told me to climb out by the trail as there was quicksand ahead. I don't know why he insisted. As usual, I asked about saddle blankets. An old squaw brought me one, but I disliked the crude, un-Indian design. She was nettled and made jokes about me. Another Indian dressed in stripped cloth showed me some arrowheads, but they were imperfect. An old man said he had a blanket at his hogan, a mile upstream. I told him I would buy it if I liked the design, so he caught his horse and started up. My neckerchief slide slipped off (I was wearing the small black silk scarf), and I was some time finding it. I trotted the horses to overtake the Indian. It was more than a mile to his hogan, situated on a hill in a side canyon. His daughter, Philip's sister, was just adding the tassels to the blanket. It had a uniform design of diamond pattern in black, brown and white. I rather liked it though there was no unique pattern. I offered two dollars, then 2½, but he wanted 3. I told him I had only ½ more to buy grub, but he was adamant. Then I went off and his next door neighbor showed me his blanket which was crudely patterned with garish colors. Harry Price had showed me a blanket too, orange and black checkerboard! I went back to the first blanket, offered three dollars if some meat were included. He had none but I drank some sweet tea, ate tortillas, and learned that my host was Dillahtsi, old yellow mustache. Last year he had passed me and Pegasus on a big black horse with a tail that swept the ground. Little Curly had barked at him and we had laughed.

Mummy Cave was in view from the shade house. I gave Dilatsi the 3 dollars and he gave me a pound of sugar, of which I was destitute before. He asked me where my wife was, how many children I had. I asked the young fellow, our interpreter, to take a picture of us all. The woman refused, but at the last moment stepped into the picture. I put the blanket on my saddle for a cushion and rode joyfully away. I think the blanket was well worth the price, tho a trader might get it for less. I certainly wouldn't try to make one for that price.

I watched two crows chasing a screaming hawk. Opposite Mummy Cave, at my old campsite, I stopped. There was no grass. The dwellings did not please me much this time. The horses were exhausted but I rode further. Whity drank at almost every crossing. Two men driving a pack burro passed me. I passed two families, then I came to the last camp, which was deserted. I stopped at the old hogan. The stone seat I had made against a pillar was unchanged. The walls were washed thin. I wandered up and down but the sheep had eaten all the grass. I led the horses on the high bank opposite. Five sleek burros were there. I arranged the interior of the hogan to suit myself, spread out my new blanket with possessive joy, read and cooked. An Indian passed by, returning from Schili.

After the rice, the cocoa, and the poetry, there were the long, long thoughts. In the dark I bruised my toe very severely so that I could not sleep. Some rodent gnawed holes in my rice sack.

July 21, Thursday

I had wanted to sketch the shadows but lay late. As I was frying rice cakes, an old Indian woman and her pretty granddaughter came up with the sheep. She talked very earnestly in Navajo. Bay had come down without hobbles & lain on the sand. I walked quietly up to him, stroked him gently, and put new hobbles on him. I gave some fried apples to "est sa." The baby girl played with her lovingly. The old woman taunted me for using the summer hogan for firewood. Then I was in peace. Finished "A Dream of John Ball," and stopped with a chapter of "Romeo and Juliet." Lunch and long thoughts. I think I have seen too much and known too much—so much that it has put me in a dream from which I cannot waken and be like other people. I love beauty but have no longer the desire to recreate it. Ambition is distasteful to me. The Bartons almost gave me confidence in myself, but familiarity washed it away. Too bad I didn't give them Curly. Everyone disapproved of my going off by myself. Actually, I am nearly satisfied with solitude, but I refuse to give up the independence I am used to.

Physically I feel weak. I would not be surprised to hear that pernicious anemia had hit again. A slight bruise has taken three weeks to heal. My injured toe will pain me for weeks to come. Diet more trouble.[20]

[5 lines erased]

I thot of Robinson's lines,

> Who goes too far to find his grave,
> Mostly alone he goes.

In the evening I shook off my melancholy, gathered flowers under the red cliffs and chanted poetry in the hogan. I wanted to write, but the words would not come. Now and then a donkey would bray, or some sand would trickle through the roof. I kept gloating over my blanket.

I decided to call Whity, Nuflo after the mischievous old guardian of Rima in "Green Mansions." Bay I named Jonathan because he is so sweet tempered, meek and gentle.

JULY 22, FRIDAY

I fed the horses plenty of oats, then started up the side canyon under the high-perched cliff dwelling where I found the necklace last year. Then I found the up trail, steep and rough, and started, as I thought, to leave Canyon del Muerto. It was so steep that I led Nuflo, and Jonathan had to be urged. Finally he fell or lay down at a rough spot about half way up. I thwacked hiim but he would not rise, so I unpacked him there. The milk had spilled out, everything was topsy turvy. When I pulled out the pack saddle, Jon slid off the trail, turned

---

20. For comment on Everett's pernicious anemia, see the editor's introduction.

over three times on the downslope and tottered to his feet. I led him up, put Nuflo's saddle on him, packed Nuflo, and slowly descended. I did not mount Jonathan, but tied Nuflo's lead rope to the saddle horn, and we went on at a good clip. After we had gone a mile past the hogan, upstream, he began to pull back. I halted several times to see if anything was wrong. In a couple more slow miles we came to my last campsite and stopped under a cottonwood. I unloaded and led the horses on the bank where the grass was very sparse. I didn't hobble Jonathan. He went around in circles and didn't eat. I washed a cut on his leg and he stood still for awhile, then staggered sidewise and fell into a clump of cactus. He got groggily to his feet, tottered again and collapsed. Then I prepared myself for the worst and began looking at my map to see how near a railroad was. In a little while, I looked at Jonathan again, and he was dead—eyes glassy green, teeth showing, flies in his mouth.

So for me, Canyon del Muerto is indeed the canyon of death—the end of the trail for gentle old Jonathan.

I've decided to cache my saddle in a cliff dwelling—perhaps the one where I left the baby board last year. Now I am on foot once more and old Nuflo is my beast of burden. Black clouds are above—dirty weather ahead.

I saddled Nuflo and galloped for the last time in my saddle. I led him half way up the steep slope, then shouldered the saddle and climbed. I was utterly exhausted and dripping with sweat when I reached the dwelling. I found the baby board, spread my old blankets on the floor of a small store house and laid the cradle and the saddle over them. Two of the blankets are from Grand Canyon—many a mule has had them on his back. Cynthia and Percival knew them, so did bronco Pacer, and Peggy, and Wendy. There was the quilt from Spurlocks, and a blanket made of a dozen gunnysacks from Superior. I wrote a note, put it under the saddle and started down the slope. By the time I reached Nuflo it was raining violently. I was wet to the skin when we reached camp. I stood there for awhile, looking at the muddy torrent, the cascades on the cliffs, and the still form of Jonathan. The skies seemed about to open wider, so I donned my poncho, loaded Nuflo, and splashed upstream. The cloudburst drenched us, but we plodded resolutely forward, and soon I was in unknown country. The rain stopped. We crossed the river a thousand times. The canyon changed from red to pink, to gray, to yellow. Several times we had slippery scrambles over rocks that blocked the way, and there was some quicksand. Pines and firs were on the canyon floor, and there was one clump of aspens. At long last the canyon walls were lower, but we did not find a way out. Finally I saw sheep tracks, the print of bare feet, and when I found a dry cave, I stopped, for we were both very weary. There is good grass for Nuflo. I climbed out and saw a range of purple mountains and buttes—doubtless the Lukachukais. An Indian was whistling a herd of sheep. I found a trail leading out of the canyon and returned to camp. It was late. The skies were murky, and I had not eaten since morning, so I fried some mutton and sweet bread. Then I read Browning, and pondered. How strange is reality! In the morning I shall not ride. I don't think I'll buy another horse. I haven't the money and one will do. Having only Nuflo, I'll care for him more solicitously. He'll have more oats, there'll be no more rope hobbles. I put the saddle cinch on the pack saddle and left the other in the cliff dwelling.

If I had not attempted the steep hill, Jonathan might yet be serving me, but he behaved strangely the last few days. I suppose the Navajos will steal his shoes.

I sang tragic songs, looked into the coals of my campfire, listened to the song of the crickets, the murmur of the water, the clatter of Nuflo's bell (yo tsoyee) and the sound of the grass being munched. Somehow Jonathan's death has not disheartened me. I feel better for accepting the challenge to proceed without him. His death was certainly dramatic. I shall never forget how he ran sidewise, as if groping for something to lean on, found nothing, crashed to earth, and rolled over.

I don't think anyone will find the saddle. The baby board was where I left it last May, except that the hoops had fallen into the bin. My printing on the board—Evert Rulan, etc.—was almost obscured. The rain washed away my tracks. The saddle is well cached. The ghosts of the cliff dwellers will guard it. I don't think I'll return for it tho.

The clouds have gone. Stars gleam above the fir tops. It might be Christmas.

July 23, Saturday

At Schili, sheep were being dipped. There were two white men who paid me no attention, and gave me the wrong directions for spite. An Indian set me right. Later on I got mixed up in some cornfields and fences. I wearied of pulling Nuflo and drove him at a lope for a while.

After that we went slowly enough, for there was such a stiffness and soreness in my limbs as I had never known before. My shoulders seemed bruised and my thighs ached piercingly when we climbed. At eleven o'clock I reached Greasewood Springs,[21] a large trading post with three long, low barns and a dozen other log buildings. Carl, the trader, said I could stay for dinner and gave Nuflo some hay, which he did not eat. An Indian brought a rug and saddle blanket, for which he was given a hundred pounds of flour, coffee, candy, baking powder, velveteen, and the like.

Dinner was very good. I ate heartily. Then I purchased supplies. 2½ pounds of cookies, cigarettes, peanuts, breakfast food, oats, and the like. He charged me well, probably including the dinner, but it was worth it. There are two children, empty headed creatures.

I stuffed my pockets with cookies and went on. We crossed Lukachukai Creek and came to the store. Here I sent notice to Chinlee P.O. and inquired about saddle blankets. There were no good ones. Soon or late we were at the foot of the mountains and entered a red walled canyon. Then my poor bones began to creak in real earnest as we began the toilsome ascent. I saw the aspens and praised God for them. I had to have someone to thank. We halted under gloomy firs beside a clear stream. There was not much grass. I was too weary to cook, so subsisted on cookies. I fed Nuflo several pounds of oats, then slept fitfully on the bank.

JULY 24, SUNDAY

Found that my limbs had <u>not</u> become lithe and supple as a cedar bough overnight. The cookie bag is much lighter now. We trudged up the canyon and entered beautiful glades of aspens. It seemed I would never reach the side road. Finally I found one, but after I followed it half a mile, it seemed to turn south, so I went back, but in a short distance we came to the edge of the mountain, with a sweeping view of the tawny desert and two lonely buttes. I think one of them is Shiprock.

I went back the side road, into the forest. I saw a big brown bear ambling off, but he bounded away when I tried to take his picture.

At length we came to a broad lake, and being weary, I stopped under six bent oak trees near a pine. There are no aspens by the lake,

---

21. Everett had climbed out of the head of Canyon del Muerto and had traveled north about five miles to Greasewood—a different Greasewood than the one Everett had passed on July 3.

but the mountainside above is green with them. I tried to fill my canteens at the lake, but the water was murky, and though I waded out, I could not find a clear space. Then I bridled Nuflo and rode over the hill till I reached a clear, dark lake. I flung both canteens across the saddle blanket and climbed up in front.

It began to rain and hail, so I covered the kyaks, put on my poncho, and walked along the rim, examining some deserted hogans, looking off on the desert, and walking around small lakes. Then I carved some cliff dwelling designs on my kyak.

JULY 25, MONDAY

I finished "As You Like It" and read "A Midsummer Night's Dream." After eating and eating till there was nothing left, I rode Nuflo towards the mountain top, passing many dark lakes and deep glades of aspens. I saw a herd of sheep, then turned back, driven out by the bloodthirsty mosquitoes. Two horses were shoulder deep in a pond, eating rushes. A Navajo wagon with aspen boughs and a white canvas for shade went by.

I went swimming, made popcorn, and wrote a good letter to Bill. While there is life, there is hope. I still think at times that the future may hold happiness. I shall wait a while and see. I have waited three years already, and not in vain. If for no other reason, I'll wait to hear more music. I never can hear enough.

I've a good meal inside me. The air is still, I feel like a man again and look at the purple and gold and azure of the sunset.

JULY 26, TUESDAY

All morning we traveled thru the forest. In the heat of the day, we left the Lukachukais behind, to greet the sands of New Mexico.

At Redrock I asked the way and was told to take the Rattlesnake Road—that I couldn't get off it. I was not out of sight of the post when the road forked with no indication of which was the one. Shortly after that it forked again and again. I'd had no lunch and was very weary, so at a grassy spot near deserted houses I stopt. I had only a quart of water and I drank most of it and suffered all the tortures of death by thirst, looking for a spring. When we started again, steering for Shiprock, I was almost too weary to move, and my legs ached horribly. It was only a short distance to a well and cement trough. I filled the canteens and investigated four hogans until I found the one that suited me. It was very large, with ten pillars, and a roof blackened with smokes of many fires. Intending to rest all next day, I slept.

JULY 27, WEDNESDAY

Thot of home. I gave all my paints to Haskel, who will use them better than I did, but I'll not be able to paint without spending 15 or 20 dollars on materials. I'd have to wash the car, I suppose. I'd do some of the cooking, listen to all the good music on the radio. Perhaps Waldo and I could do a few things together. I'd like to play tennis. I'd have no way of earning pocket money. I'd use the library extensively.

[8 lines, erased]

Solitude in the city is worse than solitude in the desert, enforced in a harsher way.

My legs are weaker than ever. I'm filled with a violent desire to go home. Locomotion is very painful. If I can get to Mesa Verde, I may be able to persuade some California tourist to take me back for a consideration. The skies are black, but I cannot hope that it will rain before tomorrow. Nuflo has two sores on his back that have been there since we started. I think they are from the wrinkle in the old saddle.

My khaki shirts are both in shreds—my tennis shoes are full of holes—my overalls are torn in several places—the leather hobbles are almost worn out. Most of my equipage is well past its prime.

I smoked half a dozen cigarettes, watching the beautiful spirals of blue smoke, blowing rings, and looking at the fungus on the rafters.

JULY 28, THURSDAY

I ate a cold breakfast and made an early start. We continued down the wash, passing another spring with two cottonwoods, a deserted hogan, and a burro and colt. Some vivid green lizards scurried out of my path. Finally we gained an eminence from which we could see the whole of Shiprock, with cinder cones at its base. I saw a distant rider galloping furiously—the first person I'd seen since leaving Redrock. I saw the smoke of Rattlesnake[22] and it seemed that the town was only a mile away, but we were hours in reaching it. The Lukachukais were shrouded in black storm clouds. I was shocked to find a golf course at Rattlesnake! I thot I saw a black-robed hag gathering wood, but it proved to be a mech-

---

22. Rattlesnake refers to the large Rattlesnake Oil Field, where the oil company had established a village with several amenities for their workers and families.

anism on an oil well, bending and lifting. There was a tennis court and a football field in the enclosure where all lived in identical cabins. I learned to my sorrow that Shiprock itself was several miles farther. I told a passing Navajo I would give him a dime if he'd let me ride behind him, but he refused. I loped Nuflo awhile but had trouble stopping him—he felt better than I did. I was weary and lame when we approached the river. Nuflo is a recalcitrant beast—stubborn as a donkey. We crossed the bridge over the San Juan River, which was a mighty, muddy torrent. Then at a camping place, I unbridled and tied Nuflo, bought two candy bars, and set out for the [Shiprock] post office, a mile east. The passing truck drivers would not give me succor. There was only one letter, a good one from Mother. She told me the advantages of home, told me where I could hear symphonies, and described the advantages of home, urging a return. I told her about Jonathan, and that after Mesa Verde, I would look for a way to return. Then I sent Bill a letter and a note to Ray Stevens, asking for my share of the postcard profits.

At a large trading post near there, I loaded up with civilized foodstuffs, priced sensibly. I bought three loaves of whole wheat bread, candy, cucumbers, butter, sweet potatoes, forgetting raisins, eggs, and breakfast food. Well loaded, I trudged back as it began to rain. I covered camp, then had supper in the chuck wagon of the road crew. I didn't eat much—just tomatoes, grapes, and a glass of milk, and another seized the last slice of pie before I could. Then I gave Nuflo a double handful of oats, and packed him up, filling the canteens. I did not feel as out of place as I usually do with a pack outfit in town.

Altho I had felt lame and very leg weary when I entered Shiprock, reaction now set in, and I whistled symphonies, and sang at the top of my voice, blithely whacking Nuflo. The Navajo horses were very frightened at Nuflo, with his big pack and banging canteens. Nuflo obstinately scraped his pack on a barbwire fence.

As we left the town behind, my spirits soared again and I sang and sang. A Navajo with a wagonload of wood came by. He couldn't speak English, but I climbed in back, sat on the firewood, and tied Nuflo to the wagon. It irked him to be obliged to step along at a proper pace. I looked at Shiprock and the Lukachukais, the green banked San Juan, and the sunset fires. The Indian finally turned aside to his hogan. I crested a hill and camped in a draw. There is excellent grass. The skies are completely covered with clouds, but it does not rain.

July 29, Friday

In the night, mosquitoes tortured me mercilessly. I could not sleep for thinking of the future. I was sure I wanted to go on thru the Carrizos to Kayenta and Monument Valley, Betatakin, Keet Seel, Inscription House, Rainbow Bridge, and Grand Canyon. I felt I'd never forgive myself if I went away without seeing more of the West. There was a light shower, then the stars appeared. I twisted uncomfortably until prima luce, fearful that Nuflo had broken his hobbles.

In the half light I found his trail, followed it to him, and rode back to camp. I ate bread for breakfast, loaded my white devil and was off just as a Navajo came driving a herd of sheep.

This highway, 666, is the first I've been on since Holbrook. It is wide and level, covered with gravel that hurts my feet.[23] We went for hours, it seemed, before we met any one. There were two comely girls who slowed their car to look at me. One, in red and black velvet, looked quite nice. Then there was a Louisiana car, with a haughty young fellow with black mustache and sombrero and a longhaired black beauty beside him.

The gnats and heat were fearful. The country was the most barren I've traveled in—not a sign of a tree—only monotonous yellow flats and hills. Clouds made a shadow for a few hours. I overestimated my speed, and was shocked not to arrive anywhere. Finally we topped a ridge and saw tawny brown buttes on all sides and a few green trees in the distance—probably Mancos creek, I thot.

The heat was too much. I stopped for lunch. Nuflo would not eat the grass—stood stupidly. We came to the Colorado state line and left New Mexico behind. Then I took a trail, searching for the Mancos Creek Trading Post. With difficulty, I found it.

The trader was a jovial, but good natured fellow. I bought a little grub, drank cool water, and asked about the trail to Mesa Verde. He knew nothing about it, but I asked a Ute who told me a few things about the way. I couldn't find out much. I bought half a watermelon, tied the purchases on, and started upstream. I'd gone a quarter of a mile when the trail led along the edge of a bank in a quite narrow pass with the high bank above and below. I supposed it was passable because it

---

23. By 1932, only a few major highways in the West had been paved; U.S. 666 was not among them.

was there. Nuflo went ahead, scraped safely by, but around the turn, the ledge was narrower. There was nothing to do but go on, and Nuflo was with a few yards of safety when at a particularly narrow spot, his kyaks pushed him out and he began to slip off. He lunged up, but once more the pack pushed him off. He clawed the ledge frantically, then fell down into the current of the muddy Mancos. It was deep near the bank and he floundered about and wet his pack. When the kyaks were full of water he could not lift them, and he floundered miserably and floated downstream several yards. He could not stand up. The pack became thoroughly wet.

I stood on the bank, looked to right and left, and exclaimed, "Oh, for God's sake, for GOD's sake." Then I leaped into the torrent, up to my waist, and tried to help Nuflo up, but he floundered worse than before. I had only fastened the breast strap by the neck strap because of a sore spot on his breast. The thin neck strap broke. Nuflo squirmed and struggled like a dragonfly casting his skin, and finally stepped out of his cinch. He started off across the creek, but I led him back and tied him to a young cottonwood. Then I wallowed back to wrestle with the pack. I flung off the things tied on top, canteens, groceries, camera, then unhooked a kyak, bore it to the bank while the muddy water sprayed out at the bottom, then got the other. The saddle blankets were heavy. One of them, a red and gray one from Grand Canyon, disappeared. I suppose it will come out at the Gulf of Mexico.[24] I flung the other and the saddle on shore, then heaved at the bedroll. It weighed like lead. I had to try a dozen times before I could get it on the bank.

Nuflo had skinned his legs a little, but already he was uncon-cernedly munching grass. I hobbled him and took stock of the catas-trophe. The camera was soused. The film was wet. I unrolled a little and found that some was dry, so tied it up and put it away. The pictures of Jonathan were on it.

I hung the saddle blankets and sleeping bag on a fence, and wrung them out as best I could, but the alkali hurt my hands. Then I spread out all my spare clothes on the ground, opened my sketch case—sorry sight! and spread some of the papers to dry. Most of them are spoiled. The oatmeal was quite ruined. The flashlight batteries were mushy. I tied my lash rope to the lead ropes and strung a line. There was only one tree to tie the end to. The fence runs east and west, did not get the

24. Actually, the Mancos, San Juan, and Colorado Rivers drain into the Gulf of California.

sun. Finally found a prop that raised it a little. Two women came by—smiled, but did not offer to help. The wreckage was strewn all over the field, drying, but clouds came up and it began to rain. Hastily I piled everything in a heap and threw the tarp over.

I put on my poncho, and chewing wet candy, walked to the post. There is a footbridge that sways alarmingly and has no side rails. I told my story to the trader. He is a native of North Carolina but has worked in Zuni and Phoenix.

I bought cigarettes, candy and a comb. In the evening a supply truck came and I helped unload watermelons.

I wanted to buy a rug. There were several that I liked, very reasonably priced, but the designs were monotonously regular, and I could not bring myself to buy them. I borrowed a pair of socks, a rug and canvas to sleep in, and returned to camp. I ate watermelon and peanut butter sandwiches, then turned in. Though I had not let it show, I really felt overwhelmed by what happened.

July 30, Saturday

Slept poorly. Awoke somewhat sick. I see Nuflo just crossing the river. There is much more grass on this side, but the old fool won't believe it. My Colt 25 was rusty already. I cleaned it the best I could, then poured oil all thru the mechanism. There was little sun, and things dried out somewhat. I ate Grape Nuts, and turned things over. A white man and a Ute began to fell the cottonwoods to make a dam. I cut one tree down. I think they have no right to cut them—there are so few.

Toward noon I returned my covers to the trader, bought flashlight batteries, and waded after Nuflo. He tried to run away from me once. The pack is still heavy with surplus moisture. We took a wagon road to the highway. Five horses in a field ran back and forth looking at Nu.

Then we took a little used wagon trail on the left bank. I finally lost it, and wandered two or three miles out of my course trying to cross crevasses. At length we found a good trail. Nuflo persisted in trying to leave it. We stopped for a late lunch under some maples by a pond. It proved to be aswarm with ants, so I didn't stop long.

The trail was not plain, but I continued on the left bank. Soon the entrance of the canyon was hidden by turns. The trail became steeper—the sort I delight in. I met a Ute in a blue-green shirt—the first rider I'd seen. Then in a grove of cottonwoods I stopped. While I was getting water, Nuflo spilled the oats. There was not much grass. I saw that there was plenty on the mesa above, and by reconnoitering I found a trail, patiently made with stone steps.[25]

It was dark when I started supper—bacon, and a fried peanut butter sandwich & beans. I would hear Nuflo's bell, & hoped he wouldn't try to come down.

July 31, Sunday

Four Navajos passed by. Nuflo's bell sounded close, but he was on the mesa, close to where I had left him. I know he had plenty to eat last night. We kept on the left bank. The canyon was monotonous. We went thru a gate. I met two Indians with a packhorse. I stopped between two maple trees, and rested in the shade, eating bread and jam. I took my camera apart and wiped the mud off, but the shutter didn't work and I couldn't get at it. The flashlight does not work either. Yesterday I was laughing at myself for feeling so crushed by the wetting, but it was not the last laugh. My photos are all stuck together, the matches are all wet, the soap is soggy, the baking powder is muddy—so on down the list.

I had expected Mancos Canyon to be narrow and rough, with many fordings necessary, but not so. Also I expected Ute Canyon and Navajo Canyon to have running streams, but again no. Finally I reached a Ute Camp—several tents. A boy herding sheep told me the way, up the next canyon past two fences. I went up the canyon. There were a few pools in the creek bed. I came to a fence, as he said, and began to look for the next, expecting to camp at the foot of the uptrail. Nuflo was exasperating. If I tried to lead him he pulled back like a burro, and if I drove him, he was constantly turning around and leaving the trail. His bulk prevented me from seeing what was ahead. We went on and on, passing a herd of horses. There was good grass. The canyon forked and I took the left fork as the Ute directed, forgetting or being unconvinced that this wasn't Navajo canyon. The trail soon thinned out. I saw a large dwelling on the right, and in a mile I saw another on the left, with tall, yellow

---

25. The usual route, followed by most visitors today, is from the north over the high crest of the Mesa Verde, then descending south toward the major cliff dwellings located in canyons draining into the Mancos River. Everett was taking the backdoor route into Mesa Verde by following up the Mancos River Canyon, then into the side canyons and up to the ruins, eventually to the mesa top. This lower route, on the Ute Mountain Ute Indian Reservation, is now closed except to charter groups led by Ute Indians.

flowers. The trail had disappeared, so I climbed up to see if it was under the cliff. It was not, and I couldn't quite get to the dwelling, so I descended and turned Nuflo round. I saw that there was no trail in the other fork. I stopped not far from the mouth, where there was a pool of water, filled a canteen, and camped under a pinyon on the bank. Nuflo's back is sore in several places. I looked at my map and decided that the trail must be somewhere in this canyon. Determined to rest here tomorrow. Fried sweet potatoes with bacon and onions. Smoked, peered into the fire, stargazed.

AUGUST 1, MONDAY

Finished the grapenuts and sauntered down, looking for the trail, but finding it not. I went to the Ute camp, and met the same boy, who told me that the trail was indeed half a mile above the gate. I sat in the shade house a while. There are two women and a baby with brown hair and blue eyes. They showed me an arrowhead. I had an early lunch with them of coffee, tortillas, and mutton. Then I went back, and found the up trail within three yards of the trail that goes by my camp. One of the Utes stopped on his way to catch a horse. Then it was peace. I bathed and washed clothes, did more work on my equipage, dried the rattlesnake rattles.

I am in no great rush to reach the park. It will mark the termination of my wanderings—my independence. I can't even see the dwellings independently. All tourists go together in an auto caravan with a ranger. I don't see how they get more than a glimpse in this fashion. It may not be so easy to find someone who'll take me home. I'd like to arrive in Hollywood with some money in my pocket.

In the evening I watched the fire with beating heart.

AUGUST 2, TUESDAY

Up early in the cold dawn. There were many things to discard—rice, macaroni, wheat, sugar, etc. I caught old Nuflo and rode into camp, giving him a nosebag full of oats. I packed him and let him finish eating, then we climbed up from the shadowed valley to the sunlit cliffs and Mesa Verde. I paused several times in the shadow to rest Nuflo and myself. The trail was very good.

Once on the mesa we rolled along thru the pinyon juniper forest, I singing and whistling gaily. Soon I came to a road, and then another,

82

and another, until I met a party of motorists who told me how to reach the park. It was only two more miles. I passed several Navajos working on the road. At headquarters I talked with a young ranger who was friendly. All the rangers are courteous and sincere—a good lot.

I unloaded Nuflo on the edge of the campground. There was a little grass among the pinyons on the rim. I hobbled him out, then returned to headquarters. There I obtained a park pamphlet, and found that there was no mail.

I strolled down the foot path to Spruce Tree House. A large, well preserved ruin. There I met a young couple who had just arrived, and offered to take me with them on the auto trip. I went thru the museum —which is a beautiful building, but houses a small collection. Most of the finds were removed by pot hunters or sent to the Smithsonian Institution or Colorado.

The Missouri tourists next to me invited me to lunch and I tried to soak my films apart. Then I went with the young couple on the afternoon trip. We went to Balcony House first—a very interesting ruin, excellently situated and well preserved. Some of the tourists were rather stupid—physically feeble & the party seemed too large, but I enjoyed myself very much. We visited Cliff Palace. I intend to make a painting there. I had supper with my tourist friends, then met one quite interesting party in the community house porch overlooking Spruce Tree House. I talked a good deal. Then I heard the supt. give a good talk at the camp fire. The Indians danced.

[At this point Everett's written journal for 1932 ends but is followed by six pages of poetry quoted from Benet, Yeats, Masefield, Shelley, Whitman, Wilde, Nietzche, and others. The typescript of the journal, however, continues with the following:]

AUGUST 9

Had breakfast in mess hall. Alberding marked my map. Watered Nu at Spruce Tree Spring. Saw Buzzard House. Read "Hiawatha." Rain. cooked bread soufflé. Read "Ranch Romances" by flash.

AUGUST 10

Late up. Clouds. Had a bath, then packed and off in afternoon. Went down to Jug House—large ruin. Shower. Camped above Song House. Sketched. Fixed up supper for Herb—pineapple, eggs, cocoa, popcorn. He has been in 17 parks, tramping. Geology in college. Moonlight. Owl in tree.

AUGUST 11

Cooked cornmeal. Went to No. 16. Upper terrace well preserved. Fine doors. Fondled skull. Frisky work on ladder and shaky wall. John Wetherill 1890. Herb heard buzzard in Song House. Tried to scare him out for pictures. Finally I caught his wings and held him for a picture. Climbed down tree near cliff. Saw No. 12—well preserved back rooms. Fine pottery shards. Pine tree inside. Straight facade and kivas. Lunch and rest. Over to No. 11 and No. 13. Over to Double House. Way down very tortuous, two miles around. Made camp and I cooked rice pudding.

AUGUST 12

Very early up. Found Step House—early basket maker. Wandered up and down. Lunched under a pinyon. I have poison ivy—aflame already. Miserable prospect. Full moon. The Mancos was only eight inches deep and almost clear. Dense foliage above.

AUGUST 13

Left eye half shut—sad face. Rode through stiff brush and reeds to river. Clear stream for a mile. Camped under a shady ledge. Juniper and pinyons and sage.

AUGUST 14

Could barely see the light. When heat and flies were intolerable, took canteens and walked a mile to water. Sat motionless on a rock beside pool for hours. Coyote came below to drink. Wet when I reached camp. Slept. Pain.

AUGUST 15

A little better. After rest, went upstream with canteen. Rain. Sat under a rock and read Hiawatha and Lamb's Tales, also about Park.

After dark, the moon rose, thin silver cloud-bar, and all was entrancingly beautiful. I felt better, kept opening my eyes to look at the moon. Admired my saddle blanket more.

AUGUST 16

Up as hot sun penetrated. Oatmeal. Then sketch case, camera, and canteen. up sweating copiously, to Wild Horse Mesa (I think).

On mesa soon ran into pottery chips. Went up and down washes looking choice pieces, gathered a pocketful. Saw flint chips and found a perfect little arrowhead—gray obsidian. Delighted. At peace with everyone. On around mesa but no dwellings.

Up right for weary trailing. Skies black and muttering. Rain imminent. Became soaked. I pulled Nuflo down steep places—wet, slippery rocks. Rode awhile. Too rough, so I led him. He ran beside me, head next to mine. Water holes all muddy—didn't fill canteens. Nu drank deeply. Rode to camp. Grand when he loped up hill. Bed not very wet, but I moved it under rock across stream, with the kyaks and supper also. Fire in my shallow cave. Cloudburst was just coming! Muddy lava-like stream, rolling sticks and trash. Dry stream bed below—brown torrent above. It rolled down and splashed away, deep and fierce. Good supper of spotted dog [rice pudding]. I thought floods might maroon us, but river abated and skies were not quite so black.

AUGUST 17

Slow start. Trotted down canyon and came to Mancos at noon. Loped on level stretches. Up Navajo Canyon and saw Inaccessible House with square tower. All I could do to keep up with Nu. Arrived at Spruce Tree before the post office opened.

[In a letter to his father dated August 18, Everett stated that he had been staying at the ranger quarters, apparently a bunk house at Mesa Verde. His last letter from the park was dated August 25, after which he released Nuflo into the wild. Then he hitchhiked his way to Gallup, then to the Grand Canyon, then to Needles and finally to Los Angeles.]

EVERETT HOLDS BOW AND ARROW, WITH MOTHER AND FATHER SEATED. BROTHER, WALDO, LOOKS ON. ABOUT 1924.

EVERETT IN KINDERGARTEN, BROOKLINE, MASSACHUSETTS, 1920.

A SERIOUS EVERETT RUESS, ABOUT 1925.
RIGHT: EVERETT IN A BOY SCOUT UNIFORM IN VALPARISO, INDIANA, ABOUT 1925.

Everett stands with his mother, Stella, beside the family sedan, while brother, Waldo, looks out the car window, about 1929.

Everett (standing), and his brother, Waldo, at the Craters of the Moon National Monument, about 1929. Below: Everett, Waldo, Christopher, and Stella Ruess on a camping trip, 1929.

Everett with bedroll beside the family sedan, 1929.

EVERETT, HIS FATHER, CHRISTOPHER, AND HIS GRANDFATHER IN LOS ANGELES ABOUT 1930.

YOUNG EVERETT AT THE PAINTING
EASEL, ABOUT 1930.

STELLA RUESS, APPARENTLY DOING AN IMITATION OF
ISADORA DUNCAN, IN LOS ANGELES.

88

EVERETT WITH HIS DOG, CURLY, AT HOME IN
LOS ANGELES, 1931.

EVERETT AND CURLY ON BURRO PERICLES, 1931.

EVERETT ON THE TRAIL NEAR MOGOLLON RIM IN
NORTHWEST ARIZONA, JUNE 1932.

EVERETT (RIGHT), FRIEND BILL JACOBS, AND
EVERETT'S DOG, CURLY, SET TO BEGIN THEIR
BACKPACK TRIP INTO ARIZONA'S SUPERSTITION
MOUNTAINS, MARCH 1932.

89

IN CANYON DE CHELLY, EVERETT RIDES NUFLO, WITH HORSE JONATHAN CARRYING THE BURDEN. SHORTLY AFTER THIS PHOTOGRAPH WAS TAKEN, JONATHAN SUDDENLY DIED.

SHIPROCK, 1,600 FEET HIGH, RISES MAJESTICALLY FROM THE DESERT OF WESTERN NEW MEXICO, IN THE NAVAJO NATION. EVERETT PASSED THIS PROMINENT FEATURE IN LATE JULY 1932.

CLIFF PALACE, MESA VERDE NATIONAL
PARK, WHICH EVERETT VISITED IN 1931
AND AGAIN IN 1932.

OLD NAVAJO IN CANYON
DE CHELLY. PHOTOGRAPH
BY EVERETT RUESS.

1933

C A L I F O R N I A

For the summer of 1933, Everett planned to enter Sequoia National Park, explore and sightsee at a leisurely pace, then slowly make his way northward, through today's Kings Canyon National Park, the John Muir and the Ansel Adams Wilderness Areas into Yosemite National Park. He accomplished his goals, but barely departed the high country before being driven out by winter snows.

MAY 27, SATURDAY

I arranged the pack and played some Sibelius. Bill Jacobs did not call, so I called, and his mother said he was asleep, having decided to go some other time. She sounded heartbroken, but I was relieved. Waldo called from the office where he was a temporary stenographer, and when he came I began to load the car. The one misfortune was that in the heat, the waterproofing smeared out of my tarpaulin. I almost forgot to bring the bed. After parting from mother and Mrs. Meinen, we swung up the avenue, elbowing between the cars across Hollywood to Franklin Circle where Waldo got Betty.

Soon we left the city behind, and roared up the Ridge route and down the hot, flat valley. Betty and Waldo necked at fifty per. Waldo was stung by a bee, but refused to notice it. At last in the evening heat, we turned towards the snow crowned mountains, driving thru carefully tended vineyards. Betty seems a good sort no matter what she does.

[Four lines erased]

We went thru Visalia and reached Three Rivers at last. I found Earl McKee and unloaded there. Betty played with the puppies, then she and

Waldo drove up to Sequoia. I saw Charley Blossom and will see his burros tomorrow. My camp was under some apricot trees. After supper I had ice cream and cake and swapped anecdotes with Earl. I showed the family my photographs and prints. They have three dogs, three pups, a cat, chickens, and a Shetland pony. Earl has 200 head of cattle, as well. We talked about pack trips until 11. The new moon had risen and set, but the open sky was ablaze with stars. I saw a flaming meteor, rolled and tossed, and hardly slept.

MAY 28, SUNDAY

Up shortly after sunrise. I walked over to the Kaweah River and watched the water leap and toss like white maned chargers. It snatched at the boughs of the trees and bent them under. I saw a handsome, leonine, buckskin mule. Earl hitched up the trailer and took a horse to the fair near Fresno, taking the family with him.

Charley came over with Jim, an old fellow with seven snag teeth who seldom works, but complains when he has no job. We borrowed two of Earl's saddles and caught three horses. Charley rode a handsome five year old black, which pranced and curved, holding his head like a war-horse. I rode a bay mare, and Jim rode Keeno, a bony twenty-year old. It was very hot, so we walked the horses up the South Fork road, pausing to drink on the way. I was glad to be on a horse again. We crossed several bridges, and Charley hailed all the ranchers. Seven miles up, we turned off, and rode on with a whiskey-packing, verse writing rancher.

I had a great thrill fording the river. The water came up over the saddle blankets. I put my feet on the swells and we plunged through the foamy, buffeting snow water, rolling like a ship in a heavy sea. We climbed a steep hill, went thru another gate and started up a canyon. We had only gone a few hundred yards when we came upon several of the burros in a dusty spot under sycamores trellised with grapevines. They ran like jack rabbits, but we chased them into the fence corner. I had borrowed a battered old sombrero, belonging to Charley's mother. It blew off once.

We sat in the shade on the hill slopes and looked over the burros. Two had not been found. Of those left two or three were small colts, and a couple were old. A black five year old jenny was the best animal, although she was not large. Charley said he would sell me two and a

93

pack rig for fifteen dollars. I decided I would like to get a saddle and ride one. The other burro was ten or twelve, bobtailed, pale tawny gray with a brown shoulder stripe. There was another red burro which bucked, and one of the two missing burros was a good one, but we did not know where to find it. The rancher told us of his days in Arizona, and how he rode an avalanche down the mountain.

We drove the two donkeys down to the ford and I got a picture of them crossing. The black jenny almost went downstream. The rancher got a picture of me riding the bay and leading Keeno, in the middle of the current, with my feet on the swells. We met four or five other riders and cowmen, and conversed in the shade awhile. One rider with a handsome black horse, a trim black banded Panama hat, and a moustachio looked quite picturesque, suggesting a Mexican vaquero.

We rode on, occasionally loping and again circling thru the brush to head off the donkeys. They are both fat. Charley was quite interesting. He is six feet one, eighteen, with a bad cut over his eye that narrowed one eye by the swelling. Jim on Keeno could not keep up with us.

The burros scuttled into the home pasture, and we had lunch. Charley showed me his rabbits, calfs, and chickens. I learned that it takes exactly 31 days for a rabbit to produce young.

Charley wanted to give me a pack saddle and a riding saddle, if I would paint the black horse he rode. There was not much rigging. We found a little saddle with both stirrups and one leather gone. I decided it would be enough, if completely rigged. I could pack the bed and a few odds and ends on it on the uphill and when I was heavily loaded. The rest of the time I could ride.

Baldy Loverin, seventeen year old son of Ord Loverin, the packer in Giant Forest, came in to visit Charley. Charley's mother and two sisters wanted to go to Lindsay, near Visalia, to tell a man to get his horse which he had left on their pasture a year ago.

After considerable argument, we all drove down. We rode thru olive and orange orchards, returning before dark. Baldy had to take a horse to his brother on a fence building camp up South Fork, so we all saddled up and started off by moonlight. We raced a while, smoked, and looked at the stars. I showed them how to find the North Star. After several miles we left the road and started up the mountain above the river. Baldy and I rode up a steep cliff. None of us knew the trail, but Spider, Baldy's horse, had been up before and we found our way up the darkened mountainside scraping thru branches and brush. It was a steep trail. We struck matches and found an old camp, then groped our way to an old cabin. There was no lantern, but we struck matches, devoured a can of peaches, and waited. After a while, Wes Loverin and Britten came up and we had some bread and apricots. I like Wes. He had a delicate, handsome features. We three went along the edge till we came to a spring in some buckeyes, filled pails, and climbed back. About midnight we started down the mountain. The moon was gone, and we groped in the dim starlight. It was a glorious experience for me. We lost our way time and again, and the mare did not keep the other horses in sight all the time, but at last we reached the road again. Then we unwound. The mare fairly flew, and Charley and Baldy couldn't come near her. Rat-a-plan-clap-clop we galloped over the darkened road, racing thru tunnels of grape festooned cottonwoods.

[Four lines erased]

It was good to be called by my name and made one of them. The mare took out again and passed the other horses on the edge of the cliff. I was too drowsy to enjoy it fully, but the mare loped beautifully. At two in the morning we reached the home pasture, unsaddled, and turned in. I agreed to go with Charley on his milk route in the morning. I was so pounded and tired that after striding proudly to my camp, I fell asleep at once in my bed on the hard ground.

MAY 29, MONDAY

I was up before sunrise and no one else was awake. I watched the cats, kittens, and pups until Mrs. Blossom was about. She shouted to Charley and milked the cow. I carried in the milk, and in half an hour, Charley got up. We drove down to the dairy farm, took a huge can of garbage and poured it out for the hogs, and left a few bottles at the road camp. Then we went up the Middle Fork and crossed to the North Fork, stopping at Baldy's. Next we went all the way to Ash Mountain, the park entrance, on Middle Fork. We drank a quart of milk on the way back. Breakfast was good, including waffles, tomato syrup, milk, eggs, and bread. Then Charley rode up with Baldy to help him haul wood for his father.

I helped Blanche McKee drive some horses into pasture. A gate had been left open. Then I sat on the porch with Mrs. Blossom and her daughters, Nora and Dot. Mr. Blossom was killed in an auto wreck, and Mrs. Blossom has a wooden leg.

Charley finally came back. I wrote a letter home to ask for my hat. We drove down the road to see about a stirrup leather, but no luck. I helped Charley heave a rabbit hutch on his trailer to take up South Fork. Compared with him, I am a Kentucky gentleman in the courtesy I show his parents.

Waldo and Betty came by, and told me their adventures. They had bathed in snow, in snow water, and sun. Betty was brown as a berry. They hurried on but said they'd send the hat.

Charley, his mother, and I drove up with the hutch, inquired for stirrup leathers and ate some figs. I had further opportunity to study the Western method of asking for a thing and replying. I showed them some pictures after supper, then we drove up town, Charley paying bills as we went. Charley treated us all to ice cream. I bedded down under the apricots. The burros were in the 2 acre orchard next to me.

MAY 30, TUESDAY

Slept like a dead man until considerably after the cloudy sunrise. I vacillated awhile, deciding what to pack where, but at long last, I threw the hitches and we were away. I thanked Earl for his help and started up the road, leading the black jenny. The gray was tied to the pack.

The post office was open, so I told Britten to send my hat on to Sequoia. Some hunters tossed a cottontail to me as they drove by, but I decided not to chance it in the summer. Tourists waved, but I crossed the bridge to North Fork. Baldy Loverin raised from his bed and books to wish me luck. I drove the donkeys at a nice pace. The black turned off the road once, and stretched the tie rope until it snapped.

Soon the ranches were fewer, and at the last one, a shaven-headed, chubby old German farmer stopped work because he just wanted to talk to me. He insisted that I must have wealthy parents to be traveling this way. He estimated that my burros cost me 30 dollars and the saddle 10. He was a funny little fellow, just like a fictitious character.

On and up we went, climbing high above the white water of the Kaweah. Yuccas were in bloom. The burros would keep on going when I paused. I found a terrapin cuddled up in a little streamlet where I drank. I picked him up, thinking I could get a comical picture of him and the burros. Soon it was terrifically, muggily hot, and the climb so arduous that I was all played out and stopped by a stream with a little meadow. I unpacked in the shifting shade of a sycamore and staked the black burro to a tree, tying the gray to a log. They fell to munching grass at once, but I was too tired for anything but relaxation. I put the turtle in the stream where he burrowed into the sand and turned into a wet rock.

After awhile I ate some prunes and peanut butter sandwiches, and read two chapters of "The Golden Ass." I was rather disappointed in it. Then cloud shadows made it cooler, and I bathed and packed again. This time I rode the gray and we went proudly along. I thought how perfect everything was, what a nice outfit I had, how beautiful the distant rushing river was, and I was constantly delighted anew by the flowers. There were beautiful four petalled orange ones with crimson centers, also red ones with shirred edges. Snake tracks curled across the road.

My burro walked right on the very edge of the road, where the grassy cliff fell sheer away. I missed one road and went half a mile out of my way down to the reforestation camp on Cedar Creek. I talked to the ranger and turned about. The boys in the camp were not working very hard. My way led higher and higher in and around the hollows, and beside buckeye trees with curving white blossoms. We passed an old ranger station and a little farther on I got off and drove the donkeys. The black snuffed the dust once or twice, and showed signs of wanting to quit. Finally she lay down, but I whacked her up at once and we went on merrily, under arching oaks. About sundown we came to the Cedar Creek bridge and station, where I made camp. The ranger came by then. I staked the burros out near a patch of grass, and started a fire. I burnt my supper but downed it, read the map by firelight, made cocoa, and so to bed.

May 31, Wednesday

Awakened considerably after sunrise, moved the burros to new grass plots, arranged the load, ate two prunes, packed, and away we went. The burro stepped on a gorgeous coral king snake. I caught it and tied it to the saddle. It will make a most superior hat band for my black Stetson. I found a scorpion by the road too. A truck was unloading wood down the slope. A genial, grizzled old ranger asked me What port? He said scorpions and tarantulas were numerous up to 8,000 feet. The burros stood on the outside of the road when the truck went by.

We trundled on up the hill to another summit where tall pines towered and the distant snow peaks sat silently regarding us. I picked a beautiful five pettalled white flower tipped with ultramarine and purple, and put it in my blue shirt front. After awhile I came to the old Colony Mill, where I drank and looked at Moro Rock.[1]

We took the cut-off trail around the next mountain, stepping definitely over the path of pine needles. When we reached the road again, everything was downhill, and we bowled along at a smart pace. I found a blue jay feather which was delicious to my senses.

We passed some road makers eating lunch, and in another hour we reached Marble Fork Bridge. Green water rushed and foamed gloriously over the gray granite boulders in its narrow rock walled channel. After a short debate, I turned the burros up the hill with a little plot of grass enclosed by fir and spruce. I staked the gray and hobbled the black. She acts as if she has never been hobbled before, turning to bite me and threatening to lie down on me. I went down steeply to the river, pushing my canteen under the buffeting water. Climbing up, I leaned back against a huge pine, munched and reflected like the burros and at last bent to the task in hand—skinning the king snake. I turned him inside out, then fleshed the edges toilsomely, rolled it up and peppered the edges. It is red, buff, and black, irregularly ringed.

I led the gray down hill when the sun was half high, hoping the black would follow, but I had to return for her. I crossed the bridge to the Sunset Rock trail, and then the fun began. The trail ascended steeply, and the burros pivoted round and round instead of going up. I got them part way up when the black went off on a tangent. Then she ran all the way back down, and raced me up the road and then back across the bridge. The gray was patiently waiting on the trail. Finally we were fairly started and then there was little trouble.

The trail was steep and we crossed a good deal of fallen timber. The black led the way, and wouldn't go under or around one log for a while. Soon we came to a big patch of snow with broken bushes all across the trail. I tested the trail by a log at the edge, but it was not good. I led the gray part way, but she would not come down, and after slipping once, she bucked right thru the brush and snow, fell to her knees, and plunged up on the other side. The black braced her shoulders and plowed dauntlessly across. I stroked their chins and we wound up among the redwoods.

1. Moro Rock is a giant granite monolith rising from the edge of the Giant Forest. Sometime after Everett's visit, the Civilian Conservation Corps built a 400-step staircase to the top. The spectacular view from the top is one of the best in Sequoia National Park.

There were many more snowbanks to cross, but with a little persuasion, it was accomplished, and towards evening, we clattered out on the great, bald surface of Sunset Rock. There were two bent pines on the edge, and the burros unhesitantly followed me to them. I took their picture.

We went a little distance down thru the campgrounds. There was no grass and I knew the ranger wouldn't want me to keep my burros in the camp area, but after a while, we came to a little meadow off the road, and I brought the donkeys around back of a giant redwood, camped in a hollow between the roots, and pastured my animals. They munched contentedly while I arranged my camp ideally. I brought in a log and laid it in the forked trunk of a pine. This was my saddle rack. I made my bed close to the wide redwood trunk, under the arching roots. I put the kyaks together, hung up the bridle and lash rope and made things shipshape. It is really as delightful a camp as I've ever had. Deer browsed beside the burros, chipmunks scolded and the wind rustled in the tree tops. A tremendous tower shaped boulder is nearby, and parallel is a fallen redwood, of proportionate girth. I had something to eat, watched the light pale and the moon increase in brilliancy, looked up the smooth, classically proportioned trunk of my redwood, and sauntered thru the moonlit forest.

I walked down to the store with a job hunter, bought cigarettes and candy, sat by the campfire with some tourists who had seen five parks in two weeks, and so to my redwood.

June 1, Thursday

Slept late but the burros were right by. I returned to a symbol of my old life—oatmeal for breakfast. In the afternoon I saddled the black burro and persuaded her to take me into the village. We went over to Beetle Rock, and I stopped at the ranger station. An artist named Chris Sciberth was painting signs and we discussed the profession awhile. Three boys, sons of the park janitor, went along with me and I let them ride to my camp. The oldest gave me a good bridle rope, and they helped me put a rope between two trees and hoist up my grub sack, out of reach of the bears.

I fried some bacon and read "The Golden Ass." Jack Sinclair, a gray shirted ranger, suggested that I find a better pasture for my burros. I went over to the Ranger station and talked to a young fellow from the forestry camp who is night assistant. Then I stopped in the Curio store and talked with the manageress, who liked the burros. She told me about the flowers and the winter life.

June 2, Friday

Frank Dawson, the janitor's son, came into camp when I was thinking of rising, so we saddled and bridled the burros and rode about. We found a potato in a garbage can & fed it to the donks. We rode over to hanging rock and climbed Moro Rock. After a bite of chocolate we came away thru the forest over a snowbanked trail. We got pictures of jumping the burro over a log and standing bareback riding. We sang and frolicked thru the woods, saw an old bear and some deer, and finally came out at the bear pits, where we watched the cubs. Half my films were blank—the shutter did not work. I lost the one of myself fording South Fork.

Sinclair suggested I move to Crescent Meadows, but I wanted to see Lodgepole and Tocopah fir, and Sam Clark said Kerr would find a place for the burros there, so I leave in the morning. There was no mail.

Frankie went over to my camp and we went over to Sunset Rock, where I made a pretty good painting of a twisted pine. A chill wind blew up from Marble Fork Canyon. We ran back to camp, and I went over to the village. I talked to the fellows building the gas station, walked around camp Kaweah with Harry O'Neal, the night assistant. I had a cup of coffee in the restaurant, bought a loaf of bread at the store, and met Lincoln Hobson, a young ranger, who pleases me most. He is really intelligent. A Stanford graduate. We talked, and Harry and Sinclair told about the forestry camp and the navy.

June 3, Saturday

The morning was cold and cloudy. I looked at the burros and considered getting up for an hour or so before I crawled out. I had a fire and was getting breakfast when Frankie and his brother came over. They helped me break camp and pack. Frank advised me to pack Grandma (the gray) and ride the black. He took two pictures of the caravan and took the film to be developed. He also took custody of my calfskin strip and sheephide for me.

I rode uptrail toward the Sherman Tree.[2] I couldn't make Blackie go between two logs on the edge of the trail, so I led Grandma, who is quite tractable, and then she came. We trotted up to the largest and oldest

---

2. The General Sherman giant sequoia tree stands 275 feet high. Its circumference is nearly 103 feet. The tree is estimated to be between 2,300 and 2,700 years old.

living thing in the world, and continued toward Lodgepole Camp on Marble Fork. We topped 7,000 feet, with a cold wind blowing shivers from the snowbanks. The sun obscured himself like a magician hiding behind a veil to concoct a new necromancy—snow crystals perhaps. I sang all the sea chanties and cowboy ballads I knew.

At the ranger station I tied my saddle burro and chatted gravely with Kerr [Irving Kerr, District Ranger] and the other ranger. Kerr was really a good chap, as Frankie said he would be. He told me to camp across the bridge and it would be all right. I made camp under a massive yellow pine, hobbled Blackie, and tied Grandma to a light log, lunched and read The Golden Ass.

Later I wandered thru the campgrounds to the upper bridge. The sky was so dismal that I went no farther, but had some cookies with a tourist. Later I smoked with a petroleum engineer from Taft, and he gave me two rainbow trout, hook, line, and worms. I made a blaze under my yellow pine, and at once I felt better. Trout fried in cornmeal with fried cheese sandwiches widened the horizon considerably.

Then [Lon] Garrison, the ranger, came over and sat by my fire.[3] We talked for several hours. I like him very much. He has been in Idaho and Alaska, is married to a girl in Alaska. He went thru Stanford. He told me about the bear he killed here a few days ago, and of the one he was gunning for. The deer ate the bacon bait. They have nibbled on my saddle too. Spoke of a preachers definition of heaven "where you slide down rainbows into tubs of honey." He enjoys his work immensely, and says it is his choice of all the jobs in the country. He is color blind and doesn't read much, but he knows the woods wonderfully well.

JUNE 4, SUNDAY

After oatmeal, I wandered up the Tokopah valley, stopping to help the cookie tourist dig under stumps for grubs and bait. I continued up to Tokopah falls, watched the green pools below, lunched well, and later helped Garrison put up some signs. I had supper in his shanty. We ran the gamut of intellectual topics, discussing the philosophical and gastronomical aspects of life.

---

3. This was Lemuel A. Garrison, nicknamed "Lon," a seasonal ranger at the time. Garrison spent his career in the National Park Service, serving as chief ranger in Washington, D.C., and later as regional director of the midwest and northeast regions. See Lemuel A. Garrison, *The Making of a Ranger: Forty Years with the National Parks* (Salt Lake City and Chicago: Howe Brothers, 1983).

Then Kerr came in and told Lon [Garrison] he could climb up to Heather Lake tomorrow and put up trail signs. I said I'd go with him if he liked, so he arranged. I found an old pair of trousers with which to make hobbles & went up and down until I saw the burros. Little black Betsy stood docilely to have her chin stroked, but Grandma circled around and would not let me near her. So I talked to her and fondled Betsy until Granny came up close and I caught her. I had one hobble on, but when I moved over to fasten the other, she got frightened and leapt away. It began to rain then, so I went back to bed.

JUNE 5, MONDAY

An hour after prima luce I went out to see the burros. They were close by, and the hobble was gone, so I left them. I had my oatmeal and covered camp, hanging my saddle in a tree for safety.

Lon was just up, and he spilled an egg and some water to start the day. We put things together and Irving drove us up Wolverton creek to the forestation camp. We left him there and struck off thru the timber, sliding down the snowbanks. We had to dig and probe in three feet of snow to find some signs which were broken off by the snowfall.

Then it began to snow, and we kept climbing higher and higher. We went thru a grove of dwarf aspens that were writhen and contorted like tortured snakes.

The willows had a beautiful coppery sheen on their bark. Lon showed me how to tell the red fir from the white, by the needles and the bark. Also he showed me yellow pine and lodgepole and chinquapin brush. We followed some big bear tracks and saw other tracks we couldn't name.

It snowed more and more heavily. We climbed to an altitude of 10,000 ft., where only lodgepole and red spruce grew. Then we slid down a vertical slope to Heather Lake. I got my shoes full of snow. The lake was beautiful. Most of it was covered with ice and snow, but there were patches of emerald green, and the red trunks and green boughs of the spruce contrasted against the white snow and gray glacial boulders.

After several attempts we started a fire against a big rock. It smoked and flared, but finally cooked the beans, which we ate, while the snow sifted down our necks. We had a reel and line and earthworms, but Lon had forgotten the hook after I laid it out for him, so we had no trout with our crackers. Just as we left, the fire roared up almost as fast as the snow hissed down. The sun glowed for a moment and the snow was blinding. Then we climbed the ridge and slithered down the slope to another buried sign which we recovered and set up. The snow was three feet deep, with about two inches of new snow. After that we used our shoes for skis, finding it difficult to control direction, however. Once my foot went thru and I jumped up, sat down, bowled Lon over, and fetched up against a tree. The long slides were great fun. We came off the ridge into Lodgepole, wet thru by this time. I went thru camp, saw the burros leaning up against the trees with the water dripping off their ears, and rejoined Lon. I put on some old clothes of his, and made some biscuits which we ate with salmon and tea.

While I wiped the dishes, Lon told me that my dish towel had been used to cover a corpse. Lon had been sent to care for an invalid of the Sierra Club, and after a few days, he died. Lon was in charge of the outfit which brought her down the mountain on stretchers. Lon guessed I was 23. He is 29. After much talk I went home. The tarp had kept my bed quite dry. There was a beautiful full moon.

JUNE 6, TUESDAY

Half the day we were in the clouds. They puffed by, veiling the hilltops and making patterns of the trees. Lon and Irving peeled a lodgepole pine for a flagpole. With much repartee and ironcracking we decided where to put it, but we hit rock and had to dig another hole. We had the pole up and balanced, ready to put in, but it fell over and knocked us down. The next time we did it.

I talked with some campers, wrote, ate, and read, also searching vainly for the burros.

JUNE 7, WEDNESDAY

I got up too late, and Lon went by on his way up Clover Creek. I rushed back and forth, pounding up and down the hillside, but I did not find a fresh trail for an hour or two, when I caught them at Silliman creek. I rode up Kings river trail to the ridge above camp, and pastured the burros in Willow Meadow. Then I went on up the snow trail like a steam engine, hoping to catch up with Lon. The sweat ran into my eyes, burning like fire.

At noon I reached the ridge and met two electricians putting up the telephone line. One of them gave me a sandwich, and I went on to

Clover Creek and the cabin. Lon was gone. The snow was melting and I couldn't track him. I explored the cabin, and sat disconsolately in front. I fished half heartedly and lost my hook. Finally Lon came back from Twin Lakes with five fish. We went down together, I carrying his Alaskan pack made with two sticks and cross braces. He showed me the incense cedar and pointed out some peaks. At the road he left me, and I went on to camp, where I made some pop corn.

I read in "The Golden Ass" about Lucius and Fotis, and how she changed him to an ass instead of a bird by mistake.

JUNE 8, THURSDAY

In the cool of the morning I tossed some things in the pack and started for Giant Forest. I stopped at Lon's and looked in his catalog of fishing tackle. I filled out a blank intending to send for a rod, reel, line, hooks, gut, and salmon eggs, but on my way down the road, I decided I would never make a fisherman and that fishing would waste and divert too much time from other things. Also, there was the outlay for tackle and license to consider.

A driver from the Clover Creek construction gang gave me a ride into headquarters. At the studio I got my films, which were not very good. I succeeded in trading my print of the eucalyptus for a convenient hip flask to carry water for water colors, and .75 cents credit in photographic work. At the post office was a 5 dollar order from father. The clerk wanted to see my signature so I showed it to her on some of my prints. She was interested and said she would buy a picture by the end of the season. A C.C.C. boy saw me showing them, and wanted me to show him how to paint signs. He was in the ranger office. I showed him the H.T. Fay technique, and painted a couple of signs, "No Hiking Along This Stream," and something else. He said he would save part of his lunch for me. I went over to Beetle Rock and then to Frank Dawson's place. I gave him the picture of himself riding the burro. I watched the small boys playing games, then went back and lunched with Leland Johnson, the new sign painter. He was swinging the brush skillfully. We argued about business and ideals for an hour or so, getting nowhere. My Stetson arrived in the afternoon mail. I put it on and felt like a man again.

Then I talked with Hobson. I like him well. He knows all the best music and is ardent for Sibelius. He used to feel that he would live a hermit life and be well rounded by reading books, but now he feels that we live only when we influence and are influenced by others. I lent him "Green Mansions." His young wife is quite an extrovert. We discussed Sinclair. He has an appealing drawl, and slow, heavy manner, and seems genial at first, but later will not even answer questions. Sam Clark is a good natured ranger, though he can't spell. I bought a map from Spigelmyre, the assistant chief ranger. He marked the High Sierra trail on it.

[Seven lines apparently erased]

I bought groceries and candy at the store, filled my pack sack, and started up the road a little before sunset. A truck of Citizens Conservation Corps men passed me on the way to Wolverton.

Finally a couple from Hollywood stopped and drove me up, though they had meant to turn around. The man was a studio worker who told me that the Wetherills had started to make a picture of Laughing Boy at last. I showed them my stuff, but made no sale.

Then I talked with Lon and Irving a while and built up my campfire. I made a prodigious quantity of tomato, peanut butter and rye sandwiches, and ate them while I read Rabelais, concerning the advent of Gargantua. Later I sat by the fire.

June 9, Friday

After books and breakfast, I washed clothes at the riverbank and had a tingling bath in the clear, green water.

I watched some men fell a dead pine, chop off the bark, and burn the pine borers. Then I talked with Lon about some trails. I may have been too forward with him. He says the government only allows outside stock to stay two days in one spot.

Then an old fellow who was watching the pine borer fire showed me his map of a gold mine, given to him by an 80 year old cronie who had it from a prospector killed by an Indian in Visalia. It is at the foot of some peaks near Frying Pan Meadow, at the forks of Kings river. He said he would like to go over there with me when his dollar a day job gave out.

The sun is warm. Above, the snow is rapidly melting. The colors are brilliant. A shaft of light touches the patch of green lichen on the trunk of red fir. A doe is circling my camp. Below, the snow water rushes and pounds thru its rocky channel, tumbling frothily into lucent green pools.

With great enjoyment I read the gusty, unrestrained exploits of Gargantua, Granzousier, Picrochole, and the monk. I wrote a letter brim full of exuberance, sending it to Lawrence by some chance tourists. I stretched the king snake skin and admired afresh its glittering contrasts of red, buff, and black. I read and ate in Gargantuan fashion, sat by my fire, and sang for sheer exuberance. Then I made tomorrows lunch, and prepared everything for an early start, lit a pine needle flare, and curled up beneath the stars. I woke in the night when two deer were beside me. The full moon gleamed searchingly.

June 10, Saturday

When the sun was just up, I woke, but it was so cold that I slept an hour. Then I made ready in haste. I found a lady mouse in my uncovered kyak. She had been nibbling my bread, for the third night. I was sorry to dispatch her, for she had a beautiful little nest of my clothes and papers, shredded neatly.

I swung up the road, past Silliman creek, Clover creek & the construction camp. Singing blithely, I came to Halstead Meadow, where I took the trail above the stream. I slipped in some soft snow by a log, but saved myself. Purling brooklets splashed down the slopes. Red snow flowers were growing by the water. At length I topped the ridge. Below I heard the frog chorus of Colony Meadows. I slid down the snow banks, and below the meadow I stopped to sketch a rock pile. It was a miserable sketch and I froze my feet the while.

On I went, losing the trail and following the granite slopes of Dorst Creek, a large powerful stream. I clambered from rock to rock until I came to a picturesquely contorted old pine, which I photographed and painted with fair success. Then I went down to the river, where it plunged into a deep pool about forty feet long and fifteen across. I plunged in and flailed about me, then tried to get out, but the sides were so steep and slippery that I barely managed it. After a rest, I swam across it and about, then dried in the sun, lunched under my pine, and went downstream till I found the Cabin Meadow trail. I startled some deer that bounded off like springboks. Then I tromped down the ridge into the lush green of Cabin Meadow. There was smoke rising from the cabin, and I found Lon cooking lunch. He had been almost to Giant Park with the contractor. There were plenty of covers, so I decided to stay over with Lon. We went up Cabin Meadow Creek posting "no fishing" signs. I saw some gooseberry bushes, cherry, willow, and chinquapin. Leaping dexterously across the stream we went down a mile or so to Dorst Creek, where Lon fished in the pools. We had no luck, and were about to return when Lon tried the first pool again. He caught twelve fish, 4 of which we threw back. The others were small. We used salmon eggs, earthworms, and a grub which I caught. Lon caught two at once, one time. I cleaned the fish and we went back at dusk.

The cabin is hand made, the shingles are split with an ax. We had cheese sandwiches and sardines.

JUNE 11, SUNDAY

We climbed Stony Creek Ridge to the park boundary, breathing in the fragrance of sun warmed pine needles. Then we packed down to Dorst Creek, and fished awhile. Lon caught three, then I plunged in the deep pool under the rock and slid downstream a hundred feet or so. The water froths and bubbles into the pool, and two pointed streamers of foam drift downstream. Beyond, scattered white bubbles fleck the glassy green surface, where the stream goes under the willows. We went south and west till we came to the trail where the road would be. It was a very narrow, uneven trail along the face of Little Baldy. We reached the derricks and steam shovels, and as soon as we came to smooth road, we pounded on like steel muscled giants in full stride.

Exhausted, we reached Halstead Meadow. There we drank and met Irving [Kerr], who took us on in.

I ate a Gargantuan mess of sandwiches and fried yams while I read about Pantagmel and Panwage and how they discomfited his giants. While I was away the mouse's mother chewed a horrible hole in my best Navajo saddle blanket. When the fire faded, the embers took on a more intense glow, the trees loomed higher, and the starlight poured straight down.

JUNE 12, MONDAY

It took longer than I liked to break camp, but by 9, I was off for Giant Forest. I trotted up to the crest and strode down the hill. One car passed, and finally, when it had reached Pinewood, Spig gave me a ride. He was driving with a mechanic, testing his car, and he forgot to let me off, so we drove over to Bear Hill and back. At the studio I met Steve, a U.C.L.A. student who clerks in the grocery store. We talked about the school for some while.[4] Then Mrs. Brann, partner with Mrs. Gaddis in the studio, introduced me to her daughter Lillian. She is a good sort, and had been two years at Otis. She wanted to see my stuff, so I showed her, and we talked a while.

I tried to write in the studio, then again in the lodge. I talked to John, who clerks there and is studying medicine at Stanford. Then Mickey McGuire, the information girl, came in for a while. I couldn't write there, so I went back to the Post Office to wait for the mail. The Postmaster and his wife looked at my pictures, and then I talked for an hour or so with Mrs. Disbrow, who lives on government hill. She is a happy woman with a sensible philosophy. It was delightful to sit in the shade of the redwoods, watch the flag flutter and the men digging in the sun, everyone happy and smiling, working, conversing or watching. The whole atmosphere was of spaciousness, peace, and contentment. In the city I sometimes wonder if one has a right to be happy when all around is such strife, discord, misery, and undeserved suffering. Here the thought never intrudes itself.

In the center of the square is a towering sequoia, very lordly, rearing his green crest high into the upper sunlight. It seems to dominate everything and all the other trees aspire to it.

I talked with Scheffer, an artist painting signs for the park. Then with Chris Seibeirth, who was installing some ingeneous figures he had contrived with redwood cones and clay. I admired his oils and showed him my work. He knows his stuff, and gave me some good criticism. I like him too.

Then I had an illuminating talk with Sam Clark. It seems I have to use some psychology on Lon. We and Mickey talked about rattlesnakes awhile. Then I went over to Sunset Rock.

I sat on the granite top in the shade of the bent pines a few moments, when I was startled by a mischievously hurled stone clattering on the rock, and along came Lillian. We sat talking a while, and I unburdened myself somewhat. We discussed the profession, and she agrees with Hobson that every genius gets his energy from a subconscious attempt to make up for the unsatisfactory elements in his life. If he were living a well rounded life, he would have no promptings to ambition. In other words, genius is a defense mechanism. Lillian expects to marry soon, and she was telling me about her house plans.

---

4. Everett had attended UCLA for one semester, 1932–33.

Then her young brother and his friend came by, and we discussed camping trips and Sierra lore. They went on, and I angled about the bent trees, taking snapshots and deciding where to paint. I made a drawing from below, finishing just as the sun went down behind Little Baldy. I talked to some well wishing tourists and started back. I stopped at Frankie's place. He and his sister Rita are down in the valley, but I talked to his older brother, the bronc breaker, and showed my pictures to his father and sisters. Mr. Dawson cordially invited me to come all day and stay for dinner some time.

I saw Harry ONeele and his friend Ike at the R.S. [Ranger Station] and they were jolly. Then I got my pack in the studio (Mrs. Gaddis kindly permitted me to leave my package there), and went to the store where Steve served me with groceries. I loaded up on fresh fruits and sallied forth, forgetting to pay for them. Steve forgot too, but I remembered and dashed back. We parted smilingly. Then up the starlit road between the pillared redwoods. I munched chocolate and sang at the top of my voice when I passed the camps. I drank at a stream, and strode gallantly up, singing some Dvorak melodies, putting all the volume I had into them. The forest boomed with my rollicking song. Then the transmuted melodies of Beethoven, Brahms, and the Bolero rang thru the silent forest. I rocked from side to side of the road, spun round in circles, looking up at the stars, and swung exultantly down the white pathway to adventure. Adventure is for the adventurous. I am young and a fool. Forgive me and read on. I thought that there were two rules in life— never count the cost, and never do anything unless you can do it wholeheartedly. Now is the time to live.

I stopped in front of Lon's. Everything was pitch dark. I wrote him an invitation to a royal repast tomorrow and crept to his porch, but his trained woodsmans ears heard the sound. I heard a hollow, throaty, Hey——goin? which was inimitably Lon. I fumbled under the door and scuttled off like a thief after leaving the note.

June 13, Tuesday

I slept little, and waited for dawn. A mouse or chipmunk started to nibble at my groceries, next to my head. I jerked around, and it scuttered off with an indignant churr.

I dozed awhile and then saw a Douglas squirrel or Sierra chickaree on my boulder. He pussyfooted along, climbed the tree, looked at me, and made such a ridiculous noise that I burst out laughing, rather offending him, I think. He sounded like a toy rubber dog being squeezed.

After reading a while, I went upstream and watched a foaming waterfall, then talked with Kerr, who said I could keep the burros in Willow Meadow another week if I liked.

Then I read, cooked rice pudding and made sandwiches. Lon came over, sat on a pine needle cushion and talked while we ate. A friend of his, philosophy professor of Stanford, is coming in two weeks, and might want to go along with me for a while. We conversed till dark, then Lon went home, taking a jubilant letter I had written to Jack and Alice.

JUNE 14, WEDNESDAY

I read about Pantagrual while I ate a pile of sandwiches. Then I trotted up the trail to Willow Meadow. The burros were soon found. Grandma had skinned her legs with the hobbles, so I changed them. Then I lay on a rock under the aspens, which were just putting out their pale waxy leaves that glittered in the sun. I looked and looked and could not be satiated. After a few hours, I came down again, and made sandwiches of all that was left in camp. I read Rabelais while I ate to my utmost capacity. At dusk I finished the book. Up to the trail makers camp I went, and looked at their two stout burros. One of them is black all over—the first burro I've ever seen with a black nose.

JUNE 15, THURSDAY

I prepared to hike to the watch tower, and stopped at Lon's to lend him Rabelais. He was just preparing to go to Heather Lake and the Watch Tower, so I went with him. Kerr drove us to the foot of the trail at Wolverton. I decided that the best way to hike was to take short rests and keep plugging. After a hard pull we reached the crest, and went down to Heather lake. Lon put up a sign, and we went a mile to Aster lake where Lon caught nine trout, fishing in a hole in the ice. The snowy glare was blinding. I went up to Emerald lake and sketched a splendidly whirled fir. After a while Lon came up too. We circled the lake, then he nearly fell thru the snow once. The water is very deep, and makes the snow look green. We ate on a rock shelving into the water. Then we climbed back above Heather in the soft snow and slid down to Watch Tower. I cut my leg when I snagged on a rock. The watch tower is a narrow cliff separated from the main cliff on one side by a steep, sheer chasm. I cant imagine how it was formed. It does not seem glaciated or faulted. The drop is 1,500 feet. We studied a nest in a cranny in the face of the cliff opposite to see if it was an eagle's. There was a bird in the nest, very hard to discern. I climbed out on the rock, then sat on the edge again until late.

We strode down the trail, past the same twisted aspens, which were now quite green. We went right down the ridge into Lodgepole. I cooked hurriedly and read "South Wind" until dark.

June 16, Friday

Early up and down toward the village. After a mile, I got a ride on a truck to Sherman tree. I took the trail past Chimney tree and Congress group to Circle meadow. This time I really saw and began to appreciate the redwoods. The meadow was extravagantly lush. I found the bears bath tub—a pool in a recess of a sequoia, very cleverly contrived. I went thru a burnt tree called the Black Causeway and down a delightful little stream where I stopped to bathe and refresh myself.

I went over a rocky knoll and through some aspens. I heard something squeaking and scraping under a log and turned it over, finding some boring beetles and a glossy-coated red millipede, which I kept.

Arrived in the village, I went to the museum where I talked with Powell, the naturalist. The museum is not yet officially open. I met Hobson and Atwood, and then Earl McKee drove up with Ord Loverin. I shook hands with Earl and exchanged news. Loverin is an ugly looking old sot and he is impolite. He said he didn't know if he would bring up his stock this year, there was so little business. Later I learned that the concession had been taken away from him and given to Earl.

I found a good letter from Laurence. Cornel has left home without telling his parents, and Benny Ershoff is very ill with Peritonitis. Laurence is sick of the city. Some of my films were good, but three were worthless.

I talked with Leland, and with Ashton Brann, Lillian's brother. He means to be an entomologist, and he showed me his beetles in his tent at Paradise Camp. Steve and another fellow came in, and we argued angrily about the world and affairs. Steve contested everything I said. Pitkin's book on Human Stupidity is his bible. They got to talking discolored humor, and I thought less of them. Ashton told about a fellow who was galloping towards a fork in a road. He leaned one way and the horse went the other way, and he was left behind. I told them about the time Clark went in the stables beside a big bay horse. He was standing with both feet together, and the horse stepped on them and wouldn't budge. Clark was helpless for a few minutes.

In the village I wrote a letter to the family, loaded up with groceries and went up the road. After a while, a tourist stopped for me. It was a teacher from Oakland, named Wilcox. He was hiking up to Twin lakes tomorrow with his wife and daughter, to stay two days, and wished he had a burro. He drove me all the way into camp, and asked me to come over to see him after supper.

I read about the island of Nepanthe, concerning Denis, the Duchess, Saint Dodekanus, Don Francisco, and Count Caloveglia.

At dusk I found my way to the Wilcox camp. They were just eating, so I sat down to a second supper. I talked to Ann Louise, their daughter, a round cheeked lass just out of high school. She likes dancing and admires Mary Wigman. She read my poems and liked them. I said I would pack them up [using burros] for three dollars, but they thought they would hike after all. I found my way back in the darkness.

June 17, Saturday

The Wilcox's didn't come thru camp, so I read awhile, then hearing voices on the trail above, I covered camp and rushed up, taking my bridle and rope. Finally I caught up with four fishermen. My friends had gone early. Arrived at Willow Meadow, I stepped up to the burros who looked like wild things belonging there. I rode Betsy to the creek, but she would not cross, so I led her. On the down trail I met an odd little fisherman, bound for Twin Lakes. I hobbled Betsy and turned Grandma loose so they could nibble the grass, which was now plentiful. They munched and lolled in the shade. I assembled my outfit, then went over to see if Lon was still there. He was, and was preparing to move his cabin to a rivulet up the road. I helped him a while, and we had lunch— soup, sweet potatoes, and loganberries, rather elaborate for me. Lon showed me some interesting letters he had received, and I showed him mine, also giving him a photograph of himself in the snow, digging out the trail sign. My camera has been behaving erratically, or else it has been mishandled.

In the early afternoon, I packed and saddled the burros and started for the trail. Betsy plunged and bucked, but I kept her under me. Grandma pulled back, so I fixed a comealong. It was a thrill to go up the steep hill without any effort on my part. I argued with Betsy a few minutes before she would cross the first snowbank. We forded Willow Creek without trouble. The burros turned their heads and long ears to look at the deer. It was very pleasant to ride up the forest trail.

Betsy wouldn't cross Silliman Creek, so I led Grandma, who is usually more tractable. Then I rode Betsy across without trouble for she didn't want to be left. We circled a steep ridge and went up Cahoon Meadow. At the top, the snow was deep and somewhat soft, so I tied Betsy to Grandma's pack and led them down to Clover Creek.

Here we stayed for an hour. The ford was easy, but the snow crumbled at the edge, and Grandma took fright. I tried another easier ford, but she was still obdurate. I strung out my rope and tied her to a tree on the opposite bank, then broke my persuader to no purpose. In despair I went up further leading Betsy, and we crossed on a narrow snowbridge which I expected to collapse at any moment. Betsy brayed for Gran, who still refused to take the ford, so with my heart in my mouth, I led her to the snowbridge. I wondered that it held my weight. It was undercut by the stream which leapt hungrily below. Granny, 650 pounds with her pack, crossed with dainty, mincing steps. My feet were very cold with the ice water, but on we rode, to the Clover Creek cabin. The stream was just as deep there, but the ford easier, and we crossed without difficulty.

Then we followed a path that led around the mountain. In a mile or two we came to Pattee creek. We crossed some snow, forded the creek, and stopped in a thicket of young firs between two fallen trees. The sunset was splendid, where tall firs stand on the edge of the meadow where it drops off.

I built a blazing fire at once, changed my shoes, pealed yams and onions and went to the burros with some tidbits as a peace offering. I explained to them that the chastisement had been in the line of duty, nowise affecting my kindling sentiments toward them. They went up the slope. Later I thought I heard a scream like a cougar's. The burros came galloping down the hill to my fire, then wandered off.

I read and wrote by firelight, dreamed awhile, as is my wont, roused myself finally, and went to bed.

JUNE 18

The meadow here is still in the first stages of spring, although here and there are flowers growing. Melting snowbanks line the east bank.

I was awakened in the cold dawn by the burros coming in to camp. It was so cold that I slept another hour. There was a cake of ice in my dish pan. I could not see the burros, but concluded that they must be nearby. I put the bed across the kyaks, and logs over that. Snatching up my sketch case and camera, I went off thru the forest. At the Clover Creek crossing I picked up a rope I forgot yesterday, then I climbed the steep trail past Staircase Falls to Twin Lakes. There I came upon Mr. Wilcox cleaning fish. The family was just preparing to depart. They had caught two limits of fish. They gave me a surprise loaf of bread cut lengthwise and filled with various condiments. Also five trout and a pair of snow glasses. I promised to send them a letter with a poem for Anne. They went down at noon, and I climbed up to Silliman Crest, looking off into the Sierras. Below was a mysterious, glass green lake, edged with dark, brooding firs. I hurried down again, took the fish out of the snow and put them in my pack, and started home. I love the snowglasses. They make the sky green, and suggest an approaching storm. They kept out the light so effectually that I lost the trail, but found it later. The burros were cropping grass at the lower end of the meadow. I fed them more delicacies, with a good response.

I fried the fish, built up the fire, and sat up against my log to read "South Wind," concerning the Locri Faun, the Bishop of Bampopo, Madame Steynlin, and Peter Krasnejabkin, Keith, Eames, and Van Koppen. The book is delightful. I read Keith's defense of Miss Wilberforce, and enjoyed the descriptions of drunkenness at the clubs.

A bird sang sweetly and long at twilight. I read for an hour or so by firelight, sat back in reverie while the flames leaped.

JUNE 19

I crossed the park boundary, following a trail northwards, upstream, but the map must have been in error, for I failed to find a cross trail. The rocks were spotted with red and vermillion. I came down a granite ridge between two creeks that converged in Pattee. At noon I was in camp again, and the burros were sprawled complacently on a bare slope. Finally I finished "South Wind," enjoying the final Bacchic scene. It is truly amusing to me what people say before they pass out. Everyone should have the experience, I think. Ending the tale of the sirocco, I brought in the donkeys, fed them some scraps, loaded Granny and set out for better pasture at Cabin Meadows.

I rode only a mile. The snow impeded the way, and the trail was sometimes hidden. I reached the ridge above Bolong Meadow, hearing plainly the frog chorus. Lon told me about the colony. It was a social-istic experiment that worked for many years, until the railroad company broke it up.

The trail was obscured, and I went down the steep slope until the way was impassable, turned about and came down another way. Soon we were out of the meadows, and the stream ran in the trail. Finally the blazes on the trees stopped and we were lost again. I circled until I found a trail, and we followed that thru the snow until we were lost once more. I led the burros across a wet meadow, past the snow to a rocky hill. After reconnoitering, I made camp on a flat space between rocks, a dying fir, or dead fir, and a live tree. There is not too much grass. I cooked eggplant, gave the peeling to the burros, and read Tomlinson's "The Sea and the Jungle." So far, it leaves me cold. It is too niggling, making much of small things. Granny came in, nosing up to me. I relented and gave her a crust, then demonstrated to her where the grass was. I got a picture of the burros laying down. The fire burns meagerly and the frog chorus swells in volume.

Ominous detonations recurred for a quarter of an hour, sounding like artillery nearby. The contractor is attempting to put the road thru in a few weeks, according to contract, but he has two or three miles of unfinished road and untouched trail.

Sunset threw long, long shadows on the sparsely forested hill. The tree trunks glinted goldly. I watched the red sun go down.

JUNE 20

I woke early after a sound sleep. The burros were right by, and after breakfast, I tightened the breaching on the pack saddle, burdened by burros, and led them down a little-used path which I had found. We crossed the brook, slid down some brown slopes, and reached a cleaner trail, which led us to the top of Colony Meadow! I can't imagine what the last two streams were, but this is Colony Creek.

The meadow was much nicer than last time, and not too wet. Grass was up everywhere, and the burros fell to with a will. I decided to stop, and selected a space between eight tall firs. My camp was laid so that I had the sun in the morning and evening, and shade at noon.

I went for a short ride on Betsy, but Granny persisted in coming too. I couldn't dismay her. When I tied her to a log, she brayed dismally, then came charging along with it, breaking her rope when she crossed the stream. Then I tied her to a tree. I saw where the trail went down. I may not get lost this time, because more snow has melted. Then I rode across the creek and up the farther hill, to a spacious view of many hills and canyons, with granite ridges above them.

I read further in Tomlinson and began to enjoy his description of the jungle. This book somewhat parallels Hudson's "Green Mansions," and Beebe's "Jungle Peace."

Three willowy young school teachers with glasses on passed on the other side of the stream. Apparently they did not trust me, for they would not reply to my greeting. I am again mistrusting myself in relation to other people.

[18 lines erased]

The girls came back, and I crossed to meet them, speaking to them as I crossed the brook. They went right on in silence, not to be outdone even in ill breeding and insolence. I went straight up the hill as if that had been my intention. I climbed on a good rock on top of a vaster one and surveyed the forests and canyons below me.

Later I read additionally, bathed and made a sorry black and white version of the bent pine. I gave the burros some more delicacies. I couldn't find any 3D brand on Bobtail, but I discovered a 3H brand on Betsy.

I foolishly built the fire on the upstream side, and at evening the smoke blew in my face. I ought to be a better woodsman.

When the evening detonations went off, two bucks came bounding down the ridges as if shot. I never cease to enjoy the fanlike fronds of the firs. A tiny chipmunk climbed the fir tree opposite. I climbed the hill at sunset and watched the waterfall.

June 21

Early up. I climbed the hill to look for the burros, but tho I went far, I couldn't find where the tracks led off, so I returned and had corn meal mush for breakfast. I read a chapter of "The Sea and the Jungle."

There was a really excellent description of city slavery, concerning an English clerk. What a miserable apology for existence those clerks led. Then I read about the Rio Madre de Dios, Rio Japua, and Rio Madeira, the blue morphs butterflies, and the quinine and fever. There were three colors there—the yellow of the river, the green of the jungle wall, and the blue of the sky.

Then I climbed the hill again until I came across burro tracks. I followed them up and down like a hunter after his quarry, until I heard the faint metallic tinkle of the bell. I crept up behind a rock, meaning to confront them unawares. Suddenly I gave my imitation of a mountain lion. They swung their heads around and cocked their ears at me. I sat under a tall sugar pine for an hour or so, watching them crop the short grass. I enjoy watching their movements, the play of muscles, the flux from form to form. On second thought, Betsy's brand must be 2H, but I am not certain. I climbed out on a granite point, and regarded my surroundings a while, keenly enjoying the sense of height and remoteness, the warm tang of dry pine needles, and the wind in the fir tops.

At length I climbed on Grandma and led Betsy down the hill. The way was rough and the burros were obstinate. I led them past the old camp, rode them a ways, then tied them together and drove them. Once they went on opposite sides of a tree, and didn't have the intelligence to untangle. Again, Betsy got one foot hung up, but she leaped quite nimbly over logs when Grandma jerked the rope.

It was midafternoon when we reached camp again. I was assailed by an unreasonable hunger, doubtless partly imaginary, but the pangs forced me to dig into my slender supplies and make a soup of split peas, rice, onions, corn meal, and a few sticks of macaroni. I finished Tomlinson. The book ends with a violent relief at leaving the wilds for civilized food and for home. Not a good suggestion for me, now. I am not as superior to food and creature comfort as I'd like to be.

[One line erased]

I read Lafcadio Hearn's "Chinese Ghosts." Learned the derivation of kaolin. I tremendously admire the incomparable Chinese vases which I have seen with their superb glazes of ruby and blue. Hearn took his name from Leucedia, one of the Green Ionian islands, where he was born.

At dark the deer came in to drink. I made some tea, and some most satisfactory cocoa, which made me pleasantly drowsy. Some time when

I am in the mood, I will list all my possessions and the romantic places of their origin. They have come from all parts of the world, and temporarily they are in one place.

Almost all of my camps in the Sierras have been close to running water. The sound is entering my subconscious. The firs are very tall and sparsely leafed.

JUNE 22

Earlier up. I found the burros at the head of the meadow and brought them in closer. I left a can in the doused fire. The only trace of humankind I found here was the lid of a can, marked Copenhagen snuff. We went to the edge of the waterfall, then began the steep, long descent. Finally we came out below the waterfall, and I looked up at the solid front of forest. It was luxurious to sit back in the saddle and look at the trees and flowers while the other burro carried all the load. The burros forded the streams and I did not even get my feet wet. The trail led thru the forest, and I missed the rocky Dorst Creek gorge, where I found my twisted pine. I'm glad I missed the trail that day.

We went thru a meadow with bear tracks on the trail. Down and down I rode on steep, narrow trails, until we came to Dorst Creek. I led Granny across. The water came up breast high. It was beautiful to see her carrying the pack across the stream. Then I climbed on Betsy, and rode right through the water, with my feet at angles. I picked up Gran's rope and we jogged up the hill, arriving in Cabin Meadows at last. The fence was up and everything was glowingly green. I heard a bell ringing, like a child pounding a triangle, and saw the trail crew's burros. Their paraphernalia was hanging about the locked cabin. I went up the trail a ways and met them coming in for lunch. They are a young fellow about my age, and a short, red-faced, middle aged fellow who is quite a personality. They invited me to lunch, and I had bread, butter, jam, cheese, and coffee with them. The older man has been all thru Yosemite, and in his youth was a nervy daredevil, climbing up Half Dome on hands and bare feet, spending the night there, and later balancing on the Hanging Rock. He told me of a tornado in his farm home in Kansas. The suction drew all the cobs in a corn bin out thru a knot hole, leaving the corn inside. Like Lon's story of the fur fish which have fur lined stomachs to digest the ice worms. In the winters they nibble their tails, and if the winter is too long and hard, all but the biggest ones eat themselves up. Like the salmon in Grand Canyon in the Colorado, who swim backwards to keep the mud out of their eyes. I asked them how they fastened their donkeys in the meadows up here. I told them I used the aspens (ass pins).

I showed them my pictures. The elder, a family man, said he always wanted to go to Grand Canyon, and the cliff dwellings.

They are hard workers, and went off after lunch to fix fence, dismissing my offer of assistance.

I saddled and packed, and crossed Cabin creek. Soon I ran into the road crew, chopping logs, sawing trees, and burning trash. After some coarse donkey humor from the boss, I left them, and at Dorst creek I had more fun. After several false starts, we forded the main stream in fine style, but when Betsy and I were half across a sidestream, Gran tried to back out, and we nearly pulled her in head over heels. Once across we took the trail to the Muir grove of Big Trees. It took us to a very lofty perch above Dorst Creek, which foamed far below us in the granite. The trail was clear and I let the reins drop and smoked a peace cigarette. I lost the trail once but found it soon. We climbed a high ridge and went in and around a long canyon, winding like the Tonto Trail. At the top on the far side the redwoods began. The noblest of all was on the top of the hill. It was not unusually tall, but very massive, of splendid girth, towering hugely.

The trail led down between the sequoias and I hardly saw the trail, I was staring so, looking and looking at the huge red trees. Some were straight and smoothly rounded, like pillars in a Cyclopean cathedral. Others were ridged and knurled and fluted. All, sadly, had been touched by fire. The ferns grew luxuriantly.

The burros speed was well suited to my desires. Visually and spiritually I was filled with a slow delight that grew in me till I almost burst.

At last we left the pageant of redwoods behind, for groves of pine and fir. The snow on the slopes had bent the firs low across the trail, and many trees were fallen. We brushed under and over the best we could.

Then we came to another grove of vegetation. Gorgeous, flowering dogwood was around us, and the black oak, for which this trail is named. In one place I had to brace up a tree while the burros went under, and they gave me a hard fight to put them thru. Then on a rock ledge at a dripping waterslide, I led them over logs and then I rode under two big ones. Just after Granny got thru, the big one fell with a crash onto the trail.

The breaching strap on Gran's pack saddle broke twice and her pack slid forwards. I fixed it at last.

We entered a tall forest of yellow pines where the grass covered the trail. I began to doubt my way, and after the path led backwards for some time, I unloaded on a rough, overgrown slope, for it was late. I went the other way to fill my canteen, and found a glorious camp spot on the edge of the cliff above the waterfall.

The stream is quite small and there is a riotous profusion of green plants. There is a thick pine needle carpet over the rock, and stately young pines and sequoias grow with sunflowers at their feet. The partly obscured trail goes right thru.

I was almost overcome, but I rushed back, clearing the trail of fallen timber as I went, and flung the saddle on Betsy, loaded Grandma and flung a square hitch, and down we rode on the edge, with the bell tinkling on Betsy and the hobbles clinking on Gran's foreleg. I dismounted in the pine needles by some gorgeous snowflowers under pines and young sequoias, well spaced.

I loosed the burros across the rivulet, and had a glorious bath while the sun was sinking behind a saffron cloud. I had a fire and some supper while the sun set, and thanked my soul profusely and unrestrainedly for such beauty and delight.

JUNE 23, FRIDAY

Luxuriously I lay back in my blankets for two full hours after I awakened. I looked up at the silvery green of the pine needles, flashing in the sun. I watched the moving patterns of light in the forest above, and I rested my eyes on the russet of the needles mantling the granite. A bluebird fluttered above, and a hummingbird hovered over me, then drank the nectar of my scarlet snow flowers.

After breakfast, I was unable to resist the lure of the trail that beckoned round the corner. I went several turns, and, heaving mightily, I pitched off all but one of the fallen trees.

Then I went down the waterfall, exploring. There were many beautiful little pools and two other falls. I climbed down to a ledge at the foot of one fall and above another. There was one redwood, and a tiny pine, and I sat in their shade watching the white cascade, and the fluttering butterflies. They were anglewings, I think. They and the mourning cloaks are the only species I have seen.

Climbing up again, I followed the stream up above camp, then came back, feeling that mine was much the choicest spot.

I tried to write a letter to Carl, but failed, and climbed the hill to see the burros. They were nearby, but Grandma hasn't learned anything about hobbles. She tries to move both legs in opposite directions, and skins herself miserably.

I sketched a rock pinnacle on the other side of the canyon, and rolled a boulder down the waterfall. Just then my solitude was completely shattered by the arrival of a trail patrolman. He was mounted on a big black horse, on a handsome red leather bronc saddle with a gun on one side. Chained behind were two white pack horses, well loaded.

The patrolman wouldn't talk, but he gave me some insulting admonishments about my fire and about rolling rocks. He put up a sign, "Skayway Crossing, Black Oak Trail," that shattered the wild note. Yesterday I thot how sadly the new road was spoiling the forest.

I watched him change the box hitch on the last horse, which was carrying shovels on both sides, atop the tough canvas panniers. Then he went off, without attempting to smooth over the break in my silence which he had so rudely made. Thus far, I've had only two days of undisturbed solitude.

However, I knew the patrolman would at least partly clean the trail.

I had my first mess of good, familiar spotted dog in many months. The burros came down to drink at sunset, and I snapped them, sunlit against the lush grass, dark water, and shadowed forest.

Then out of curiosity I went down trail to the obstinate fallen fir. The intruder had lopped it off neatly. I counted the rings. The tree was 19 summers old, just as old as I.

My shoes are wearing out, and the sole flapped off one. I bound it on neatly with a copper wire. Then I had a cup of tea.

June 24, Saturday

Today I tied the box hitch for the first time and got it right. We were out of Skagway Crossing before the middle of the morning, riding happily on the edge of the steep trail. Before we topped the farther ridge, there was a splendid view of Skagway Falls, the three cascades, and my little redwood on the ledge.

Twice I dismounted to lift trees from the trail, and at Hidden Springs I turned down. The ranger station seems to have been burned up. I climbed a hill and saw the horses running here. There was a brown mule with a glistening, satiny coat, a handsome sorrel, and a lustrous steel grey.

We missed the trail twice, but then all was well. The trail was steep, both up and down. I admired the engineering and the rock masonry. The woods were very dense much of the way, and I was delighted to watch the tiger and zebra swallowtails, as well as the flowers. We crossed Cascade creek, and the burros snatched at some thistles as we rode by. I saw a ruffled grouse and the crested mountain quail. Lizards scuttled on the rocks.

Up a steep slope through manzanita and pine we toiled, until we saw the ranges spread out before us, and on our left, Cave Creek and its cataracts. Then down we climbed, past flowering dogwood, brushing against the ferns. I missed the cutoff to Suwanee trail, and we emerged at last on the tame, dusty North Fork Road.

Gran pulled back all the time, though she had no load to speak of, so I made her a nose loop, which taught her nothing. Betsy lay down once in a soft dusty spot, but after that we went on to Marble Fork bridge, looking up at Sunset Rock as we went. At the bridge we turned and climbed the grassy hill where we camped before, and I tethered Gran and hobbled Betsy.

The C.C. Camp was below, and a boy scout camp above. I started in for Giant Forest to get mail and provisions, as my grub box is empty, but it was too late for the mail, so I turned back.

I watched the flag lowering at the scout camp, but I could not bring myself to go thru the crowd of roystering boys, and I turned down to the C.C. camp. The captain was gone, and I couldn't buy food, so I went again to the scout camp, where I was directed to Mr. Lucas. He found some food and very generously gave me all I could carry for 60 cents. For my supper I had my fill of brown bread and baked beans, which promptly stopped my long clamoring apetite.

At dusk I returned, and the boys all gathered about me asking questions and asking me what kind of snakeskin I wore. They invited me to their camp fire where I told them some of my adventures, some tall stories, and sang them the song about the old woman who lived all alone, also a sea chantey and a burro song.

They had their court of honor, a story about the Dawn Patrol flights in the war, and some scout songs. Three bear cubs scrambled up a tree.

A C.C. boy, once a scout, led me down to my camp, and we stopped to talk awhile. The first thing I knew, he was doing his most to convert me to Christianity, and telling me what the Lord had done for him. I couldn't hurt his feelings, so I took his misdirected persuasions in good part, and finally he departed. He is on K.P. duty.

JUNE 25, SUNDAY

At Prima Luce I arose and attired myself in my finest raiment, after refreshing my features. After awhile I thought I would attend the scout camp's sunrise services. They had not started, and so I passed an hour or so in answering questions for the scouts. The chaplain did not arrive, so I went down to my breakfast.

I made everything ready, then went back to the camp. I helped peel potatoes and took the peelings for my burros. Then two boys went down with me to take my picture. I loaded the donkeys, got a couple of pictures and rode off for the Suwanee river.

Towards noon we came to a little rivulet in the big trees. After insane vacillation I chose a poor camp site, where the slope was wrong and the sun came thru at the foot of two redwoods. I hobbled Betsy, and after she ate a few mouthfuls of the grass which was plentiful here, she started back the trail with Gran. I drove them back, and they went off the other way. Then I tied Betsy. I read the Yosemite Park circular, and was very irritated by the tone of the editor. Soon I could stand it no longer and packed out. The pack slipped over on the trail, and in fixing it I tumbled on the double triangle hitch. Before long, we came to a larger stream, with a grassy place, and there we stopped. There was plenty of grass there, and almost none on the ridges, but the donkeys went first one way and then another, in spite of my teachings. In desperation, I tied Gran, and all night long, Betsy was going back and forth, each burro braying to its mate, until I tied Betsy too. The beans made me sick, as they always do. I was a fool to let myself be persuaded into buying them. Altogether my musings were of the darker sort, although the firs towering to the stars were beautiful.

JUNE 26, MONDAY

Rose early, took a bath, and washed all the dirty clothes. I loosed Grandma, and she stayed by. My blue mood departed with the night, and I plotted my course for the next two months to my entire satisfaction.

I was looking at a government map of the park when Grandma thrust out her muffled jaws and took it gently from me, munching philosophically. Betsy couldn't bear to be left out, so she had a corner too. They ought to be able to find the trail now!

I didn't bother about lunch, as I had had a late breakfast of oatmeal on toast, very tasty.

I packed Betsy and rode Grandma. Betsy is a much better lead animal, and if only she were bigger, this arrangement would be fine. Birds called melodiously. In a short time we came to Halstead meadow and the Suwanee river. The grass was high. I camped near some aspens, and answered Laurence's letter.

I tied Betsy in some tall grass, and from time to time, when Grandma went too far off, she would bray dishearteningly. I remembered in the "Golden Ass" a description the donkey gave of his torments. He said the boy that loaded wood on him would pile great stones on the light side when the pack did not balance. I was guilty of the same offense in my wood packing days.

June 27, Tuesday

I was up before sunlight, had breakfast, shaved clean, and when the sun was an hour high, we were off for Tokopah. I rode and sang, and met Lon at the campgrounds. He invited me to lunch and told me to camp where the trail crew used to be, and feed the burros some hay. He was riding a black horse, looking very much in his element. There were two other horses in the corral.

I was just about to take the burros up to Willow Meadow when two friends of Lon came over. They were Marshall Mason, a genial doctor, and Melvin Johnson, a real estate broker, both from San Jose. They wanted to go up to Pear Lake for fishing, and wished to use my burros. I said I'd enjoy going with them, so Melvin drove me down to the forest for my mail. Waldo has a job at San Berdoo [San Bernardino], working for the Metropolitan Water Co. It must have been a wrench for him to pull up stakes. He sent my boots. The last roll of films developed beautifully, except for one flaw in the film.

I met Inger, Lon's beautiful Alaskan wife, and we all lunched. I gave Lon the picture of himself looking at the eagle's nest.

We brought everything over to my camp, and Lon brought two more kyaks, which we put over the saddle. I left out a quantity of my things, and we packed their grub and the three beds on the burros. At about the same time Dickson, a visiting park naturalist, went off with three boys carrying packs and a well laden mule, to study Nature near Twin Lakes.

We sent the burros trotting up the road and were soon on the trail. Discussing philosophy, science, religion, work, and suicide, we reached the top above Heather Lake. They admired my kyaks and took a skyline picture. We climbed up the steep path to the next ridge, and then came down over jagged rocks and melting snowbanks to a fine camp site a little above Aster Lake.

Soon we had a roaring fire, and while the clouds covered us, we had dried apples and ham, pineapple, tea, and chocolate. Then for a few hours we sat in the firelight.

JUNE 28

We climbed the next ridge to Pear Lake, and I fell thru the ice into the water. Doctor fished me out, and I spread my socks and trousers on the rocks to dry, while I clambered about barefooted. I looked down from a ledge into the clear green water, and pointed out the fish to Melvin and Marshall. Marshall had the best luck.

Before long my clothes were dry, and I went to the other side of the lake to make a painting of some twisted firs in a notch, against high piled clouds. When I was quite exhausted by my rather futile efforts to materialize my vision, I went round to my friends to suggest lunch, for the afternoon was half gone.

On the way back, the Doctor let me cast with his rod, and I caught two trout. It really was fun. We caught 25 altogether and returned thru the clouds. I took some pictures in the mist.

Betsy and Grandma were close by. We fed them some scraps, and stirred up a fire. After supper we discussed medicine.

JUNE 29

Melvin and I planned to go to Alta Peak this afternoon while the doctor went down to Tokopah, as he was not interested in the climb. However, the morning's fishing at Pear Lake lasted till evening.

I saw a snake catch a fish in the water, and holding it in his ugly reptilian jaws a few inches out of the water, it swam ashore.

I used Melvin's rod a while and hooked ten or twelve fish, but couldn't keep any of them on the line. One got away just on the edge of the bank. The doctor caught 22, and Melvin only one. He fished again at Aster, unsuccessfully. We went up to Emerald lake together at sunset. I watched the sunlit crest of Alta Peak reflected in the water, and Melvin caught one big trout. We watched the moon awhile, then returned to the glow of the fire. There was a wonderful gleam on the opposite cliffs.

JUNE 30

Melvin took a picture of me flipping a flapjack, and one of the burros eating oats. I showed them my pictures and they were very appreciative. Marshall found a tiny nest of goldfishes, full of delicate miniature goslings. The coffee was good.

We took the fish out of the snowbank, and packed them on Grandma with Marshall's bed. Betsy fell thru the snow onto some sharp rocks, but was not injured. I took them down by way of the Watch tower, where we looked over the 2000 foot drop at the long, glittering cascade of Marble Fork, and at the eagle's nest.

It was afternoon when we reached the parting of the trails. Marshall went on down with Grandma, while Melvin and I steered for Alta Peak.

We crossed Panther Gap and circled the mountain to Alta Meadow. There we lunched, but Betsy ran away, hobbled, and we lost an hour in catching her. She ran like a deer.

It was four o'clock when we took the summit trail. In an hour and a half we reached the top, and the world was spread below us. We saw distant Mt. Whitney, the lakes, and the valley, and even the coast range. Tharps Rock towered splendidly above a snowfield. I wanted to paint it. On the way down, I heard the weird, wild lunatic quaver of the coyotes. The moon was bright. We watched it while the fire flickered.

JULY 1

Betsy brayed at dawn, feeling very lonesome for Grandma. The peaks opposite were magnificent with the foreground meadow fringed with firs. I wanted to paint it. We were off to an early start and reached camp at 9, as Lon was packing off to Clover creek for the day. We shaved and showered, and lunched with Inger. Lars is the baby. Melvin and Marshall each bought a print for 2 dollars, and Marshall took my shoes to be repaired. I was glad they had enjoyed the trip so much.

I talked with some S.F. [San Francisco] campers near by. One of them, Walter Lamb, an architect, had worked with Uncle Emerson. There were three couples, two black shirted men, and Marjorie, Lydia, and Ruby Lee. Marjorie was quite attractive to me. I had supper with them.

July 2

I took the burros to Willow Meadow at dawn. The meadow was beautiful and green. I walked part way to the forest when Aston Brann stopped for me. He envied my wanderings, for he is working in the curio store. There was a letter from Laurence, who had received his inheritance from Belgium, and expected to join his cousin on the Standard Oil tanker.

My films had been ruined in the developing and printing, tho there were some beautiful shots. Mrs. Gatos sent them to another place to see what could be done with them. The pictures of my outfit were all blurred and useless. It set my teeth on edge. The milling herds of stupid tourists also frayed my nerves. I visited Dawsons, who had asked me to lunch, and they didn't remember the invitation at all.

I went over to McKees. They have good horses and a new corral. There are 19 horses and 6 burros now. Earl was cordial. I bought a good pair of spurs from Lee for 2 dollars, to give to Lon. They jingled nicely and it was a pleasure to possess them.

On my way toward Sunset Rock, I stopped at Hobson's shack, and met his wife, Lee. She is quite delightful, reminding me of Elinore. She is exceptionally well read and understands art. She told me about her wanderings on horse among the pueblos near Tucson, when she was at the university. She asked me if I knew the work of John Sharlow. I said no, but later I asked her if she was familiar with Jean Charlot's stuff.

She enjoyed my pictures and poems, and invited me to supper. Later, Lincoln came in. I gave them a print of "Radiation." Lincoln preferred the eucalyptus.

Supper was most delectable, consisting of spaghetti with mushrooms, salad, beer (not legitimate like yesterday's), jello, coffee, mentholated cigarettes, and delicious cake. We discussed the futility of effort, and the vagaries of tourists. One had tried to take Lee's table today.

Lincoln went to work, and we talked awhile, then washed dishes.

They have an old sock for a dishrag. Just before sunset I swung up the road, considerably mollified. I got a ride to Pinewood from the first person and to Sherman Tree from the next. Then I had one to Lodgepole from the catspinner of Wolverton. I gave Lon his spurs, and later on I had a sandwich and tea with him while I showed some pictures to Inger. It was 11 when I crossed the river on a log and came in to camp. The tourist nearby who had driven me out with his radio was silent at last.

JULY 3

I talked with the man who drives the caterpillar here. His is a highly paid profession, but he is barely making out now. He told me how he once inherited 35,000 dollars and spent it all in two years, traveling about the world. He says it is impossible to get a day's work from a CC. boy.

After a mile, I rode in to the village. I brought Ashton two beetles for his collection. McKee thought the High Sierra trail was still impassable. Lee had gone to Hamilton Lakes by the River valley. I found that an octopus is an eight armed cephalopod, while the cuttlefish and squid are ten armed cephalopods, but I convinced Ashton that obsidian is not flint. I read about the forests of the Sierras and learned that the fir cones fall to pieces before they touch ground, and that the climatic record of the big trees in the Sierras corresponds closely to that of Asia for the last 3,000 years or more. I escaped the crowds to Beetle Rock, then wandered to a ledge below Sunset Rock and slept on the pine needles under a silverly glinting sugar pine. I slept on a ledge in the waning sun and the scent of the poppies is with me yet. In a drowsy haze, I climbed up the rock without seeing the tourists, and walked on like one in a dream.

At Hobsons I stopped, and rode over with them to the Pageant, While Sequoias Watched. The Creation scene was amusing. Then the Indians and the Colonists were dramatized. It was done under a fine redwood. There was much singing. It was quite late when I went back. I had a ride to Sherman tree and one to Lodgepole, on running boards. Some new tourists had moved in right next to me.

JULY 4

I wandered downriver away from the crowds, and lay in the grass near a mossy wet granite near my old camp. Then I watched the bathers in the pool, and Inger sewed my snakeskin for me. Lon convinced me that the juniper grows here. I swapped yarns with Rube, the cowboy head of the fire patrol. There is a good natured, lazy, fearful, old, Kentucky negro in the crew. Ken told me about the 1926 fire.

A deer ate some of my bread, and I attended the campfire.

JULY 5

Early up. I went to see Olson, the tractor driver, who had my bell. The deer had eaten the leather, if he hadn't. His neighbor drove me down to Sherman tree, after I had collected some juniper to show Rasmusen. Steve took me the rest of the way in. I looked at the films, and they were vastly better. Mrs. Gaddis kept them awhile to show the manager. She is making a test case of me. I talked with Ashton, and I like him better all the time. He wants to come with me, but can't. I took what supplies I had and then bought 5 dollars worth in the store. The money didn't go very far, but I eked it out with a can of George Washington coffee essence.

Then I talked again with Ashton, about the trails and the life. He was so good as to discover a roll of film for me.

I wrote to Anna Louise, the family, and Melvin. Then I lunched on the rim of Beetle rock, and went over to Earl's to see if I could get a louder bell. He couldn't find any of his, but I had almost no money anyway, so it was as well. I talked with one of his young guides who was just back from King's river, and he showed me the trail from Bear Paw Meadow to the River Valley.

I stopped in at Lee's to show her the pictures and talked to her brother Ben Miles. Then Bissell, a ranger naturalist, showed me his photographs of the high country, and saw a few of mine. I showed him and Powell the tree toed (toad).

Then I talked to Lillian awhile after buying two rolls of films with what was left. She is working in the restaurant. I gave her a black lady bug for Ashton. She gave me a milk shake, pineapple, for the fourteen cents I had left. I gave her the print of the live oaks. It turned out that I only had 13 cents, but the cashier let me by.

Atwood, the ranger, bought the letter head of Percival, Curly, Cynthia, and me for the price of another roll of film.

Just before sunset I swung up the road and after Pinewood. I had a ride into Lodgepole with my friend of this morning and his wife and daughter.

I got a large box of groceries at Lon's. He was arguing with Inger that he should order 26 inch handkerchiefs instead of 16 or 22, and he won.

My costume today was boots, jeans, my dark, Lincoln green sweater, my pale, luminous green neckerchief, and the black Stetson. It was very effective with my swarthy countenance and scowling brows.

After supper, I went up a ways to a campfire where were three couples and a pile of dunnage. A big fat fellow, Phipps, told me they were going to King's River for two weeks, and asked me if I thought they could pack everything on their two mules. I answered many questions for them before I found out that they were kidding me from start to finish. Buck Doran was the owner of most of the stock. Phipps had introduced the wives of the wrong husbands, and they had 6 saddle horses and 7 pack mules. One grey horse had a rattlesnake bite, but was recovering.

They invited me to have some beans and gave me some excellent cake.

JULY 6

Up at dawn again. I worked with my pack a little and brought over the other package from Lon's porch. Then I watched my friends pack. There was one interesting saddle of black and yellow leather, with oval stirrup leathers and a very low cantle. I told Buck I could show him an easier way to throw the diamond hitch, but he insisted that he had packed for 20 years and couldn't be shown. At last they were off in a swirl of dust. They did not tie the mules, for they followed right along. Most of them carried 200 pounds or more. They used canvas panniers entirely.

Betsy and Grandma came down, evidently driven out of the meadow by McKees mules. I rigged a pack for the saddle, using the pack sack, seamless sack, and a gunnysack. I rode a few turns on Betsy, and it was delightful and luxurious to be in the saddle again. Then I concentrated on arranging things, and there is not so much grub after all.

I found all kinds of delicacies for the burros in the garbage can. They ate plaster of Paris, grapefruit, orange peel, bread crusts, beef, and bath salts, following up with bunch grass.

It was ludicrous to watch them roll over in the dust, switching their tails, and scratching themselves on the trees. They are not in the least self conscious. The bell is now barely audible.

It rained awhile, slanting silverly against the evening sun. I wrote to mother and Mrs. Meinen, entrusting the letters to two small boys who stopped to talk. A park service man came in leading 6 pack mules to take fish fry up to the lakes tomorrow.

JULY 7

While the stars paled, I broke camp and packed the burros. We went up the Wolverton road toward Sherman Tree. On the way I met Pop Myers, a school teacher from Visalia, who is staying here till September. He said he would buy my burros anytime for what I paid. He used to be in Oakland, and has been thru these mountains. He offered to drive me down to the valley for groceries when I came back.

We took the trail of the Sequoias to Circle Meadow, then to Crescent meadow and the High Sierra trail, after the burros had jumped a creek. I had to stop and adjust Granny's pack. We went thru swarms of butterflies, and crossed streams at every turn. We passed the Redwood Meadow and River Valley trails, and then I was so exhausted I had to stop. We had gone by Bearpaw meadow without realizing it. After something to eat and a dash of cold water, I felt much better. The trail became rougher and steeper, being cut right across the face of the cliff. We lost sight of Cathedral Peaks. Lone Pine meadow was two miles off side on a rough trail, so we went ahead, crossing a ford 75 feet wide without trouble. Then we went right up the cliff to the edge of a big waterfall. A sign showed that we had come 22 miles, so that explained why I felt tired.

For some reason, the burros wouldn't take the ford above the waterfall. The water was shallow, and they saw me walk thru, but they wouldn't come. Gran jerked back twice when I had her half way over. I tried persuasion in vain, and after half an hour or so of exertion, I used force on Betsy, getting her across. Even then, I had a hard time with Gran. At last we were over, and we climbed up between very picturesque junipers, some of them a yard wide and no higher. We went thru a gate and camped on a grassy hill between junipers, above the stream, and the lake. There was excellent grass, so I turned the burros loose and after watching the fish, I took a plunge in the deep green lake, swimming out to a rock and back.

I felt vastly better, and set a stew of split peas, rice, carrots, potatoes, and onions to cook while I read the Arabian Nights, concerning Shahryar and Shahrazad.

Then I watched the stars fall and the moon glowing on the jagged tips of a splendid perpendicular while cliff above me. The wind rushed down the canyon.

JULY 8

The stew made a good breakfast. I climbed the hill above camp, following an old trail, and kept on going. I passed some glassy quartz and a fine picturesque pine tree. I circled the upper lake and found two good ropes. The mosquitoes nearly drove me wild. I saw a snake in the water, and plenty of fish. Back I came by the new trail, and it was now too hot to arrange camp. I read the Arabian Nights awhile. Then two couples came up, back packing. I had a bite of chocolate with them and showed them where to fish. Raymond Ager and his wife Margaret attracted me. I watched Raymond land some fighting trout with a dry fly. They went to the upper lake. Three men rode by with a pack mule, and fished illegally. Raymond was unable to appeal to their sportsmanship. At evening I climbed the hill above camp once more, and photographed a splendid juniper with a conical mountain above it. Also the spiry white cliff. I rode Betsy to the upper lake. Grandma followed behind. After much maneuvering, I snapped [photographed] the pine tree against the white cliff, and felt bound to paint it. I rode briskly back to camp meaning to paint the juniper, but the Ayers invited me to chip in on their trout chowder, so I decided to stay another day. I brought an onion, a carrot, and some spuds, and ran back for some pots and pans. They are camped under towering red firs on the other side of the lake.

We had chowder, biscuit, and baked fish, which seemed tasteless to me, and some tea I brought. I showed them some pictures and gave Mrs. Ager the Ballad of the Lonely Skyscraper. We sat by the fire till late, then I went home stumbling once in the dark.

JULY 9

The moon was paling with the first flush of dawn when a black horse, a brown horse, a mule, and a buckskin mare came by with the burros. After oatmeal I climbed the hill looking for good junipers, finally sketching the pine near the upper lake which I liked before. I came down to the camp of the two tourists and talked with the guide, one of McKee's men. He looked at some pictures and asked if I'd scare the horses up his way. In camp I was unable to read or thing, being driven frantic by mosquitoes no matter where I sat. In a little while I lengthened my bridle and went down to the horses. They were standing with their noses over the gate. I bridled the buckskin mare, because I have always liked buckskin or palomino horses better than any other color, though I also like a jet black horse or a white one, and a strawberry roan, and sometimes a chestnut bay. I like a handsome sorrel too. I routed out the mule and horses, riding the mare bareback to my camp, where I put my little saddle on her.

Then we capered briskly up the trail on the heels of the mule, who occasionally lashed out at us. The mare hardly felt my weight. It was a gay ride while it lasted, but soon we were at the camp.

The men invited me to breakfast and we had fish fried in butter, grapefruit, and peaches, ham, and coffee. I helped saddle the horses, scoured some pans, and packed the mule. Charlie (the packer) brought me a box to stand on, the pack was so high. I flung a good diamond hitch, and they rode off, leaving me some bread, butter, and milk. I shouldered my saddle and went into camp, having my last banana sandwich enthroned between the shaded roots of an old juniper. The Ayers went by after awhile, and there was solitude again.

I climbed along the precipitous shore till I was near a waterlogged, narrow raft. After a few minutes I mustered courage and took the plunge, swimming out to the raft. It almost sank when I sat on it, but I paddled about in the water up to my neck, over the green depths. I touched at the other side, then swam the logs back. Though refreshed, I was very cold, and could not get warm for a long time.

When it was still early I painted the juniper above camp. I made a good drawing and the colors were careful, but not quite strong enough in spite of my efforts. It was evening when I uncoiled from my sketching position. I hastily saddled Betsy and rode up to the pine tree. Granny followed soberly behind us. She looks like a Quaker. I just send a picture of her to Mrs. Meinen.

The light was leaving, and I worked furiously while the mosquitoes tormented me fiendishly. I could not do my best working against time and torment, but I got a good sunset effect. Then I shook off the mosquitoes and capered gladsomely down the hill, saving the still damp sketch. Poor Betsy was patiently standing with her hind foot in the stirrup. I helped it out, thrust the sketch into my leather case, donned my blue scarf, and singing throatily and chanting lustily, we scampered home, Grandma preceding this time.

The mosquitoes were still swarming so I made a smudge, heating some beans, fried some cheese and peanut butter sandwiches, and made cocoa in the new pot which I bought for 35 cents in Giant Forest to supersede the tipsy little one that Clark gave me when we parted in Tonto canyon. The new pot is capacious and nests nicely into my pans.

Then I indulged in a favorite pastime—map reading. Tired and content, at last I lay down and looked up at the cliffs and the stars.

JULY 10

I did not wake early as I planned, but eating and packing hastily while I fought mosquitoes, at length I was off. With a little persuasion the burros crossed the creek, and went up the steep trail. It was hard work pulling the burros across the snow banks. They fell thru now and then. I gathered some plants that looked like onions, but the roots, tho large, were bitter. Around a bend we came to a suspension bridge and my heart grew heavy with apprehension, but Betsy, after bumping her kyaks once, went right across.

We crossed hundreds of streamlets, and some icy lakes at the foot of sheer cliffs. Near the summit there was a long, steep stretch of snow. I led Grandma, who is much better than Betsy for snow. The edges of the snowbanks were undercut and treacherous, and the burros fell thru time and again. We crossed a grassy, rock walled plateau with shallow lakes and reached Kaweah Gap at last. Not far below was the Big Arroyo. Black Kaweah and Red Kaweah were on the horizon.

There were two bad snowbanks to go down thru. The burros stumbled and slid, constantly getting tangled, and going every way but the shortest way. I led them over steep, smooth rocks and they stepped cleverly. At the last bad place, the snow was deeply ridged, and the burros jumped and fell. They are downright fools when in trouble. They always tangle together with their heads across one another's necks, so that their packs prevent them from moving.

Grandma fell down once, and Betsy stood over her so that she couldn't get up without breaking a leg. Fortunately, she slid down to the edge of the snow and then stood up.

The arroyo is a level valley, grassy, and thinly forested. I lunched near some columned trees while the burros munched grass. Then we went down further, crossing a stream on a snow bridge, till we found a good camp spot on a big rock by a rivulet. I pastured the burros, and camp was in shadow when I started the blaze and put on the carrot stew.

The peaks above were radiant in the evening glow. I remembered the feverish, triumphant melody of the scherzo in Tchaikowsky's Pathetique. The wind began to turn. It is interesting how the canyon air currents fluctuate. The wind always pours down at night. I remembered a canyon gale that swept thru my camp on the Mukuntuweap in Zion Canyon. Then I thought of the unnerving night in the deserted buildings at Hermit Ranch, when the hot blasts swept eerily down, shaking the buildings and blowing out my lamp, leaving me in the hot, empty, low-ceilinged rooms with scorpions.

July 11

I went up and down and up and down looking for the burros, finding them at last in a meadow below. The bell is inaudible at a distance under the roar of the stream. Then too I have a fixed hallucination about bells. It started when I was 16 in Yosemite. I was walking along near Vogelsang pass when I thought I heard a burro bell. Determined not to be overtaken by a pack train, I hurried along, but all the rest of the day I thought I heard the bell just behind me. So it is now. Whichever way I wander, searching, I seem to hear a bell.

The stew was highly successful. I read at length in the Arabian Nights, wading uncomfortable thru the "poetry" but delighting in the descriptions, and words like "cark and care," "with goodly glee," and "lullilooing," "parqetted," "purfled."

Finally packing, I drove the burros across the stream to the trail on the other side, and led them down thru the peaceful, grassy valley. There was no sound but the occasional reassuring creaking of the kyak boxes. We got thru some very boggy spots and reached a maintenance cabin at the fork of the trail. I unlatched the door hasp and peered into the dark cavernous interior. Everything was on the floor.

We forded two branches of the stream and went up a very steep trail thru stands of well-formed lodgepole. After miles we topped a ridge and came down at the marge [sic] of one of the Little Five Lakes. By the edge of the water I camped, and climbed the farther hill, exploring. I met two men, the trail crew, with their horses and mules. They intended to dynamite and dig thru the snow on the trail to Kaweah Gap. They said I was the first one over it with animals this year.

I climbed to an upper lake, then down and around to two more.

There were fine clouds, but I could find nothing to paint.

The bacon was mouldy. I fried yams and made tea, then heaped up the fire and read Burton again. The burros strayed.

JULY 12

I went down to the lower lake, but the burros had turned uphill. The lake was glorious last night at sunset. Black and Red Kaweahs were magnificent. But, as it happened, I did not paint them. I found the burros in a soft, dusty spot, reclining. I rode back on Betsy and packed hurriedly. The sun was up. We went down trail at a great rate, but Betsy's pack slipped to her shoulders, as the breeching had been adjusted for Grandma, who is larger. The saddle pack is always a mess anyway. We forded again and went up a couple of miles out of the arroyo when we met a man and woman from Alameda, with horses and pack mule. The trail was narrow and steep walled, and there was difficulty in crossing. A mile further we reached the top and passed a shallow lake when I discovered that my slicker was lost. I could not understand as I had driven the burros all the way and would have seen it fall. Some things had fallen on the other side, but I replaced them. I unpacked the burros, tied Gran, and drove Betsy, saddled, down trail at top speed, shouting encouragement. Sweating and panting, I reached the bottom without catching up with the couple. I thot they would find the slicker and carry it on.

On the bank between the two streams, at the edge of the water, lay the silver-gray slicker. This was the one place where I hadn't followed behind the burros, having detoured to cross dry shod on a footbridge. What luck it had not fallen into the water and been swept down stream.

Then I met the travelers, who had been circling about. Earl Wells was the man. They have camped out for two weeks and are returning by Black Rock Pass. They told me the mosquitoes were insufferable at Moraine lake, and to camp at Chagoopa Creek.

I sat tiredly back in the saddle, and Betsy nobly brought me up the long hill. I crunched graham crackers with apple butter, then on we went, on the edge of the plateau. We passed some beautiful meadows, then took the perhaps wrong fork of the trail, in a sandy, barren field. We followed the rim of the arroyo, then turned slightly and arrived unexpectedly at the lake. We had missed the Chagoopa creek trail. How I longed to swim in the lake! It was very dusty on the trail and the sun was hot.

We went down and down for long into the canyon. It was hot and there was the dank smell of vegetation as in places in Grand Canyon, but firs, juniper, pine, and fern bordered the way. The trail was alternately excessively dusty and full of sharp rocks. I found a very strange flower.

At length we reached the river, and I camped by the edge of the pasture, upper Funston Meadows. After unloading, I turned the burros loose in the pasture and went to look at the other end of it.

On the outer edge of the rocky trail, a rattlesnake was coiled, and he sounded his rattle that is the bravest battle music I know. I hurled some stones, but as usual, I did not at first find accuracy, and the snake went off the rocks into the dense brush and brake.

Furious at his escape, and hearing the war cry of his warning rattle, I leaped into the brake above him. Stones were useless, and I could only find a stick about a foot long, but with this I poked near the stirring, thrilling, deadly dry rasp of the rattles. Peering intently, at last I saw him, and after a few attempts made a jab, pinioning his tail. His head wove in and out and I nervously broke another stick and poked down between the boughs and branches, finally stabbing his middle. Excitedly moving the sticks, both hands full, I got his head at last, pushing it into the soft earth.

Then what to do? The brush was almost impenetrable. Taking my life in my hands, I reached down and caught his tail. Loosed the makeshift spear, and whipped him out on the rocks. He was very much alive, but after a few tries, I mashed his flat head and cut it off. He was reddish brown with veins of buff. Only six rattles and he is not long, but what a fight we had. It was true sport.

Hunting rattlers as I do comes nearer to real sport than almost anything I know. It has the necessary element of danger, for it is not sport unless opponents are somewhat evenly matched, and the quarry can turn the tables on the pursuer. By comparison, fishing is a diversion for senescent bachelors.

If I had painted the picture, I would not have encountered the snake, so I wonder it is not best to leave all in the hands of Fate? A hard question.

The pasture was long, and the further gate was of no avail against burros, so I took the bell and hobbles and went in search of them. They had hidden, but at last I apprehended them and belled Gran.

Then the fresh luxury of a bath! Then fire, and cheese macaroni with butter and brown sugar while I read The Tale of Kamar Al Zaman.

A grey moth flew bang into my face, then fell into the pot of water where it swam and fluttered for ten minutes. I had no idea they could withstand the water as well. I leaned back securely, looking into my fire of alder logs.

As I was walking back to camp swinging my rattler in one hand, his rattle would slap against the ferns and there were echoes of the battle song I love to hear. Bishmallah! Ishallah! Alhamdolillah! I chanted victoriously! The hunter has not failed today!

JULY 13

The moth was still swimming, so I let it out and it dried and flew away. Then I did my bimonthly washing. There were two other burros in the meadow—huge, black creatures like young mules.

After lunch I met the couple with the burros who were camped on an island. They were Mr. and Mrs. Jory from San Francisco. They invited me to supper, which consisted of dehydrated carrots, spinach, and soup, with beans, fish, bread, and nuts, all preceded by a cocktail.

Mr. Jory works in a bank. The two have taken pack or camping trips to different places every year. They enjoyed my photographs and Mr. Jory said I should try my prints at Gump's in San Francisco. They told me to visit them when I arrived there. We talked ourselves out by the fireside, and they gave me some fish. Mr. Jory held his flashlight while I crossed the stream on a log, and I found my way home.

JULY 14

Fish breakfast and a late start. We crossed the Kern on a new bridge and went up the dusty canyon trail, passing Chagoopa falls. At Kern Hot Springs, I ran down to have a look, and was astonished to find two boys camping in the bath house. They were Ned Frisins and Charley Hixon from Hollywood High School.

I had a hot bath and a plunge in the river, then we went up the trail together. Ned has some intelligence, but Charley is rather callow. Ned is a fundamentalist, intending to become a medical missionary in Africa, where one of his brothers has preceded him. He tried to convert me, and explained that the earth and rocks were here for thousands of years before the 7 days of creation.

[Four lines erased]

He told me about his horses on his father's ranch at San Diego.

We camped at Junction Meadows and put up their little tent when it began to rain. They shared their figs and cheese while I provided graham crackers and pineapple. For supper I made them a grand stew of split peas and a dozen other things. We had to chase the burros three miles back, and finally I tied Betsy in the meadow on the river bank. She and Granny brayed back and forth. I invited Charley and Ned to circle up to Reflection Lake, Kearsarge, and Whitney, and they decided they would like to.

JULY 15, SATURDAY

For breakfast we had three fish which Charley caught, some oatmeal and pancakes, which I flipped. I lashed their pack on top of Betsy's and we went up river in the rain. It poured hard, and then sleeted. We forded several streams, passing waterfalls on the other side. The top pack slipped several times. Juniper gave way to sugar pine, and that yielded to lodgepole, which in turn was succeeded by red fir and the alpine pine, with its fine short needles.

We meant to reach South America Lake, but the climb was long and strenuous, and we were quite gant [sic] when we came to the first lake. We looked at the map and saw that ours was further, so we climbed on up grassy passes between rock walls, with rivulets running downstream. We passed lakes on each side, then reached a fair sized one which we thought must be South America. We camped by some Alpine pines, and after lunch of cheese, dates, and powdered milk, it appeared that Charley's sweater had slipped out of the pack. In a little while, we all went back to look for it, Charley grousing all the while, but we found it a mile or two back, and climbed cheerfully back. Just a little before sunset, we reached camp and all prepared for a swim. I was the first into the water, and I swam all the way across the lake, in the cool, enfolding water.

Then I concocted a rice pudding, which was a delight to the palate, and after, read to them by firelight the story of "Ali the Persian," from the Arabian Nights. It is a very extravagant tale, and we all enjoyed it. Then I read the Rubaiyat of Omar Khayyam.

July 16, Sunday

I woke at sunrise and saw the light creep down the peaks, then slept until my comrades stirred. The mosquitoes were upon us at once in swarms, and in airy battalions, endlessly attacking. Betsy, tied to a log, brayed to Grandma, who returned the salute. It sounded like a buzz saw hitting a nail and ended pitifully. I imitated it humorously. However, a burro always has the gift of making you feel that you are a bigger ass than he is.

Charlie and Ned read the Bible under a mosquito netting. We had an early lunch and laded the donkeys. After a few steps, the pack slipped hopelessly, and I made it over again. We climbed by a steep, rocky trail to a pass, then descended to the shores of a large lake with barren shores. This was probably So. America Lake. Then the trail disappeared but there were occasional ducked rocks [trail markers], and we followed these while Ned made more ducks. Finally we reached Harrison Pass, and scouted about looking for a down trail, but there was none, and the slopes were almost sheer. So we turned back in disappointment, and traveled down a rough valley until we reached timber at sunset. I unburdened the burros by a huge granite block in the center of the meadow. We used a sprawling dead tree growing in a granite cleft for our firewood. I fixed them such a mess of macaroni, corn meal, potato, onion, rice, cheese, and milk as made them forget all their troubles. Then I read the first two voyages of Sinbad the Sailor, concerning Rukh.

July 17

Early up. I flipped pancakes of my own inimitable mix with surpassing dexterity and gusto. I tied Grandma to a log, and we were off before the mosquitoes swarmed upon us. We back tracked to the summit, looking for my leather jacket, which the Southards gave me at Grand Canyon, but found it not.

Then we scrambled down from rock to rock and rock to snowbank till we reached two green ice pools which we circled, then followed a turbulent stream course that plashed [sic] downwards between rocks and springy turf. Charley grumbled about his feet, and I bent some of the nails in his boot. We found a trail that led from a little grassy basin past the margins of shallow lakes, then down to the main stream. I saw a man on a horse and rushed down to accost him. There were two, looking for a stray white horse and bay mule. They were likable chaps. We found their camp and four more men. I had a cigarette, and they invited us to hard bread with syrup and Roquefort cheese, which Charley loves. A can of pineapple followed, and they gave us two cans of beans with some odds and ends.

Ned and Charley fished the stream while I went up to Reflection lake. It was not the remarkable place that had been described to me, and there was nothing to paint. I saw four horses tied in the shade and stopped at the lakeshore to talk with two women. They were rather common, but cordial, and told me about their horses and husbands. I had another smoke. They had a big leaden weight on their fishing lines, and casting was easy.

I went down and met six other common people who had just come in. The place lost its charm for me. Ned had caught two tiny fish which he gave away. We ate some figs and peanuts and climbed up the mountainside, seeing several clumps of tiger lilies. I explored two more lakes while Ned fixed a blister on Charley's foot. It was a hard pull over snow and rock to the top of the pass. We were constantly making puns.

We looked again for the jacket, and Ned and Charley circling around while I retraced the last tracks. I reached camp first, made fire, and started a big mess of spotted dog, or rice pudding. They came in at dark, empty handed.

I read the Third Voyage of Sinbad, concerning the apes, ogres, and serpents. "By Allah," quoth Sinbad, "this is an abominable way to die, as the serpent swallowed his companion. Better would it have been that I had drowned in the sea, rather than to be eaten by this viperish monster." But he escaped from the valley of diamonds, met friends and voyaged from seas to sea, and from isle to isle, and from city to city until he reached Bassorah and packed to Bagdad, with wealth five times greater than before. Then he gave largesse and alms to the poor, and ceased not eating and drinking in all joyance of life until he had forgotten all the suffering that had befallen him, and the old bad man in him awakened, and for greed of gain and pelf and filthy lucre, he set out, again from Bassorah city, with bales and baggage of rich stuffs to trade.

JULY 18, TUESDAY

The mosquitoes were up before us, but we breakfasted well and packed skillfully so that the pack was evenly built and well balanced in spite of the six gallon cans.

We journeyed down stream, circling lakes, and fording brooks, till we rejoined the old trail, then singing each a discordant song, we continued down the Kern in all joyance of heart. Betsy's breeching broke again, but I fixed it with wire. We saw a fine camp with all appurtenances and a lush meadow on the other side of the stream, so we drove the burros across and disembarked. Charley put up the tent while I built a fire and cooked the beans with bread and wild onions. This we ate with peanuts and Roquefort cheese while the afternoon rain streamed down. Charley read Sinbad very amusingly.

"Voyagers and pilgrims declared that this beast called "Karkadan" (the rhinoceros) will carry off a great sea elephant on its horn and graze about the seacoast taking no heed of it, until the elephant dieth and its fat, melting in the sun, runneth into the rhinoceros' eyes and blindeth him so that he lieth down on the shore. Then came the bird Rukh and carrieth off both the Karadan and that which is on its horn to feed its young withal."

He also read about the ogre who snarked and snored like a cow with its throat cut.

The lima bean mess was not quite done, so we had rice and cheese.

JULY 19, WEDNESDAY

Away once more with a lighter load. Part way up the Shitney Trail we met two men I had met at the Scout camp, traveling with a pack horse. We all stopped in the same meadow at Wallace creek for lunch. One of the men caught a golden trout at his first cast. It was gorgeously colored beyond all my expectations. I borrowed Charley's rod and caught one too.

Then we climbed upward in a hail storm. It rained and hailed violently for an hour or so, and then, singing boisterously, we topped the ridge into Whitney Creek and Crabtree Meadow, above which we camped. I tried to fish, but the mosquitoes drove me wild. For supper I made a delicious sugared squaw bread, with rich cocoa and rice pudding. We went to bed early, I sleeping with them in the tent at their behest. I slid out of it, however.

JULY 20, THURSDAY

Charley woke us up at the crack of dawn, and we had oatmeal, and we staked Grandma, covered camp, and went up trail towards Mt. Whitney.

Ascending steeply, we passed two lakes before the sun touched us. I cached my blazer, and we came to Twin lakes, unbelievably clear, so that they looked like a granite cliff below the mountains. We took the Chimney trail, which led right up the mountain side. Half way up I called to Ned for my camera to take a picture of the view of Chagoopa Plateau, Kern canyon, and the snow peaks and clouds above. I spent an hour or so painting it, with cloud shadows on the green plateaus and red granite cliffs in the foreground. Ned went to sleep near me, but Charley was above us and would not sacrifice his altitude, as he shouted to Ned intermittently.

It was easy climbing in the big boulders, stepping from one to another.

At long last we reached the top of California, when all other visitors had departed.[5] Charley counted the names in the registry book and I took pictures. In the book we entered our names and a legend from the tale of Abu Hasan which nearly made us die of laughter. No doubt coming visitors will be affected by it too.

We lunched in the stone house, and lay in the hot sun on the windy edge of eternity. Ice green lakes, valleys, canyons, towns, and mountains were spread below us. Clouds scudded by but it did not rain, for a wonder.

We went down by the horse trail, meeting the Arroyo trail crew with their mules.

Our friends from the scout camp gave us some fish for breakfast.

Ned and I talked till late. He told me all about wrestling, in which he is very proficient, and we discussed fools and fate and faith. Also recipes. I enjoyed the day and the Whitney trip much more than I had expected to. The dawn colors of pale, misty green meadows remained with me.

JULY 21, FRIDAY

I watched a Clark crow eating the fish heads, and finally roused myself. After breakfast we prepared to go our separate ways. I gave them some milk and sugar, while they gave me some salt and bacon. I also traded them two ropes for one better rope. My beasts were packed and saddled before they were ready, so we made our farewells and off I rode.

---

5. Mt. Whitney, the highest peak in the contiguous states, tops out at 14,495 feet. The climb is nontechnical, although long and strenuous. It is ascended by thousands each year.

I enjoyed the boys very much and I know they learned some tricks of the trail from me.

It was glorious to be in the saddle again. Before long we left the meadows and climbed the mountainside to the Sand Flats, a very desolate plateau. I shut my eyes and swayed sleepily in the saddle, trusting in Betsy. Then I sang Lawrence's song:

"In the Isles of the dry Tortogas,
In the sunny Carribees,
We will eat some more, and will drink again,
And will plunder the near by seas."

About noon I reached Guyot creek, where the grass was high and thick, so there I encamped, and prepared to make squaw bread. Just then, along came Hank and Leo, two L.A. boys I had met on the Whitney trail. They were lost and trying to reach Mineral King and Yosemite. I showed them the map and suggested they go down Rock Creek to the Kern. Leo gave me my pencil which he had found on the trail. They went off.

All afternoon I was deep in the Arabian Nights. I reveled in names and phrases. "It was such a night as makes a man forget his father and mother."

"And they ceased not to dwell in this fashion until there came to them the Destroyer of Delights, the Sunderer of Societies, the Plunderer of Palaces, and the Garner of Graves. Praise be to Allah, the Companionating, the Compassionate."

"Verily we are Allah's, and unto him we are returning."

At dusk I paid a visit to the burros, then watched the stars from the hillside meadow.

July 22, Saturday

I finished the Arabian Nights, the tales of Ifrits and Marid of the Jinn and Jinniyah, of Kut al Kulub and Kamar al Zaman, Sharyhar and Shahriman, Aladdin and Ali Baba, Zubadayah and the Commander of the Faithful, Maaruf and Jaafar, Shajaret and Badral Budur, Nuzhat al Fuad and Princess Jauharah, Abu Kir and Abu Sir, dirhams and kohl, Damascus, Baghdad, and Cairo.

After a walk to the edge of the ridge, I sewed a patch on my slicker, but I broke a thread and two needles.

Then in the evening, I took out the Rubaiyat and read with the greatest of pleasure. It was written in the time of the Arabian Nights, and of Jalala-din. I read about Naishapur in Khorasan, Khaikobod and Kaikhosru.

Smoking with unclouded delight, now that I had no young charges, I read aloud, sonorously and feelingly.

"Ah, make the most of what we yet may spend
Before we too into the dust descend,
 Dust unto dust, and under dust to lie,
Sans Wine, sans Song, sans Singer, and sans End."

"Verily we are Allah's, and unto him we are returning."

"Yesterday this days madness did prepare;
Tomorrow's Silence, Triumph, or despair,
 Drink! for you know not whence you came, nor why;
Drink, for you know not why you go, nor where."

I was completely swayed by Omar's thoughts, and I decided I'd certainly get some wine from Lee if I could.

Again I surrendered myself to somnolence.

July 23, Sunday

Early up. I led the burros down into Rock creek, then rode up the other side to the Siberian outpost and to the desolate Siberian Pass, where I entered Inyo forest. The stirrup strap broke, but I rode on anyhow. Whitney Meadows was not at all inviting, so I kept on till I reached a little meadow on Golden Trout Creek.

I was reading "Casuals of the Sea" over my bean stew when Hank and Leo came up. It seemed that the last quarter mile of Rock Creek was impassable. They studied my map again, then made camp with me. They had some grasshoppers, and gave me a hook and line. I cut willow poles, and we all caught fish, seven in total. We had a real supper, with rich cocoa, split peas, and pop corn. Leo is a tenderfoot, but Hank is a good sort, though younger than I. I lent them my saddle blankets for covers. Betsy got into camp and started eating my map of Sequoia Forest. I chased her half a mile before she would drop it. She galloped in hobbles with the map fluttering from her mouth.

July 24, Monday

We had breakfast together and Hank and I took a plunge and sun-bath. Then they packed up to go over Cottonwood Pass, and take a freight home. They left me some odds and ends and the hook and line. Determined to fish, I caught grasshoppers and butterflies for bait. They were very scarce, and it took about three for each fish landed. I sat on the bank under some willows and caught five fish in one hole. I lost another fish on the bank, and another took the hook. I had another, and at last I had ten fish and no more bait anywhere. I had used fritillaries, wasps, lady bugs, and hoppers. I read additionally in Mc Gee, but was not thrilled.

JULY 25, TUESDAY

After my trout breakfast, I fed the burros salt so that they put out their pink tongues at me.

Then I rode on, riding Betsy, and driving Grandma. The arrangement worked rather well, and I enjoyed the ride.

We crossed the tunnel, where the south fork of the Kern and Golden Trout are only a few yards apart. The cattlemen on one side had stolen the water from Golden Trout, but the ranchers blew up the tunnel in revenge. I registered at the rangers station. Betsy always starts as soon as I have one foot in the stirrup.

A few miles down I found a pretty little meadow with four donkeys in it. The camp was empty, as my curiosity aroused, I followed footprints upstream until I found two fishermen. They had caught all they wanted, so we went back to their camp. There I found Betsy and Gran with packs and saddles off, and if the stud burro had not been hobbled, it would have been worse. I unhitched Grandma while they tied the stud.

Then Beck, the third and youngest of the three, came in with more fish. I brought out my raisins, and they shared their Melba toast. We rested awhile, I talked with the oldest man, and showed them my pictures. They told me about their wanderings in the North Woods. One of them gave me a candy bar and another gave me a fly for fishing. I showed them the Diamond Hitch when I packed, and they all practiced till they knew it.

Then a cowman in all his trappings came riding up and after some talk, he led off and I followed down towards Little Whitney meadow, where he has his ranch.

Soon he outstripped me, and I rode in silence over grassy pastureland beside the willow bordered stream. I noticed the meanders and oxbows, and remembered my geology. Then the stream straightened and hurried down, foaming from pool to pool. The trail was right on the edge of the bank, leading under slender trunked pines.

I forded the stream, and camped across from the meadow, under three pines. There were prepared camp sites, but I found them odious with their litter and the cautionary signs on the trees.

I rode Betsy back to the pasture opening and closed the gate without dismounting. But try as I would, I could not make them cross a little stream with boggy banks. So I tied them and walked up to the ranch to find out which was the government pasture.

I heard more about the bridge over the Kern. Polite doubt was expressed as to the possibility of getting the burros across it. The ford was impossible for donkeys, they said. My companions of yesterday had been unable to make their burros cross there.

Again I opened the gates without dismounting, and found the right pasture.

In camp I cooked up a mess of spotted dog and read Casuals of the Sea. The crescent moon rose and gleamed yellowly thru the pine tops. I read by firelight, and made a couple of fumbling, stumbling, forays for wood, as there was none near. I doled out a few twigs at a time and swam thru a hundred pages in this fashion, when I had to search for more wood. It was quite late when I finished, so, as I was no slave to habit, I built up the fire, had a smoke, made a pot of coffee, and oatmeal for my breakfast. The dogs at the farmhouse howled once when I broke a dead limb for firewood.

JULY 26

I sipped the coffee and puffed away, until the stars began to pale. Dawn, and the East grew bright! I crawled into my cocoon, and slept till mid-morning when I arose, and donning my tennis shoes, cut a good willow pole and fastened my Black Gnat to the line. Upstream I fished, and the sport was glorious. The trick is to pull the line just at the psychological moment, but even then, the fish may fall off. I landed one fish in a pine tree above. He fell off the hook and into the water again. One little fish was flung into a little pool, and I couldn't get him out again. Others landed high on the bank, in the red lava rock, and flipped their way downwards until I caught them, and put them on my willow fork, tail down.

Oblivious of time, I went from pool to pool, angling for the golden trout. In the afternoon I came back to camp with twenty-one fish. I cleaned them and had eight for dinner, and a fried yam.

Then I went downstream to catch the other four. Altogether I threw back more little fish than I kept. Thunder rolled and jumbled, and the northern hills were hidden in storm clouds, but I was dry. I crept up to the edge of pools in the open meadow, and hooked five beauties. One fish I whipped out of the water with a terrific switch. I saw him gleam against the sun, high in the air, but I never could find where he fell.

The burros were enjoying their freedom. After cleaning the fish and catching one more, I went to bed at dusk, like a sensible person.

JULY 27

For breakfast, I had eighteen delicious trout of my own catching, fried in bacon grease and corn meal.

Betsy snorted as if I were a cougar, but I caught her at the gate. I never bother about Grandma now. She follows like a good burro. In camp I appropriated another rope end which will make a good cinch when un-raveled. I find short lengths of good rope almost everywhere I stop.

I led Gran this time. Betsy splashed thru the stream and we fol-lowed above it. We crossed a natural bridge, and went down precipi-tously to the Kern, past Volcano falls. At last we reached the bridge of ill fame. It was worse than I expected, for there were no sides, it sagged and swung, and the river was visible between the floor boards like the Chicago River bridge. However, Betsy went right up to it and even put her foot on it, then shied off. I dismounted and led her and she came well enough. She would come several steps, then stop, and forward again.

In the middle, the bridge rested on a huge boulder in the river. On the last stretch, the bridge swayed up and down and sidewise, till I near-ly lost my balance, but we came across, and I stroked the burros, for they had done nobly, beyond my wildest hopes. I could not possible have made them cross if they had been unwilling.

On the other side I met a rider with a purple neckerchief and horse hair hatband, who was traveling with his young son and a pack mule. We drew rein and talked for some while. At Camp Lewis, I paused again, and talked with Mrs. Conterno.

After I rode up the Kern a mile or two, I saw five horses tied, and, anchoring Betsy, went to see the strangers. There were three men, a mother and son, just finishing lunch. They invited me to have what was left, so I made sandwiches with corned beef and butter. The leader was a very jovial, hearty, fat man. While we sat on the river bank, a tall, black mother duck came shooting over the whitecaps and riffles, honking solicitously to her brood of fuzzy young bobbers. I don't know how the ducklings kept topside, but they did, and the little flotilla shot by like submarines in the wake of a transport ship.

My friends galloped off, and I followed at a more leisurely pace, donning my gray slicker, as it was beginning to drizzle. We made camp at the upper end of Lower Funston Meadows.

I sat perched under an overhanging rock on the cliff, and watched the packer come by with six pack mules. A mother and baby squirrel, dull yellow brown with white collars, crept over the rocks, the little one always a few leaps behind his mother.

I had a sumptuous repast of noodles with cheese, cream, butter, brown sugar, and cocoa, while I read "Green Mansions" for the third time. Then I bedded down on high piled pine needles.

July 28, Friday

After a refreshing bath in the Kern, I made ready my mount and my burden bearer, affixing to the patched lead rope another end I had found. We rode about four miles up the Kern to Rattlesnake creek, then turned up its canyon, following a very steep and rocky trail. I drove Grandma and she struggled slowly upwards. The valley unfolded below us, with its golden brown river threading between green jungle banks. I have found Kern Canyon rather monotonous and depressing. There is no variety. The rocks are a dull gray, and the forest is an impenetrable tangle that cuts off all outlook.

At long last we topped the rise into the valley of Rattlesnake Canyon. We crossed flats of white sage, under pale orange cliffs. After negotiating a bog, we came to a good campsite in a circle of trees, with green meadows by the creek. I thought I would make some squaw bread for lunch, then go on towards Franklin Pass and Mineral King.

In casting about for firewood I found a willow fishing pole, very well balanced. Entirely diverted from my original purpose, I fastened my black gnat to it, and at my first cast got a fine strike, but the trout fell back at the water's edge.

So it went for some time, and I tipped over wires and brush, snagged my line, and was bitten by mosquitoes. Then the luck turned and I caught half a dozen.

Coming back to camp, I fed the burros some salt which I found in a can, and went upstream. The luck was better yet, and in one pool under a big rock, I saw a dozen fish including a huge one. I sat out of sight and flicked the gnat across the surface of the pool, landing half a dozen and throwing back two small ones. At last the big fellow rose to the fly, but he didn't bite hard enough and I lost him.

The banks are very much overgrown here, and it is very difficult to land a fish unless I can get a straight swing to left or right, but I caught one or two with an overhand pull. I came into camp at dusk with twenty-two sizable trout, cleaned the largest, belled Grandma, and had some spotted dog, eating at a table.

I slept well on springy pine boughs.

July 29, Saturday

Lazy morning. Watched the clouds move over the orange cliffs, and took two pictures. Three pans full of delicious trout for breakfast. Thus I drained the dregs of piscatorial delight.

The burros were near. They finished the salt. After dousing the fire, I saddled and packed and rode joyously up trail in sunlight and shadow for some hours. I put an orange tiger lily in my pocket. At the head of the canyon my two days solitude was broken, and I met two pack out-fits with appurtenancing dudes. I had to smile as one horsewoman (!?) mounted her beast. The Franklin Pass trail was scratched (not hewn) in the living rock. I turned aside to let a pack string by and talked with the packer. Betsy fell down with me on some slick rock, but we did not roll down the canyon. She had presence of mind, and lunged with her hind feet, getting up to her knees and over the bad place. Farther on I drove them both. It was very steep and rocky. At the crest I looked down on a red volcanic mountain, veined with tilted strata and intrusions, with a deep lake below it. The trail was very rough, and the breeching strap wore thru the skin on Granny's back, in spite of all I could do. I was worried too about their feet, for their hoofs are worn down. In addition, Grandma, it is now beyond doubt, will be a mother before long. Poor ignorant creature, she had no knowledge of contraceptives!

The trail was long, rough, rocky, and dusty and steep, and the sky was overcast. At last we reached the foot of the trail, at the bottom of a sheer sided ridge. The red cliffs were golden in the setting sun.

I loosed the burros and started some split peas to cooking. It grew dark, and the peas tipped into the fire when half done. I had some chipped beef and turned in.

JULY 30, SUNDAY

In the morning cool, I prepared my pancakes and prunes. Then I had a plunge and a sunbath, sewed rents in my shirt, wrote a letter to Mother, and dressed Grandma's wound, acquired while she was on duty.

It was late when I rode off. I stopped at Phil Buckmans, and talked to a one-armed man and Jack. I had found a fish pole tip, but his party had not lost it. He opined that Granny had a month to go, and I could use her within a few days of the event, then go on with the little fellow trailing us. Burros are like Indian women, he said, and began spinning yarns. He had no burro shoes.

At the store I mailed the letter, bought candy, and talked with Roland Ross, the packer and storekeeper. He had no burro shoes either, but took the pole tip, and said he'd find me a strap for a stirrup leather if I'd wait.

I unpacked under a fig tree, pastured the burros, and went down to Roland's corral. I riveted two straps together, took some gall salve, and bought 10 pounds of oats. In camp I talked with a proud young rider of 14 or so, who had no father or mother, owned six horses, earned $50 a month as a cowpuncher, and paid his way wherever he went. He showed me how well reined his horse was, accepted a smoke, and went his way.

After being directed by a handsome tall girl in a black Stetson similar to mine, I found the up trail and rode, singing, up the mountain. I punched buckle holes in the new stirrup strap as I rode. We climbed thru manzanita and fir stands to Timber Gap and Sequoia Park.

Too proud and lordly to set foot on the ground, I rode Grandma right up to the registration box, and signed as coming from Siberian Pass and going to Yosemite. Soon it was too steep to ride, and after tightening the girth and shifting the blankets on Betsy, I drove them down Deer Creek 4 miles to Cliff creek. I leaped into the saddle, forded the stream, and camped on the hill. There was a mule and someones pack already there, but since there was no one to consult, I unpacked in a clump of willows.

Then, thinking of breakfast, and since the necessary interval of 2 days between fish was elapsed, I cut a willow pole, and went upstream. The stream is very tortuously wound up, and the banks are steep, overgrown with rank vegetation, waist high, and full of treacherous fallen trees, slippery boughs, and rocks. After a few casts, when I was wondering if there were any fish, I hooked a handsome one, and he stayed on. Much encouraged, I strung him on a willow fork, and tried again. I caught a larger one and swung him inshore, but he fell off into another pool. I fell down in the brake repeatedly, and once I went all the way into the creek with one leg, between two logs, but I jumped out so quickly that I didn't get wet.

After patient casting in a deep pool, I felt a tug on my line, and thrilled to the core, swung the pole, and the biggest fish I ever caught thudded up on the bank. I hunted five minutes before I found him in the deep brake, but he was still flopping. I could hardly close my fist on him. He was a foot long and weighed at least a pound. How I shouted! Half an hour later, after many fruitless strikes, I landed another, an inch shorter, but huge for all that. It was sunset, as I started down stream, pleased with the black gnat, but disappointed that I hadn't caught half a dozen or more.

In camp I met new companions. They exclaimed at my fish in heartwarming manner. In the course of the afternoon, one had caught four little ones, and the other none. They gave me their four to clean, and invited me to supper. Elliot Seymour was the older, plumper man, and Robert Wood, the younger, more likable chap. They are both on the threshold of the Law, natives of Berkeley. Seymour swore and fumed as he burned himself and fumbled in the dark. We had a royal feast of sweet prunes, corn, corned beef, and tomato sauce, soy wheat crackers, fruit cakes, and tea. Then we sat by the fire till 10, recounting glorious adventures with wine and song. I enjoyed the talk immensely.

JULY 31, MONDAY

We had breakfast together. I showed them my pictures and other lures in the accepted fashion, and they gave me flies, hooks, salmon eggs, dried fruit, powdered milk, and dehydrated eggs.

Robert brought down Franklin, the hefty mule and gave him his breakfast, oats and a lump of sugar. Franklin is an enormous, affable mule, ignorant of his own strength. He ran away one time from Claire Lake up Rattlesnake Creek and over Franklin Pass, with hobbles on!

I discovered the burros, led them in and grained them, and finished packing before they did. Wood took a picture of me, and I got one of the two of them with Franklin. At noon we departed, they to the left and I to the right. It was a downhill to Redwood Meadows. The ranger rode in just after I was settled. I found him very likable and versed in the lore of Sequoia. He has been here 12 years. He mapped my route to Yosemite for me.

At lunch I read Green Mansions, about Cla Cla and Nuflo and Rima. Then most of the afternoon, I talked with Ranger Fry. He is the son of Judge Fry, the retired park superintendent. He told me much about the flowers, animals, and trees. He had seen the burro who fought the panther in Battle Canyon. I learned that the Clark crow was named from the Lewis and Clark expedition, which it followed into this country. I learned that the cougar has a hard life, for the deer have keener hearing, scent, and sight than it, and are swifter. A lion killed a fawn in the meadow a few days ago. Fry is married, but his wife is in town now. He is gray haired and short.

After a good rice pudding, I read Literary Digests in the cabin while the ranger made out his reports. I heard the San Francisco news by radio, and was disgusted at the advertising and the vulgar quality of the news & sports.

Then we talked till late at night. Fry told me of his youthful days as a ranger in Owens valley, during the cattle and sheep feuds, and how he told the Basques, "No Trespassen con Borrengos." We lamented the despoilation of the wilderness, and cursed the greedy fools who wanted roads across Grand Canyon to Mt. Whitney. Fry told me that a sheep-skin on a pack saddle would keep the blankets from slipping out, so I determined to tack mine on it. He is the best informed ranger I have met, and the oldest in the park, he told me, having started Kern and the rest.

AUGUST 1, TUESDAY

At dawn I packed and finished the cold pudding. Betsy's deceptive bell had awakened me. I grained the burros and said good-bye to Mr. Fry, who was preparing for a trip to Hamilton Lakes.

Exultantly I rode down trail from Redwood Meadows. I bent in the saddle to pick up a lustrous blue jay feather, and I put it in my hat. Rejoicing inordinately, I overflowed in triumphant song, rendering melodies of Beethoven's great 9th Symphony and his 5th, transcendent bits of Brahms, Halvorsens March of the Boyars, sonorous fragments from the Twilight of the Gods, and the Valkyries, gay bits from Rossini, the valorous Scherzo of Peter Ilich's Pathetique, even "L'apprenti sorcier," and the piercing music of Jean Sibelius.

We forded Granite Creek and the Middle Fork, then it was all uphill. At Bearpaw Meadow I stopped for lunch, turning the burros loose. Two women with burros of Earl McKee's were having breakfast, and gave me bread, so I fried cheese sandwiches. They told their tale and I laboriously showed them the diamond hitch. We rode on, monotonously, over the high Sierra trail to the intersection with 7 mile hill trail. We took the last two miles of it to Alta Trail, and it was a very long two miles. We went thru meadows waist high with leopard lily, paintbrush, and sunflower. We startled grouse and gentle does. Grandma was tired. We followed the Alta trail to Panther Gap, then went down to the first meadow.

It was late afternoon. I watched some splendid 4 point bucks.

I finished "Green Mansions" by firelight. It made me feel my isolation more keenly to read of Rima's death, Abel's revenue, and his hallucinations and feverish visions in solitude. I am only too readily led into a melancholy mood.

I could not hear the burros, so I went down trail in the moonlight till I found them. I caressed Grandma and reassured her, sat silently contemplating them, as they me, then walked back, encountered a foraging hoptoad. I heaped the fire high. An infection on the palm of my right hand has been growing steadily worse.

August 2, Wednesday

The burros were two meadows below. A deer had chewed up my blue scarf while I was gone. I rode down past the Heather Lake trail, passing a herd of 50 tourists with a Ranger Naturalist. Solitude does not have the effect of making me desire crowds. I loathe them more than ever.

Garrison's cabin was empty, so I went across the stream, which was now only a rivulet, and camped below the old place. Betsy had skinned her flank somehow. I piled the stuff under some young pines and started for Willow Meadow. At the foot of the trail I met Whitey, the packer I met at Hamilton Lakes, and young Bob Malry, Lee's brother. They were waiting for someone, they said.

Grandma would not follow; I had to drive her. Soon Whitey and Lee came riding along. Lee gave a whoop, and Betsy nearly went out from under me in her haste. We went along rapidly. At the meadows, I turned the burros loose, as the mules might injure them if they were hobbled. I helped Leo to catch a horse, and put my bridle on one to lead another. I climbed on and he bucked and plunged, but Lee told me not to grip him with my feet, and I rode to the gate where I tied them outside. Then I bridled Dave, a fat white horse and led a half thoroughbred sorrel. Whitey drove the mules and I led the way down the mountain. At the bottom, Lee drove off while Bob rode and led a horse. The stirrups were too long for him. Dave has a very easy, slow lope. We followed the trail of the Sequoias and I saw a new part of the forest. It was hard riding down the steep hills, but I enjoyed it.

I had lunch with them, served by Blanche. Then I went to see the doctor; he soaked my hand in Lysol and hot water and told me to come tomorrow. I cannot bend one of the fingers. Hobson has been transferred to Ash Mountain. In my mail was a little copper burro bell, clear toned and high pitched. Also a good letter from Waldo, and many from Mother and Father, including 14 dollars. My shoes had not arrived, so I wrote a post card to Doc. Mason.

In Lodgepole I had a good talk with Lon. He told me of the several catastrophes which had occurred in my absence.

I hardly slept, the pain in my hand was so great.

August 3, Thursday

Sprawling wearily on the blankets, I rested awhile, then heated Epsom salts to put on my hand. I started down the road until I caught a ride.

This time, the nurse laid me on the operating table, and after my hand had soaked, the doctor injected Novocain and slashed and probed in four places. After more soaking, I was bandaged again, my hand put in a sling, and I was dismissed for the day. The pain was intense.

I got my films at the studio, some were overexposed, but there were some beautiful shots. Suddenly I felt dizzy and faint, as I hurried over to

Beetle Rock and lay in the sun for an hour or so. Feeling better, I went over to the restaurant and had a chocolate sundae. Lillian was not there, but the older waitress was (not old, however), and she was much interested in my pictures. I showed them to a gentleman who was the only other occupant of the dining room, at the other end, and as he was interested I moved up there. He proved to be the chaplain, a Catholic, neat and ascetic in his black dress, but very young, and a native of Ireland. We talked about poetry and music. He objected to pantheistic religion on the grounds that it had a shallow background. He was quite intelligent, however, cultured and well informed. It was a very pleasant conversation, really.

In camp I had more sandwiches with lettuce, tomatoes, and bananas, and later, when a 3 C boy passed by, I called to him, and we conversed by the fireside for several hours. He gave me considerable information, about the crew, and told me about his life in Ohio.

I tossed about until morning, surviving the night somehow.

AUGUST 4, FRIDAY

I am not a good left handed camper, but I did my best. After a mess of oatmeal and a short rest, I started for Giant Forest again. The first car, a Packard, gave me a ride. There was another nurse, Miss Jeanette Beauvais. Seeing that I would not be able to do any cooking, I bought grapes, tomatoes, and pears, had then put in a gunnysack, and found a ride back to camp. I looked up Pop Myers. He had just returned from business in L.A., and welcomed me heartily, asking me to dinner. He invited me to stay in his extra tent and use the bed. I said I preferred to be alone, bothering no one, when ill, but it persisted, and I said I'd consider.

I went over to camp after the pictures and Epsom salts. Pop looked thru the pictures, and we had supper. Then we drove as close to my camp as we could, and carried the stuff to the car. We went to the campfire, Pop showed me how he collected pine gum and balsam, and in spite of the pain, I slept fairly well in the comfortable bed.

AUGUST 5, SATURDAY

I was awakened by sweet strains on a violin. We had a good breakfast, and I took a nap, then visited the Davis family, English people, whose son Russell is the violinist. In the afternoon, Mr. Myers drove down to the village. The doctor got some black blood out of my hand, and when the treatment was over we went back.

AUGUST 6, SUNDAY

Lon stopped in for awhile. I borrowed Pop's typewriter, and rattled off a good letter to Ned with my left hand, enclosing plenty of pictures. Previously I had written to the family with my left hand.

Pop is studying law by correspondence course, and I enjoyed reading questions to him and testing my own knowledge.

He told me his life story, of his acquired skill in all branches of printing, his days with Jack London, Ed Morrell, and the others, his divorce, and unsuccessful second marriage. His wife is English, and does not like to camp out, and by his word, is jealous of his friendship with others. Pop is a good mixer, and generous, but somewhat of a spoiled child withal.

We always have tomato salad for the first course at supper. At the campfire, Russell Davis gave two violin selections, and two ministers quickly satiated any religious impulses I might have had. One of them had a very unpleasantly strained, exhorting voice.

AUGUST 7, 8, 9

Day after day, I was treated by the doctor. The blood poisoning grew worse, then remained stationary, while the doctor probed and pressed my hand. His name is Doctor [Morton] Fraser, of Woodlake. He is quite portly, and unprepossessing. Once he kept an old lady waiting for an hour, while he played two games of chess and treated me. Lillian was in for some heart trouble once. I wore my dirty blue shirt all the time, covering it with my green blazer. At the library I drew out a book on Applied Psychology. Father sent a letter with the August remittance. I helped Pop with the questions on Wills. I wrote a good letter to Wilvin Holther. Then my hand began to feel better.

AUGUST 10

Early up. After breakfast, at 7, we drove down to Visalia, 52 miles. Pop ranted about the heat and the highway. His pet word is "spasm." He does everything by spasms, and he calls everyone Buddy. I saw Hobson for a instant at Ash Mountain. We reached Visalia at 9. Already the temperature was miserable. Pop drove me about, then I had a much needed haircut, but decided to forgo a shave, as I was returning to the mountains. I bought a good khaki shirt, and most of my groceries, some films, and an ice cream cone. At 11:30 I met Pop at the courthouse. We drove to the Visalia H.S. and went the rounds. I found a large sphinx moth and Pop carried it about. We looked in the printing shop, which had been enlarged in his absence. Last night Pop had decided to stay overnight here, but had no suggestions as to where I could stay. He finally said I could sleep on the floor in his print shop. Now, however, he had decided I could stay in his back yard.

We drove to his house. I met Peggy, his 14 year old daughter (not his, I think), and his wife, a pleasant woman at the turn of life. Also I met Doris Gray, his daughter. After a few moments, we went off to do half an hour's shopping, then we returned for lunch. Then the four of us drove to Tulare to see a relative in the county hospital. Doris told me about herself and her divorce. She has black, curly hair, and is not pretty, but she has the animation or the charm that means more than beauty. Pop and I shopped about in Tulare while Doris bought shoes for Colleen, her little girl. We found a few things like dried fruit that we hadn't found in Visalia.

Then we stopped on a ranch which a Portuguese had been buying from Mrs. Myers. Doris and I talked about hospitals and the Rubaiyat. She has had operations on her feet for infantile paralysis.

Supper was a pleasant affair with peaches, yellow tomatoes, milk, and cake. Mr. and Mrs. Myers drove off to see about a ranch, and Doris, who teaches piano, invited me to make a call with her, but I was anxious to hear the radio concert, and told her I hoped to see her later.

The concert was glorious. I was drunk with the beauty of it. First there was an Overture to Spring by Goldmark, which I had never heard before, but which was fine, clear cut stuff. Then the second movement from Brahms 2nd symphony, and I don't know what I have ever enjoyed more. I danced and danced in my delight, smoking half a dozen cigarettes the while. At last it ended and there was Schubert. Next was Moussorgsky's "La Nuit sur la Mont Chauvé," and I whirled and wove a dexterous pattern with my feet, reaching and maintaining a frenziedly fantastic mood until I was exhausted. Then to cool the air came Rimsky Korsakov's The Prince and the Princess, from Schaherezade.

Doris came back, then her betrothed Clarence Chaffin. Clarence was quarreling about some imagined faithlessness on the part of Doris, so I told them the story of King Sharyahr and his brother Shahriman, and their vain search for a virtuous woman. So we observed about the difficulties of love and marriage. I mentioned that the music had been like wine, and this led to a discussion of vintages. Clarence said he would find me a vintners, and we would go for a ride after the family came home. Meanwhile, Colleen was sliding about the floor in her new shoes, she and Peggy were parading about in my Stetson, and Peggy kept reading my name inside it to reassure herself of my identity.

Finally the parents returned and the three of us and Colleen sallied forth. We went first to a Portuguese or Italian farmhouse a few miles out, and Clarence asked for work.

[28 lines erased]

Doris told me how she was caught in a bog once, and how she explored an old mine shaft, and on her way out, she noticed that the dirt runnels were bigger, grew frightened, and ran. She paused at the entrance a moment, and the whole interior collapsed with an ominous, chilling thud. I keenly enjoy such vivid pictures as that, usually coming to me at first acquaintance with a friend. I well remember the lst night I stayed at Jack Becker's. . . . [1 line erased] I listened to him as he told me how he drove the tractor at night on the beaches at the foot of the sheer sea cliffs, racing the breakers, and occasionally buried by a foaming, whelming comber. He told me too how he watched the river and the sea. The river would flow swiftly down, carrying huge logs and tree trunks on its green crest, far into the ocean. Then the sea would surge resistlessly inwards, sweeping the timber far up the river's mouth.

Doris told me the kind of person she had expected to meet in me, when Pop told them I was coming. She too enjoys solitude, and scorns the shallow crowds. She told me of the difficulty and misunderstanding between her mother and herself, and between her mother and father. Her mother has been married three times, but she and Pop have known one another from infancy. She told me of the fascination India held for her, and of her childhood friendship with a Hindu. I told her she would enjoy "Candide" and "The Mysterious Stranger." She told me I'd like "Hypatia" and DeWolf Gangs stories of Africa. She looked fondly at Clarence and told me how his hair was curly. She wanted to know if I knew any girls she would visit in Los Angeles, as she goes there for some law case now. I couldn't think of any, as all the girls I know are gone to New York, Santa Barbara, Carmel, or moved without address.

[7 lines erased]

Then I crept around the back of the Myer's home where my blankets were spread on the grass. Two dogs howled, then there was silence, and I looked up at the humid moon.

August 11, Friday

At five o'clock, Pop wakened me.

[4 lines erased]

Soon it was hot again. The new road goes around 3 Rivers. We stopped at Hospital Rock, and I looked at the pictographs. Then we went right up the mountain. I got my packages of grub at the studio, and talked with Ashton anent the trip. My hand felt much better. At the store I bought melons.

We had breakfast in camp. It was quite hot, even here, and Pop was out of sorts. I was very busy packing my supplies. The bear had been in my tent, deftly nosing out the bacon from the bottom of the box, but smudging some papers in the process.

I sat the sheepskin to soak preparatory to padding the pack saddle blades with it. A fellow with "a lean and hungry look," stopped by and told us of his difficulties in finding a fit traveling companion for a mountain trip, but neither of us volunteered for the position.

I did a good job on the pack saddle, then wrote letters to Waldo, Doc Mason, and Father. Pop had gone off and it was almost 5, so I hastened down the road and stopped the first car, riding seated on the tool box on their running board. I arrived in time, received a package with two books I asked for, and mailed a box full of stuff I didn't want to carry.

The doctor was out, as Miss Beauvais dressed my wound, and I left her two prints for the doctor. She was delighted with them, but I wonder if the doctor will be. He is a patron of the arts, and for the first days work, involving only Lysol and Epsom Salts, he wanted $2.50. I said goodbye to Mrs. Gaddis and Mrs. Brann. Mrs. McKee gave me ten pounds of oats and I gave her the print of the oaks at Morro Bay.

August 12, Saturday

Up at the crack of dawn. We looked vainly for my hunting knife, which I had lost in my old camp, and hurried up to Willow Meadow. The burros were not in sight, so I walked all the way to the head of the meadow, looking anxiously for tracks. I saw only deer tracks and mule tracks. With sinking heart I went down on the other side of the meadow, and near the lower end, my diligent search was rewarded by tracks and traces. At last I came upon Betsy, switching her tail in the middle of a little meadow. Grandma was right by, and a low backed mule was keeping company with her. The mule tried to follow us, but stayed at the gate where I met Pop. He led Granny, and we hurried down the mountain. After a good breakfast, I packed and farewelled the Davises and Pop. It was hot as we climbed the trail to Panther Gap.

I met one tourist only. We stopped at Alta Meadows for an hour or two. It showered, and a high wind sprang up. We kept on, down fearfully dusty, steep trails to the High Sierra Trail and Bearpaw. Then we jogged on at a smart pace to Lone Pine creek, where we turned up, following a steep, rocky trail. We reached the meadow at starlight, but there was no pine or any grass. I camped under a fir with snaky trunk.

August 13, Sunday

I woke very tired, bathed before breakfast, and rested till noon. Then I read and lazed awhile, finally packing under thunder clouds. We went steeply up the mountainside. I stopped once to photograph a fine, writhen juniper. Betsy leaped thru a bog and Grandma went down in it. In vain I broke my prickly but fragile persuader; she could not rise. Soon, however, she wallowed over to the edge of the morass, and at last she staggered groggily to her feet. We climbed from 9,000 to 11,650 feet. The two bells, one high pitched, the other mellow, jingled harmoniously. We went thru a riotous profusion of wild flowers, and the burros were constantly stopping to nibble grass.

It was near sunset when we reached the crest and looked down into Deadman Canyon. I led them then, and we descended rapidly. I saw the last of the leopard lilies and some yellow columbines. We reached the stream and I lost the trail, but rediscovered it. The trail was rough, leading between high rocks, and thick willow brush. Before long it was quite dark. Betsy stumbled and fell once. Later Grandma hopped and fell as if her leg were broken, but it had only been caught in the lead rope. The trail was plain on the level banks, but obscure in the boulders and bushes. Finally we reached the meadow and trees I had marked out from the pass, and, having lost the trail, I stopped by some young lodgepoles, gave the burros some oats, and fried yams, bacon, onions, and egg. I was on a little island with water and bog on each side. Splendid granite towers were above. At its head the creek had flowed under a snowbank. Stars were reflected in the mysterious quiet pool at my feet.

AUGUST 14, MONDAY

Early up. The burros were grazing on the slopes. I had corn meal mush, then went out to reconnoiter. The trail was right by. It led to another drop off to more meadows, fir clumps, and a meandering stream below. On the upper edge were dry orange grass, sheer granite cliffs, and twisted lodgepoles. The stream is not large. I crossed and studied the various camp sites. Each had advantages and drawbacks, but at last I chose one with plenty of shade, on the grassy banks of the stream, with a table, fireplace, and wood pile. There were two comfortable rustic chairs. I caught the burros and heaped the loads on haphazardly. It was only a stone's throw to the new camp. When everything was nicely settled, I read the Golden Book while I munched chocolate and sandwiches. Then I started a stew of split peas, carrots, rice & potatoes, with flour, salt, milk, sage and pepper to top it off. After my writing was done, the clouds came down and the thunder rolled and rumbled. There was a let up and I had supper—stew.

I swaggered out to the edge of the drop off and chanting personal praise to Brahms, Beethoven, and Tchaikowski, watched the storm, perched on the edge of a cliff above the stream. I lolled back and made salutations to Carlogers, Haskell, and Samuel, to Clark and Zella, Harold and John, Jack and Alice, Doris and Clarence.

In camp I heaped up the fire and read Omar, also "Tennessee's Partner." Then the clouds swooped down and I had to crawl into bed.

AUGUST 15, TUESDAY

I lay in bed, waiting for the clouds to break, until I heard voices. I jumped out of bed, put on my tennis shoes and sombrero, and went over to see. There were two short, grizzled men with one of McKees black burros. We talked a moment and one of them gave me a good royal coachman from his hatband to replace the one I lost yesterday at my first cast.

I had more stew and something to warm me up, then went down and sat on a ledge surrounded by small aspens, where I absorbed beauty from the sky, the mountains, and the trees.

In camp again, I turned to find a stocky, gray haired, unkempt stranger, who introduced himself as Ferguson, the former Fish and Game commissioner. I soon found that he knew all about these mountains and had traveled them for fifty years. He was the first to bring trout and golden trout into the mountains here. He told me the derivations of the names hereby. He it was who opened the copper mine above at Elizabeth Pass. He chose a camp site at a flat rock above, and I went with him, and met his grandson, Bill Hughes, a little younger than myself. I helped him make camp and we talked awhile. Then his horses and mules stampeded. Bill and I tried to stop them. I burned my throat out trying to head them off, but it was no use. We went down a couple of miles to the lower meadow, but they were gone. There were other horses in the meadows, and we tried to catch one to ride back, but could not. Bill thought camp was a bend farther, but I showed him the spot and wagered a penny that it was there. He wouldn't believe until we arrived.

We had supper together and swapped yarns far into the night. I enjoyed the occasion immensely. The horses had been stampeded by a bare legged woman with pack burros, and as Andy Ferguson said, it was enough to scare the liver pad out of them. The burros snorted alarm and ran half way up the hillside.

AUGUST 16, WEDNESDAY

After breakfast, Bill and I took some lunch in a nosebag, some ropes and bridles, and went after the horses. They were not with the others, but we finally caught a big gray horse to ride down. He was a little wild. I was the first to climb on, and he pranced and stepped high, but I stayed on and headed the others back. Bill could not catch any, so I came back to him. As Smoky was climbing up the creek bank, he bucked and lunged. I slipped back a foot or so, and when he plunged and pitched again, he piled me. I caught him and got on again, and Bill and I took turns riding down the canyon. We passed the Deadman's grave and reached the bars. They had been left open, and the horses were gone. We met a windjamming cowboy who said he had come from Sugarloaf and knew the stock was not between.

At Scaffold meadow, a fisherman lent us a saddle and we rode down to the next fence. When we rode double, Smoky pitched. The horses were gone. We ate lunch at Roaring River, then I rode up one side while Bill searched on the other. I crossed the bridge and stopped at the

Barton ranch. It was raining, and Mrs. Barton invited me in. Smoky is her horse and hadn't been ridden this year and never bareback. He was just broken last fall. Bill came, and it began to hail. We crept inside the dark log cabin and the hail beat a deafening tattoo on the roof. Rivers ran thru the yard. Plops of mud shot out of a hole where a squirrel was trying to keep from drowning. The dog house was inundated and the dog howled piteously.

After an hour or so it was over, and we returned the saddle and started back. I rode most of the way. We reached camp at dark.

After supper we told tales again.

AUGUST 17, THURSDAY

Bill went down to Barton's to send a cowboy after the horses. Andy told me stories of his more or less checkered career. He told me he had done everything in life, and related his experiences as a preacher and as a bartender. He told me how he drove the stage up to Weaverville, and how his boys went to war. He told how the general would lead the charge, saying "Come on, boys; do you expect to live always?" He told how, with a 30 mule pack train, he had planted the first golden trout in Volcano creek (now Golden Trout Creek). One time, the only way he could get down a slick rock was to swing the mules forward and let them slide down on their haunches.

Bill came back as we were starting lunch, and after awhile, we went up to Big Bird Lake, also known as Dollar Lake. Humming birds hovered over the Columbines. We went down on the steep granite.

I cooked a pot of rice pudding, and Andy and Bill came over to join me. There was also cocoa and cheese toast. We sat by the fireside in the rustic chairs braced against the tree trunks. Andy told us of his role in politics. He fought Mather and the whole park service with its encroachments. He owns Wilsonia in Grant Park, and has sold it for private homes. Bill told about the lumber camps. I held a torch so they could find their way across the stream.

AUGUST 18, FRIDAY

Bill went down to get the horses. I sewed a rent in the tarpaulin, doing the job skillfully. Then I chopped wood and listened to Andy. I lent him some of my books. A pack train went by, and I gave them a letter for Mother.

We staked out Shorty and Daisy. Shorty is young and untrained. It was he who led the stampede. Last winter he was snowed in, and fed and cared for in his snowhole so that he became quite gentle.

In the evening, Bill and I went up to the snow to fish. I tried grasshoppers, but the fish took them off too easily, so I used a royal coachman. Each of us caught eight, and came back as the Alpine glow disappeared.

August 19, Saturday

Early up. We made ready to ride to the copper mine. I tried to catch the Barton's sorrel, but the herd stampeded, and I failed to head them off. Then I saddled Red, the pack mule, who had never been ridden, but was quite gentle. He was uneasy at first, but as long as I did not prevent him from following right behind Daisy, he was manageable. We passed the old copper mine, with its caved in shaft, and climbed on to 13,000 feet. A long pack train of 18 animals came by. Bill had tied Shorty insecurely, and he bolted. There was a glorious view of Black Kaweah, and of Lion Lake, green with an unearthly luster. A snakelike stream curved its way into Tamarack Lake.

We turned aside to the mystery shaft, which Andy believed to have been made by a superior race some thousands of years ago. The shaft was full of snow, with a windlass and slippery logs leading down into the snow. Bill and I found bits of malachite and copper. When found, the shaft was filled with granite slabs, but a miner and his crew cleared it to a depth of 150 feet, found no bottom and gave up. I crawled thru a tunnel and looked down the granite slope into Cloud Canyon, wide and bare. Glacier lake, a green pool, was beyond its walls, back of Whaleback Ridge. I looked down the crest of Glacier Ridge with Deadman Canyon on one side. I could distinctly hear the pack train at Elizabeth Pass. The mules shoes clattered on the rocks and the packer shouted at the animals. I looked again at the spires of Black Kaweah.

Shorty had gone down the trail. After lunch together, we both packed, and Bill took a picture on the edge of the cliff. He could not find Shorty, tho some people said they hobbled him and left the saddle on him. I arrived at the bars with Betsy and Grandma, a few moments after Andy. At dark, Bill came in whistling, without Shorty.

Andy made an extremely hot stew. Bill thought he had simply seasoned it and set it on the snow to boil. I ate a good portion, but Billy gave up after a few spoons full.

August 20

I rode Daisy across the creek, and Andy saddled her and rode for Shorty. Bill and I cooked breakfast, then sat on our oat sacks with our backs to a tree. Young Kinawyes came by and was followed by another pack train. We made fancy pancakes and lolled about.

Andy came back at noon, leading Shorty. The saddle had made great welts on his sides. I tried to fish, then listened to Andy. He told me some of his gunning exploits and illustrated involuntarily with lightning like flashes to his gun belt.

Bill brought in 27 fish, and I helped him clean them. He has taught me a quick method of cleaning. I've also learned that carrots keep indefinitely in moist sand. Another camp fire.

August 21

At daybreak I went after the donkeys. They had gone all the way back to Deadman meadow. We rattled back at a smart pace. Bill was still asleep.

Andy gave me some flies. I was the first one packed, and went ahead. At the Allen camp, I was invited to pancakes and coffee. Mr. Allen told me the way to Brewer Lake and gave me some tomatoes and cucumbers. Andy arrived at the Barton's first, and we sat in the log chairs awhile. Andy told more tales, of prospecting.

Betsy had shipped her pack, so I pushed it on again. Our trails diverged, but I could not find the Brewer lake trail. The forest was dense and monotonous. I read Tchekov whilst I lunched. I met friends of Melvin and Marshall, who told me where to camp, up Sphinx creek. At dusk I reached the uptrail, where they had rolled their horse. Grandma fell down in a rut and could not get out. I led her out backwards. We found some better grass above on the ledge, but it was damp, and the ground was a wreckage of fallen timber. I was trying to decide where to camp, when Andy arrived. I was surprised, and so was he.

I had a huge fire, and some hot stew, then thought long long thoughts.

August 22

A swearing cowboy drove his stock down the precipitous ledge above, and woke me with his maledictions. Then Bill arrived, looking for

Shorty. He came back empty handed and had some prunes with me. Then we went up to Sphinx lake. He avowed he would go swimming with me, but didn't. We felled a tree and built a fence. Shorty was there. Andy gave me a leader.

The burros were in camp. I caught three fish after supper, read Tchekov, ate peppermints, and so.

AUGUST 23

After an hour of circling, I found the burros up on a grassy ledge. We came down safely, and the trail was all ours. I studied the mountainside and figured where I would put the trail were I the engineer. Sure enough, there it went, only the trailmaker put in three more switchbacks than I had. We came to the mouth of Sphinx Canyon, under the rock, in which some light-headed fellow saw a faint and fancied resemblance to the Sphinx, and crossed Bubbs Creek on a narrow bridge.

Andy had said there were meadows every half mile, but we went for hours up the hot trail, above inviting green pools, before we found a grass patch. Then gladly I encamped.

Betsy nosed the kyaks. Muchly wroth, I shouted "YOU lazy beast, Go and eat grass!" Turning, I saw three bespangled ladies riding by. They asked me the way and went on.

After a long repast over Anton, I tied my line to a beautiful long pole I had cut, crossed at the waterfall, and went upstream. I pulled two big fish out of the water, but they fell back. Then I slipped and ran the hook, barb and all, into my thumb. After a painful five minutes I pulled it out. It was dark then. I met three men who had left Beverly Hills at 1 in the morning, and were now nicely encamped.

Nearer my camp were five fellows, who had caught a trout two or three feet long. I sat by their fire. They invited me to breakfast in the morning.

AUGUST 24

We had fish for breakfast, then I went up stream with Alvin and Bill, while John and Jim went down. At noon I came back with my sack flapping. In camp I read and lazed, then at evening, too late, I felt industrious. I hurried up and made a good drawing of the spires that rimmed the canyon, while Alvin watched. It was dark before I could paint. Jim and John returned at last, with 28 fish. Bill had caught four. I cleaned half of them and helped Al to find firewood. As before I found my way back in the dark, feeling the trail with my feet.

AUGUST 25

The fish breakfast was excellent. Al decided he didn't want to go up the mountain with me, and I was not sorry, but Jim Douglas was glad to go. The fish were excellent.

We took our cameras, and some raisins and chocolate of mine. Right away we began climbing over some breakneck granite cliffs. With cooperation we came safely across and found an old overgrown trail. We ascended a notch with a little stream in it. Soon we were puffing and gasping, for the way was very steep. Reaching an alpine meadow, we gained second wind, and breezed up to the crest, some 12,000 feet.

Five lakes were spread below us. We could see Harrison Pass and East Canyon, North Guard, South Guard, and their lakes and streams. We looked, then found a sheltered corner, and ate from a granite table. Jim aspires to aviation, but is timid in high places. I had him take my picture on a shaky pinnacle, then, much as he feared it, he went there too. Then I had him snap me when I was kicking on the edge of the abyss, and again when I was pushing off a block of granite. Jim pushed the wrong thing, so I cast about till I found a boulder three times as big. At first I did not think I could move it, but at last I got it to rocking, and it swung way out, then came back to the parent rock. Finally I tipped it off, and Jim took it just as it fell away, I think. I rolled a few boulders down the cliff, then we ran down the mountain with giant strides. The canyon spires, that had been hidden by the round crest above, slowly appeared.

In camp I took pictures of the rapids, then Al and Jim and I had a bath in the stream. I provided some raisins, and we had spotted dog. Again I helped clean fish, and found my way back in the dark. The white pinnacles were poignantly beautiful in the tremulous starlight.

AUGUST 26

Breakfast in camp. I packed and found the burros. The boys gave me some salt, and I packed a bag of their clothes ahead for them. I lost my two pennies.

We climbed above the falls to Vidette Meadows, then above to Bullfrog Lake. A large marmot watched us from a rock. I camped on a point of the lakeshore. Gathering wood, I started to make squawbread, became discouraged, and made pancakes.

Then two fishermen, father and son, came by, and we talked. They gave me three steelhead trout and told me of a camp across the lake where there was some food left behind. Two parties came by, one with a crop eared pack horse. He looked pitiful, and I pitied the man who could have maimed him so.

While tossing sticks of firewood down from the cliff above, I saw smears of blue and white oil paint on a rock. Some dauber had sat there. I did not like the thought.

At evening I went round the lake, finding onions, corn meal, flour, and coffee in the camp. I cast my line a few times, but it was not long enough, and I did not feel confident. I cleared up some of the rubbish left by campers and cooked a savory mess of tomato, onions, bacon, and yams.

The new moon gleamed liquidly on the dark water. The lake is in a hollow on the edge of a cliff. Tall peaks wall it in on all sides.

August 27

Early up. After trout and pancakes, I wrangled the burros. They had gone up trail a way with some horses. I heard Betsy's copper bell ring once when she shook her head, and found them standing silently on a ledge, regarding me solemnly. I rode Betsy part way back.

The burros munched oats and licked salt while I packed. I left the boys' pack sack prominently placed on a rock. It is made with a head-strap, and is very capacious.

We wound around following the contour of the mountainside. Charlotte lake, long and translucently green, was below us. Then we climbed a canyon to a circular basin with granite crags on all sides, and a pale, hauntingly luminous blue green ice pool at the foot of it. My shouts to the burros echoed startlingly. I have been rigorously checking all involuntary profanity. Swearing is an easy habit to fall into. It is laziness and unintelligent. It is evading the need of skillful description.

We passed another lake and followed a very rough, rocky trail up to Glenn Pass. I looked my last on North Guard and South Guard, with their cirques, and snowbanks, and their granite crests.

The down trail was even rougher. There were great blocks of smooth rock to descend from, loose boulders, and crevices. Rae Lakes were spread below. They did not look unusual from that height. We came down from the rocks, startling some grouse at the watercourse. The lake had all of the colors of the ocean at Carmel, except the foam. There was every gradation from melting yellow green to blue green, ultramarine, and purple. We went around on one side and followed the main trail across a neck of land separating the two main lakes. We forded the outlet and around a corner. I met the two boys in their camp. They were preparing to leave, so I stopped there.

One had been here for five weeks. They were waiting for their two older brothers to return from fishing. They had two horses with saddles, and expected to go over Glenn and Kearsarge and drive to L.A. tonight. They were complete dudes, and knew nothing about packing. They offered me some beans, and we talked awhile. Then I wrote Waldo a letter for his 24th birthday, and gave it to them. The others returned with a good string of fish. I cleaned most of them showing them the quick way. Then I improvised some kyaks for them, packed them, rigged up a cinch and lash rope, built the burden, and made a tight diamond hitch on the old white horse. They also had a meek strawberry roan, a mare. They had mounted and cinched from the wrong side. I tried the saddle once. They left me some odds and ends and cans of milk. The afternoon was half gone when they left.

Then my goodwill for them lessened as I saw what a slovenly camp was theirs. How I despise confirmed dudes, tenderfeet, mollycoddles, and sloppy campers. There are no words for my feeling. I spent an hour or so burning trash and clearing rubbish, then climbed the hill and watched the lakes and the peaks. There is one especially noble peak across the lake, and a picturesque island in the middle. Even if I cannot paint, at least I have the sense of beauty, which these and the Bubb's creek campers lack completely.

I thought strange thoughts, and looked forward to San Francisco. My longing for the desert has increased.

Spanish rice with tomato and cheese made a delicious supper, with good coffee. The crescent moon hovered over the lake.

August 28

After breakfast of Roman meal and coffee, I climbed to Dragon Lake. It was not unusual, so I came down, rubbing some bacon fat into a sore spot on Gran's back.

I commandeered the raft below camp, and paddled out to the island. I rested there on a bed of sunny pine needles, then swam back.

Much refreshed, I built up a roaring fire, and began to wash all my clothes, as there were all the conveniences. I washed ten or twelve pairs of socks, shirts, shorts, and kerchiefs. When they were all flapping on the line, I began to bake cornbread. It was fairly successful. I read Tchekov concerning Varlamor, Pelagueya, and Ivan Ivanitch. For supper I had spotted dog, very tasty, with cinnamon. Then I sketched the peak and watched the moon rise, while I built a blaze.

Yesterday I read some of the stories in "True Confessions." Tonight I began reading the "Red Lily" of Anatole France, by candlelight. I was struck by the following:

"It would be a pity if there were no God and the soul were not immortal."

"What? You do not know what to do with this life, and yet you wish to live throughout eternity!"

For a couple of hours I watched the fire. I find sleep very unpleasant. I cannot bear to yield consciousness without a struggle, especially as I sleep so poorly. I call sleep temporary death.

Andy said there must be a Creator because there was a Creation, but he took no stock in "this Billy Jeans stuff."

In a while I began feeling better. I chanted Navajo and enjoyed the thought of return. I thought of the prints I would cut in S.F. Then my soul floated out in song. Cesar Franck's Symphony carried me away, and Brahms and Beethoven followed. Finally, seeing the dreamy mists on the mysterious dark lake with guarding mountains, I succumbed to sleep.

AUGUST 29

I saw a glint of sunlight on one of the red volcanic fissures of Dragon Peak. Before the sun touched camp I had breakfasted on rice, with cinnamon and mellow coffee, washed all dishes till they gleamed, and began packing. I left Tchekov for other comers.

My pocket knife had disappeared, and I looked high and low, tracing my paths to the raft, and racking my brain for a clue to the whereabouts. No luck.

I brought in the burros and packed Betsy. As I was putting the first kyak on Granny, I saw the knife, covered with dust, in front of the camp fire. I pretended not to see it, put on the other kyak, and rediscovered the knife. Then, caroling blithely, I started the burros off. We left Fan Dome behind. I was confused for awhile, because the trail did not cross and return as on the map, but after much walking we reached the confluence with Woods Creek.

They was a little, inset log cabin, with homemade snowshoes on the wall. A bear had broken the door and plundered what food he could find. I discovered some cornstarch, however, and determined to make pudding like Mrs. Reynolds!

We forded, passed littered camp sites, and found an untarnished site under lodgepoles near aspens, with a very fine meadow. Betsy had stopped at every camp site along the line, hoping I would stay. Gran, who had been eating in the meadow, came up to be unpacked after Betsy.

I rested and read Anatole, consuming part of my diminishing provender.

At last I arose, girded my loins and strung my fishing pole, put the fish bag over my shoulders, and sallied forth. I saw a fish dodge around a rock, and dropped the fly there. He was mine and a good one. Grandfather fish hit the fly like a runaway horse. I pulled too hard and lost him. Another trout slipped thru my fingers. I forced my way thru the brush, and wet my feet a few times. As I went farther downstream, the Castle Crags were much more interesting. One of the peaks was inspiringly shaped. I mean to paint it.

The fishing was better and better toward sunset, and soon I was pulling them out at a great rate, hooking them too. The old fly lost his feathers, so I put on one of Andy's. The bag grew heavier and heavier. I caught half a dozen fish in one big pool, after sunset. One fish had white, black, and orange on his fins. I caught the last and cleaned them at top speed. There were forty!

Hurrying back, I met the burros and found camp before dark.

Supper consisted of fried trout. Then I turned to my favorite pastime of map reading. I decided that I was more than a month from Yosemite.

AUGUST 30

More trout for breakfast! Then I spread out my Navajo saddle blanket and read the "Red Lily." Therese, Miss Bell, Eusebie, deChartre, and LeMenil took on life for me.

A party came by, with a packer wearing a black sombrero in the rear. He said they came from Big Meadows.

Then my solitude was unbroken. Above, the white castellated cliffs glittered fairylike against the turquoise sky. The wild silences enfolded me unresisting.

It was all a gold dream to me, with the unreal rustling of the aspens lulling my senses, and pure and perfect colors flowing before my eyes. Everything was so beautiful that I felt a joy like rapture, then a cool, soothing, dreamlike calm that enveloped me completely. I was so filled with delight that my languorous calm gave way to the desire to tell someone, and I wrote a letter to Doris. Then I went down the trail and sketched the cliff and a writhen juniper. I filled the canteen and found the burros in the meadow over the hill, in the aspen thicket.

At last I finished "The Red Lily." The ending was rather helpless, but it was not a stirring story. The description of Miss Bell, the poetess, delighted me, however, and also Paul Vance's exposition of Napoleon.

I ate supper and wrote letters by firelight to Wilfred Abbott, Zella, Clark's mother, and Betty Owen, and her daughter. Again I studied maps by firelight, lingering over the beautiful names of some of the places. I think I shall stop at the Lake of the Fallen Moon, and perhaps hike over the mountains to the Enchanted Canyon and Disappearing Creek.

Finally I resigned myself unwillingly to sleep.

AUGUST 31

The hot sun wakened me. In the night the burros had gone thru camp, and I found them over the hill.

Down we went, long time, until we reached the South Fork of the Kings, and Paradise Valley. There I met Poley Kanawyer again, with another party. He asked me about the fishing, and told me how to find the Granite Pass trail. The women were horrified at my aloneness. I gave Poley my letters and wished him good luck.

I could not find the right place for the turnoff, and lunched moodily at a cluttered camp in the dismal dark forest. There was no grass near and all the aspens and plants were parched. I saw a dove bound off.

Studying the map, I decided the trail must be farther down, so I roused the burros from their dust baths and packed quickly. Poley said the valley was aswarm with rattlers and he had seen three big ones. I hoped for sport, but not a snake showed himself.

We found the right place, with plenty of grass. It was nearly sundown, so I went out to fish. I landed some splendid ones from deep green pools. There was one huge pool, quiet, vast, and breathlessly deep. I caught one fish from a big log in midstream. I lost three fish; one got off the hook at the last moment, another flopped back into the water despite my frenzied, frantic efforts, and another swung off the hook into the brush. I spent a futile fifteen minutes searching for him.

Trout and onion soup for supper. I bedded down on a fine mattress of pine needles.

SEPTEMBER 1

The burros came in an hour before dawn, and I called to them. They stopped awhile, then went back trail. I sank back to a confused slumber, and did not waken till the sun was high. The burros were a mile up, past all the good grass, so I rode Betsy to punish her. It was hot when we started. I led the burros at first, hoping to find a rattler in the trail, but I soon gave up. We climbed three or four thousand feet, and it was midafternoon when we reached a lush meadow on the rim. After a short lunch we went on, and the trail disappeared. After a dozen attempts, I found it again, but there were no ducks, and it forked dismayingly.

We reached a little nameless lake at last, and circling it, went on. There were ducks again, and it was fortunate, for there was no trail. I tussled with the burros, trying to drive them together, then gave up and led them slowly. We topped two ridges, then the trail was no more. I proceeded to find my way down, and we went over rocks, thru brush, and down steep, slippery grass banks in the aspen thickets. There were a few really alarming places. Gran's pack came off in a bad place. One of the gunnysacks had slipped loose, and the cinch rope from Kern River was broken too. I mended that, and at length we came out in a comparatively clear hillside, and I stopped the caravan under a tall pine. Below I discerned a duck [trail marker]. We may have been on the trail without knowing it. Above, here were healthy, ten foot saplings growing in it. Certainly the ranger service has burst no blood vessels trying to maintain it. I saw no traces of passage other then my own.

It is always hard to decide what to cook for supper, because there are so few alternatives, and everything takes a long time to cook. I decided on rice, and after turning everything inside out, I decided it wasn't there. The Roman Meal too, was missing. I could not imagine where they might have been left, so I cooked macaroni and drank tea.

Then I decided they must have fallen out up trail where the pack broke, and unable to wait for dawn, I went up in the moonlight, climbing over a batholith. After much trashing about, I found them and a can of milk as well, so I returned, light hearted. Tent Meadow is evidently below us. Once there I can find my way to Granite Pass. The fire blazed high, and the aspen over my bed quivered in the wind.

SEPTEMBER 2

The burros were right below. I could hardly see their ears sticking out of the tall grass and brake. I crossed the canyon in search of the trail, but it was not there.

I led Betsy, and Gran followed. We went sharply down three bogs, chuck holes, and thickets. Then I found an old campsite, and after reconnoitering, led the donkeys across the stream and up the other side, thru a bog. There we found the trail, and it was just in time, for the other side of the canyon was quite impassable. We went along briskly and soon found the real trail, which ascended steeply and dustily. There were marks of recent passage, and near the top, well over 9,000 feet, there was a rattlesnake, dead and docked of his rattlers, in the trail.

We topped the ridge into Granite Basin, with its lakes and streams dotting and threading the white granite that predominated.

The noon half was by the last rivulet. The burros rolled in the dust and munched grass blades, while I ate chocolate and studied the map.

Granite Pass was high and open, 10,677 ft., and the entrance to the Sierra National Forest. I looked down on a new set of ranges and whooped for joy.[6]

Then I met a lone rider, with a string of empties. He was returning from a trip he had conducted to Yosemite from Mineral King. He was only eleven days out of Yosemite, but his horse was completely ridden down. He had to hurry on to Tent Meadows, so we parted.

The trail led thru broad meadows, then down the granite. Here it was faint and hard to find, so I had to lead the burros. I don't like to tie

---

6. Everett had embarked on what is now the John Muir Trail, a 211-mile-long trail from Mt. Whitney to Yosemite Valley. It runs through the John Muir and Ansel Adams Wilderness Areas of the Sierra National Forest.

them, so I let Granny follow, but she stood there owlishly and watched us out of sight. When we were some distance down, she woke up, and I could hear her bell tinkling. She went back and forth, trying to come down the rocks, but finding no way, she grew worried and clattered back to the trail. She was a long time reaching us, but then she followed.

We made camp on Dougherty Creek by a little meadow, a little while before sunset. Cinnamon rice for supper.

SEPTEMBER 3, SUNDAY

I studied the map again, and we went until we reached a stream. I traveled the length of it, but found no lake. I half believed it had dried up into the sand flat I saw, but additional study of the map showed clearly that I had gone too far. We went almost back to the last camp, then down a little gully, around the edge of the cliff, and down a path to the Lake of the Fallen Moon. The lake was deep green and mysterious with gray cliffs rising from the other side. Junipers gangled on the ridges.

The lake is quite isolated, almost invisible from above, and there is every indication that I will find complete solitude here. There is excellent grass for the burros.

I had a bath and plunge, then ordered my camp. I set a stew to cook, explored the lake margin, gathered some mushrooms (I hope they are).

[2 lines erased]

I put on my indigo shirt and my black trousers, cooked the stew to a turn, piled my saddle blankets at the foot of a tree, and leaned back to watch the sky.

At sunset I went down to the lake margin with my willow rod. I could not cast far enough, but finally I hooked a big one, and led him to shore. He was a new species to me, purplish pink on his sides, roseate below, and green on the back.

I swaggered in with the spoils, and built up the fire, singing,

[6 lines erased]

Then the radiance of moonlight stole down the cliffs and cast a silvery sheen over the Lake of the Fallen Moon.

[3 lines erased]

I found sweet rest at last on my pine needle couch, and the night was warm, for clouds closed down.

SEPTEMBER 4

For breakfast I cooked my big fish. Even with his head off, he would hardly fit into the pan.

Then I strolled off to find the burros. I heard Betsy's bell, and followed it down the canyon, then in another direction, up the mountainside. I found an aged juniper of tremendous girth, and watched the cloud shadows climbing and dipping over distant mountains and canyons.

I had fried potatoes for my early lunch, and [rest of line erased]

The burros came in, and I led them over to a new pasture, above camp, walled in by the cliffs.

I had lima beans with all kinds of seasoning for supper, and I ate too well.

SEPTEMBER 5

Waldo's 24th birthday. I slept luxuriously, dreaming the most thoroughly delightful dreams I ever dreamt.

Scolding chickarees awakened me, and I heard the reassuring tinkle of the burro bells.

With a full heart, I lay cozily back in my covers, watching the sunlight creep from the top tufts of the pine trees to the gnarled roots and the rocks. I thought of Wilson and San Francisco.

The sky is clear and the lake is calm. The waterfall rushes musically down from the cliff. All is peaceful, and my thoughts are serene.

A marsh hawk flew to a tree nearby, where he chirps and twitters to me.

I made some apricot jam and naneskadi. DeQuincy remarks that poverty is a great advantage to an adventure, and if he suddenly were bequeathed a fortune, he would be much less careless of his hide.

Shakespeare's "Tempest" was the next thing I read. When the boat was wrecked in a furious storm, just before leaping over, Ferdinand cried,

"Hell's empty, and all the devils are here!"

Then further,

"We are such stuff as dreams are made on, And our little life is rounded with a sleep."

I sat in the sun by the lakeside, listening to the metallic rustle of the wings of fighting dragon flies. Blue damsel flies hovered over the marsh grass, and the lake was dark and unfathomable.

In the evening I sat by the fire and in the fire glow, I read old Omar once more.

"Think, in this battered Caravanserai
Whole portals are alternative Night and Day,
    How Sultan after Sultan with his Pomp
    Above his destined hour and went his way."
    "Why all the Saints and Sages who discuss'd
    Of the two worlds so wisely—they are thrust
Like foolish prophets forth, their Words to Scorn
Are scatter'd, and their mouths are stopt with Dust."
"With them the seed of Wisdom did I sow,
And with mine own hand wrought to make it grow;
    And this was all the harvest that I reap'd—
    'I came like Water, and like Wind, I go.'
    "A Moments Halt—a momentary taste
    Of Being from the Well amid the Waste—
And Lo!—the phantom Caravan has reach'd
The Nothing it set out from—Oh, make haste!
"Oh threats of Hell and Hopes of Paradise!
One thing at least is certain—This Life flies;
    One thing is certain and the rest is lies;
    The flower that once has blown, forever dies.
    "Yet Ah, that Spring should vanish with the Rose!
    That Youth's sweet-scented manuscript should close!
The Nightingale that in the branches sang,
Ah whence and whither flown again, who knows!"

I finished the night with a soulful rendition of César Francks divine symphony.

SEPTEMBER 6

Another day. The night was miserable. I emptied the kyaks, nailed leathers on the corners, and went thru the contents. I am something of a sadist, for I take great delight in making discards.

I took out my needle and thread and whiplashed the bottoms of my trousers, which were very ragged. Then I wrote to Mrs. Whitnah and to Father.

After a sunbath on the beach, I made some cornstarch pudding, which by no means rivaled Mrs. Reynolds. I read "The Travels of Marco Polo."

At evening I fished in vain, returning to the cold hearth. Perhaps I am asking too much of life.

I noticed a paragraph in the Red Lily:

"He is suffering because he realizes that no soul can see into another. He feels alone when he thinks, alone when he writes. Whatever one does, one is always alone in this world. That's what he means. He is right. One may be always explaining oneself, one is never understood."

I set less and less value on human life, as I learn more about it. I admit the reality of pain in the moment, but its opposite is not as strong. Life does not grip me very powerfully in the present, but I hope it will again. I don't like to take a negative attitude, but it seems thrust upon me.

SEPTEMBER 7

After a woeful, restless night full of evil dreams, I recovered consciousness, and had my last breakfast at Lake of the Fallen Moon. I made scrambled eggs with the dehydrated eggs, and they were good.

The packs were light. I made ducks all along the up trail, till we reached the main trail. Betsy had sense enough to go around a place too narrow for her kyaks, where I had shown her the way before. The trail was very rough, and the kyaks took many knocks and scrapings.

We climbed to 10,000 feet on a granite ridge, went over the rock, then down in the dust some 4,000 feet.

When we reached Simpson Meadows, there was no trail sign upstream, and as the map had indicated a gap in the trail to Grouse Meadows, it looked as if I would have to crash through. Downstream at Dougherty creek I camped near the bridge, and the down trail. I read Marco Polo while I ate figs and jam.

Exploring upstream, I found camps and signs, discovering that I was at last on the Muir trail, with all clear ahead.

At sunset I fished, but the trout were very wary, and there were no good places to fish from. I hooked a number, but lost them in trying to land them. I swung one in a tree, and the other stayed on while I swung him round the river. Then I lost my fly and had [was] done.

Trout and Spanish rice for supper. I decided to explore the Enchanted Canyon tomorrow, and perhaps Tehipite Dome.

SEPTEMBER 8

Up with the sun and off to an early start, sketch case under my arm.

There is a rude trail at first, and someone had been there with a horse. It was the lower fringe of the Tunemah trail, named for a Chinese imprecation, according to Andy.

I was already weary when I reached Goddard Creek, but I plunged up the hillside. The stream raced down the bottom of a deep, ragged gorge of red volcanic stone. I had passed this and was in an impasse, wearily trying to force my way thru the brush, when I decided to cross the canyon. Half way down, in a tangle of prickly brush, I disturbed a bee's nest and a dozen of them set upon me, the rest swarming out upon me. I struggled frenziedly down to the water, tearing my shirt. I had to leap down onto some wet rocks, then I climbed up on some more, pulled out the stings and the bees in my hair, threw off my clothes, and plunged into the water. Then I seemed to burn all over, and looking down, I discovered that my body was a mass of poison oak blisters! The shock nearly broke me, and I felt sick all over. When I was trying to put on my shirt, I fell into the water, and could not find the strength to get out until I was half drowned. Then I lay on a drift log in midstream, on the edge of the fall. There were no stream banks. I threw up my breakfast, and had not an ounce of strength. Before long, I began to burn in the hot sun. I tried to rise, but tho my eyes were wide open and I strained them, I could see nothing but blackness, and fell back, exhausted, dizzy, and faint. An hour later, I managed to put on my clothes, and in the late afternoon, I forced myself to rise. I staggered across the stream and endeavored to penetrate the thicket. Time and again, I fell down drained of strength, not knowing how I should rise again, in that entrapping jungle. Finally I did emerge from it, with its treacherous holes and entanglements, and with many halts, I climbed the slope and followed a deer trail down to the Kings.

At the upper camp, I searched for some lemon peels I had seen which Pop Myers claimed would cure all poison oak, but the burros were there and had eaten them. I mounted Betsy and she carried the living corpse into camp. My sweat was ice cold. At length I was able to drink water without revulsion, and finally I downed some sugar and milk. After sunset I packed everything on Betsy and rode Gran to the upper, shaded camp. I unpacked and went to bed at once. For some time I had been saying to myself,

"The worldly hope men put their faith upon
Turns ashes; or it prospers, and anon,
        Like snow upon the desert's dusty face,
        Lighting a little hour or two, is gone."

I also recalled a very piercing melody, and thought it must be Brahms, but finally recognized it as part of Debussy's "Afternoon of a Faun," which I love to hear.

At dark, a hiker came by. I called out, and it was Dwight Bissell, ranger naturalist, from Giant Forest. He bedded down beside me and we talked somewhile, I rather recovering my good spirits. Then I lay and burned until an hour after moonrise, when the boon of elapsed time was granted me, and I woke and found it daylight.

SEPTEMBER 9

I watched the light creep tenderly down the pines, white chipmunks whistled.

We had pancakes for breakfast, and Dwight decided to stay over the day. After breakfast we boiled apples and before long, we dined on applesauce. Dwight studies medicine at Lane Hospital, Stanford University, in San Francisco. I shall see him there this winter. He has been four years at Sequoia and was a school superintendent for three years. He has never been out of California except to Tiajuana, however.

We had lunch of rice and split peas, then I showed Dwight my pictures. Two men with pack and saddle horses went hurriedly by.

I went out into the meadow, with alder, aspen, and cottonwoods in rows and banks like a pastoral scene in France. Then I salted the burros. Dwight said the 15 year cycle of influenza had swung round again, and there would be an epidemic this winter. He told me much about the science of medicine. He is on his way to Yosemite too, but will continue to travel faster than I.

For supper we had applesauce with cinnamon, and a chocolate pudding, which I concocted. We talked late. The coyotes howled.

SEPTEMBER 10

Dwight was up betimes, packing. I arose in time to say goodbye. My lip was swollen as were my eyelids.

I looked long for the burros and packed laboriously, and it was almost noon when we started. I saw a little brown coyote who watched me, ears out like a kit fox. Betsy's pack was top heavy and inclined to shift. The trail was bad, and there were many places where it was hardly wide enough for Betsy's pack. In one narrow place, she gauged wrongly and fell down on the recoil from a rock. The distance to Cartridge creek seemed interminable. There I stopped, lunched, and read Marco Polo. He links up with Burton, Omar Khayyam, and Hackluyt. I mean to read Svan Hedin and some of the others this winter.

We continued over a steep trail, full of sharp rocks, blasted in the mountain side. It is clear that I could not have made my way without a trail. We reached some beautiful green pools, wonderfully deep and gloriously colored, with rapids and waterfalls between. I thought of John Muir and his solitary strolls here, long ago.

At dusk we came to Palisade creek, just below Grouse Meadows, and made camp. Two fishermen came in at dark, and one of them gave me an assortment of flies, but no coachmen.

SEPTEMBER 11

Pancakes with prune syrup started the day. I gave the burros the rest of the oats. Then I rode joyously up the canyon, between waterfalls and granite palisades, in the morning sun. At Little Pete meadows I camped, and found potatoes, syrup, and lemons, left by the two men who had gone out to Bishop this morning. I was very grateful and knew Dwight had given them my letters and asked them to leave the lemons.

I rested and read, wrote, and looked at my graceful tree and the towering cliff above, which were beautiful, but could not be painted.

I caught three golden trout at even, snagging my coachman so that he lost his feathers.

Supper and thoughts. [5 lines erased]

SEPTEMBER 12, TUESDAY

Away as the sun hit us. There was a long rocky stretch in which the trail was hardly visible, and here I realized that the burros were tenderfooted. At Muir Pass, I stopped in the stone beehive hut built in honor of John Muir. There was not water or I'd have made lunch. Gnawing some dried fruit, I drove the burros down and at Wanda Lake, I mounted Granny again. It is a vast lake, the largest I've seen in the Sierras. I rode along the edge, looking into the pellucid depths. We went down into three more lake basins, past Sapphire Lake to Evolution Lake, and timberline. We had been above 12,000 feet with snow banks on all sides. It was bitterly cold, and the burros were slow, so finally I waved my arms and ran after them. Dwight's footprints were always on the trail ahead. We escaped the storm, which blew up to the Sierra crest. In the evening, the sun came out, and we descended into the upper part of Evolution Creek, camping by a peaceful green meadow, with the stream meandering silverly below.

There was a fine fireplace, and after eating lots of rice and studying the maps, I made a big blaze and read awhile. My bed, on pine boughs, was very cozy.

September 13, Wednesday

Again we were off at sunrise. I rode calmly through the green pastureland, by the slow running river, under the smooth trunked pines. It was very pleasant.

Finally we descended over sharp rocks into Goddard Canyon, crossed a bridge, and followed the San Joaquin. We forded and went thru aspen glades, crossing another bridge at Piute Canyon, and came to the foot of the up trail to Heart Lake.

We camped by the stream. There was nothing but scorched grass, but the burros ate it. After devouring more of my diminishing provaunt, I went fishing with the flies from my friend at Palisade Creek. The gut was old, and they all snapped in the mouths of the fish. I did catch 13 rainbow, including some very small ones, losing eight flies. They were of all kinds, but the fish rose to them all.

Split pea soup completed the day, and I plotted my course for the future. Now I am ready for rest on my bed of pine needles.

I neglected to remark that the poison symptoms disappeared entirely. Either it was something else, or some powerful counter agent stopped it. Also, one shoe sole is fastened on by a piece of wire.

September 14

I lay in a pleasant drowse or semi-consciousness till after sunup. Trout for breakfast. There are several in the river with flies in their mouths. I looked some while for the burros.

With the sun well up, I rode away. The trail was most pleasant, climbing gradually thru aspen glades. After long windings, it arrived on top and we stopped for lunch at Heart Lake, 10,500 ft.

After a short halt, in midafternoon, I packed very rapidly and shoved the burros up trail. Betsy came to a log fence, a yard high, and impetuously leapt it, bursting the lash rope at the cinch. That was soon remedied, and we topped Seldon Pass. Then we sailed before the wind. Past Marie Lake to Bear creek and down beyond Hilgard creek we never once slackened, until we made camp by some aspens in a fine meadow. We had done two days travel in one day. Dwight's tracks were plain ahead of us. I wonder where he is.

In spite of the long day, camp was in good order and supper served by sundown. Sunset was poignantly beautiful. I watched in silence, wistful I know not why.

SEPTEMBER 15, FRIDAY

There were deer, coyote, and lion tracks on the trail to Bear Ridge. I saw a beautiful Catecola or underwing moth, with black and vermilion bands on his wings, reminding me of old days in Indiana.

The trail went down my monotonous switchbacks. I diverted myself by knocking the dead limbs off the pines and firs as I rode down. We reached Mono Creek at the foot of the Vermilion Cliffs. They are a very pale pink, and make me wish for the real Vermilion cliffs of Utah and Arizona.

There was a good pasture, so I decided to rest the burros.

A hunter and his wife rode by. I opened the gate for them. The man talked very rapidly, but his wife put a word in. He said he'd be back in an hour and give me some flies, but it is night now. He must have lost or crippled himself.

The day passed slowly. Marco Polo recounted how the Tartan warriors were used to staying forty-eight hours in the saddle, sleeping erect while the horse grazed, and drinking curdled mare's milk for nourishment. I read about Kanbalu and Khubla Khan, and the hordes of people who lived then. To what end? My interest in life is waning. Popcorn at star time.

SEPTEMBER 16, SATURDAY

Up before day. There was heavy frost on the meadow grass. I packed with surpassing adroitness and celerity. We went up the north fork of Mono creek and climbed out of the canyon by the edge of a waterfall. I quarreled with the trailmakers several times, but it seems they went in the best way, after all. We passed some lakes and climbed to Silver Pass, where I was "High in the white windy presence of eternity."

We descended past more lakes and lunched at Cascade creek. I made pancakes, as my chocolate and figs are all gone, along with the cheese and Rye Krisp. There were a number of wire cages, left behind by some expedition. I startled some huge grouse, but could not bag them.

After lunch, when the burros had rested and eaten their fill, I packed with great rapidity and drove the burros down at a spanking pace. We reached a fork of the trail, and it appears that the Muir Trail does not go down Cascade and Fish Valley, but up to Mammoth Lakes. Reds Meadow and Devil's Post Pile are my next destinations.

Instead of down, we went up hill, over two passes. We are now in terra incognita, for I do not have the Mt. Morrison quadrangle. In a valley below the second pass, I camped by a long lake that sparkled in the evening sun. I managed to have a bath and plunge before sunset, and felt the better for them. I salted the burros and had cornstarch pudding, lemon flavor, for supper. Now the alpine glow is fading from the mountains.

SEPTEMBER 17, SUNDAY

A high gale sprang up in the night, blowing the saddle blankets, pots, and pans away. At dawn I was up to combat it, and ate the food that was not blown away. But the lake was truly beautiful with the ripples and whitecaps scudding across.

There were three trails, and no signs, so I took the one that seemed to go N.W. Soon it dimmed, and there were trees across it, but we continued to a high pass, where the wind whistled and shrieked, making gusty swoops of extreme velocity. The other side of the trail was rocky and very steep and difficult. At the bottom we came to two better trails, and I learned that I had spent the night at Purple Lake. I chose the Mammoth Lakes trail, and at Duck Lake, I was in the saddle again, fighting a gale of the greatest intensity. The lake was very large and now quite rough. A split peak of black volcanic rock was across it. We topped a ridge, and passing a dozen lakes, including a unique one of milky green, reached a road and Lake Mary.

At the store I made a few purchases, and after lunch walked round to a corral where I bought a sack of oats. It was expensive, as none is grown here, and it had to be hauled from L.A. I had a long, satisfying chat with the packer. He gave me some hand made flies and told me how he heard a frog shrilling and found it half devoured by a rattlesnake. We agreed that the 3C boys were ruining one another and all the campsites and doing nothing for the trails.[7] The college boys annually steal all the trail signs for their frat houses.

At dusk I strolled round to Crystal Crag Lodge, where I read magazine articles about Black Mesa, Wetherill, and the Navajos. The music was delightful and the proprietress invited me to supper. I ate in the kitchen with the very pleasant waitress and cooks.

SEPTEMBER 18, MONDAY

I rode round the lake, and at the Wildgrie P.O., sent home a fine view of the back range. Passing two other lakes, I struck the up trail, climbing thru pumice gravel. Then there was a long descent thru a dense, gloomy forest of firs, into Red's Meadow campground. I camped a little beyond and went to see the Devil's Post Pile.[8] Then I went thru camp to see who was interesting. After wasting some time with a wheezy old senescent, I stopped in a camp of disappointed hunters. They were an interesting crowd. After supper they decided they'd like me to pack them back into Fish Creek or Deer Creek. First it was two, then three, then all six decided to go.

Cecil, Ray, Walt, and I drove down to Mammoth to buy provisions. After debauching on candy and cigarettes, we drove back in the dark. The lights went out when we were going down a dangerous grade, but we came in safely. I saw the earthquake fault on Miniaret Ridge. Sunset had been superlative, with a green sky behind the spires and minarets, and the rays of the sunken sun spreading fanwise behind the pinnacles. We had plenty of coffee, and Walt, Cecil, and I stayed up quite late, talking. They seem quite alert and intelligent.

SEPTEMBER 19, TUESDAY

Up before light. Ham, the likable fireman, had started the fire. Finally Vinson, the uncle of Cecil and Ray, came out in his purple shirt, and before long we had hotcakes and spuds to repletion. I grained the

---

7. A common misconception at the time. In retrospect, the Civilian Conservation Corps is considered one of the best of the depression-era programs, employing thousands of young men who built large numbers of trails, campgrounds, and other facilities throughout the West.

8. Devil's Postpile National Monument ranks among the world's finest examples of columnar-jointed basalt. The 800-acre monument also includes the 101-foot-high Rainbow Falls.

burros and fed them some flapjacks, then piled them up. There were three bedrolls, two kyaks, two gunnysacks, and a heavy bread bag, which I put on top of Gran's pack. Three boys carried blanket rolls. We started off over the frosty meadow. The burros were heavily laden, but they rolled along briskly. We followed Crater Creek, crossed it, and traveled over rocky ridges above the San Joaquin. Walt and Cecil startled a buck and doe, but missed their shot. A hunter who had just shot his second deer told me to cross Fish Creek to Pincushion Butte. Another hunter told us not to. There was much delay and quarreling, and grousing on Vinson's part. The burros had been standing too long and I had to repack. On the down trail the saddle pack slipped twice. We lunched at Fish Creek, and talked to hunters who had wounded a buck nearby. Walt caught two fish, and Red cut his finger. Hower, the bachelor, mild-voiced, shot through a yard thick sugar pine. We wanted him to try a lodgepole, but he said it was too much strain on the gun.

In midafternoon I packed again and we began the 2,000 foot ascent to Silver creek, over a terrifically steep, sandy trail. Near the top, at dusk, I carried the bread sack myself, as it was constantly over-balancing the pack. Ray led Betsy, and we sailed along on the level. It was quite dark when we reached the first crossing and a hunters camp. We stopped a little beyond on Silver Creek, laid down our guns, and unpacked. We had a fire going when Vince and Hower arrived. Ham was next, and Walt and Cecil were far behind. After ham and eggs with coffee, we felt better, and the talk was cheerful. We bedded down as best we could.

SEPTEMBER 20, WEDNESDAY

Again we rose before the sun. I made some oatmeal and coffee, and the hunters went off in pairs. Cecil and Walt were first, leaving without breakfast. Ham and Ray stayed for a couple of hours, and we had a rousing discussion.

I cleaned camp, made a trail to a bedroom on the sand, and made things convenient.

Walt and Cecil came back empty. I had a second breakfast with them, and they went fishing. I located the burros and caught 3 baby snakes. Vinson came in and we had lunch. Hower came in. He had seen a doe and fawn. We heard shots, and Ham and Ray returned. They had startled a forked point and doe, but missed. We gathered wood, and I split the ax handle. Cecil shot a grouse and the nearby hunters gave me some buck liver. Walt came in with ten fine fish. Vince returned at dark from his second trip, and Hower came in last, on his lame leg. Supper was a bonny affair, with grouse, venison, bacon, and spuds.

The gang had guessed my age all the way from 20 to 30. The fireside was pleasant indeed. We bedded down on the sand, and I had wild dreams about snakes carrying my packs, burros dying, etc.

SEPTEMBER 21, THURSDAY

Early again. When the stars paled we had breakfast. Ham felt sick, and Walt had burnt his shoe soles, so I took a deer gun, and we went around some ridges. I was in advance and found myself on the trail of the other hunters. Vince and Hower went off at a tangent. Cecil, Ray and I came in. Then Ham and Cecil went out for awhile. Ray and I chewed raisins while we discussed all kinds of food.

Hunters and packers came by with wild tales of ten point stags charging, etc.

Hower came in, dejected. He had had three good shots at a four point stag, and missed them all.

In the afternoon I took the 22 and went for a walk up a side canyon to a walled-in meadow. I saw a red tailed hawk and shot at a partridge, but missed. Coming down I met Cecil and Ray, who were sitting on a rock, spotting a thicket. Cecil shot at a marmot and missed.

SEPTEMBER 22, FRIDAY

After breakfast, I washed dishes with my Portuguese dish mop and put a pot of beans to boil. The hunters went their several ways, all but Ray, who stayed to chew raisins with me. Before long, Cecil and Walt came in, all excited. They had shot a spike buck,[9] mistaking it for a fork horn, and did not know what to do, so they had left it there. Cecil had broken his gun stock clubbing it.

Ham came in after awhile. Everyone had talked about killing a doe for camp meat, but Ham had been skittish. He had a headache and felt short winded, but he went up with us to butcher it. I took the pack sack with two gunny sacks and an ax. Ham butchered the buck hastily. I took one horn, two strips of skin, and the bag to cool my saddle horn. We put the meat in the sacks, and I carried it all—about sixty-five pounds. Cecil scouted ahead, and I hid it in the bushes near camp. I cut a few

---

9. A male deer too young for a legal hunt.

pieces for supper, and washed them. When I returned, one of the neighboring hunters was in camp, but he did not notice it. Everyone was frightened however, especially Ham, who thought he must be a game warden. We had beans for supper. Vince told how he missed some good shots at three bucks he saw. After supper three of the hunters stopped in. One of them is a sheep owner. The fourth man is sick in the stomach. He has been whooping and making ungodly noises night and day, till one would expect to see him inside out. He is too weak to ride in, but they mean to try it in the morning. After they went, Hower and the young bucks broiled strips of venison over the coals. Coyotes howled close by, so Walt hid the meat sack in camp.

September 23, Saturday

At dawn the sick man and his caretaker rode by. Everyone went out to get a buck, for then it would not matter about the spike. Hower took the pack sack and hid it upstream. Ham had a headache. He had wished to return to camp alone. I fleshed the deerskin the best I could, and covered the saddle horn.

At noon I took a bath and swam a few strokes in a deep pool, then had a sunbath.

Cecil came in with a quail, and he and Walt and I barbecued it with some venison. I talked to the two remaining hunter neighbors. One of them gave me some post cards and some sugar and cake. We had been out of sugar, so at once we made coffee and ate the cake. Our neighbors talked awhile. One had missed an easy shot at a four pointer because he left his safety on. Hower had been lost again, and Vince had seen another buck.

At dusk, our neighbor's packer came riding in with a big string of stock. He was half sea's over, but could still ride. I asked him where he was bound for. He said it was none of my business, but ask him where he came from and he'd tell me. [3 lines erased]

After a while he came tipsily back, waving a flashlight and fell into our barbecue pit. He told us his name was Bill Dillon, and began calling us porcupine bastards. He had one eye kicked out by a mule. Hower got his goat by asking him why he had two pairs of glasses when he only had one eye. Bill said he was from Tennessee. Hower told him about the Tennessean who, when someone dressed him up in a tie, stood all day by a hitching post, thinking he was tied. Cecil told of the one who got a pair of shoes and walked backwards for two days to see his tracks.

Bill showed us how he shot his gun without sightings. Finally he went off, led by Cecil, but he finished his bottle and came right back thru the brush. This time he was not even funny, and his language was more offensive than ever. We did our best to get his goat. He began vilifying my black hat and tried to trade me his bandanna for it. At long last he did go home. He heard a crashing in the brush and had a scare that he was returning. Everyone hid, but it was a false alarm.

SEPTEMBER 24, SUNDAY

I was first up and started the fire. Hower bought a few groceries from our neighbors, who were packing. Soon they went by.

Ham stayed in camp and told me about his experiences as a skyscraper riveter and fireman. He ran a restaurant once too.

Ray and I barbecued a pot full of venison, after our gorgeous breakfast of flapjacks with butter, syrup, jam, eggs, and cheese toast. Some of us were out of tobacco.

We went thru the wood gathering ceremony several times. I chopped a couple of dead trees down. I have seen two trees fall since I've been in camp. There is a huge one leaning impendingly over our table. If it fell it would knock it down and fall clear across our sleeping parlor.

One by one the hunters came in. After supper of venison stew, I went up to the Meadow with Walt and Cecil. They took their guns and I took the bridle to catch the burros. The evening sky was beautiful. Clouds were banked row upon row and the distant hills had a mysterious glow.

I tied the burros nearby, after feeding them some oats.

Vince is a great complainer. As soon as he wakes up he begins complaining that the boys are not out hunting, then he complains that they eat all the food, that they can't cook, can't hunt, and so on thru the day. This morning, Ham and Hower ragged him back so thoroughly that he lost his goat.

It began to rain softly after dark, so I covered camp and turned in. There was another pot of venison in the pit.

SEPTEMBER 25, MONDAY

Corn meal mush for breakfast. Ham was the first to take the trail, Vince and Hower followed. I cleaned camp and packed the burros.

There was an immense load of blankets on Grandma, and it wouldn't balance, but we started off anyhow. I led Betsy and Ray drove Grandma. Halfway down the steep part, Cecil and Walt passed us. Then Granny's pack shipped hopelessly. After one repack it shipped again. I told Ray to go on with Betsy. I made myself a huge blanket roll. Gran kept trying to break away and bray. Ray shouted that something was wrong below. I came on and found that a breeching strap was broken. The grade is too steep. We went on to Fish Creek and forded. There I fixed the pack sack and a small blanket roll. We went out of the canyon without much difficulty. I startled two coveys of handsome mountain quail.

At length we topped the ridge and shambled on to the mouth of Crater Creek, where we met Vince and stopped for late lunch while the burros rested. We had tomatoes, pickled pigs feet, and venison.

Vince went ahead, and we two took the donkey trail again. The bare ridges and lone sugar pines and junipers were very picturesque with the cloudy sky. The shadows brought out the color more.

I stopped to look at Rainbow Falls, and then we were in camp. I dumped their stuff and went on to my old camp, as they were afraid to have the venison around. Then I returned for supper, bringing some sugar. The mice had gotten into the rumble seat, eaten my oats and nibbled my chocolate. I passed the rest of the chocolate around. After supper Walt went to camp with me and carried back my bed so I could sleep in their tent. Ray and I had a hot bath in a square pool of mineral water.

SEPTEMBER 26, TUESDAY

Everyone broke camp. They left me some cans and odds and ends, and gave me ten dollars. Ham gave me a pack of cigarettes, and his address in the city.

After last farewells, I bent to the tedious job of making my pack. I laded both burros, and singing, went away. At Pumice Flats I left the road, and followed the San Joaquin to Shadow Lake, where I camped. There was no precedent, not even a tin can, but I did not mind. After lunch I set to work slicing venison into strips. My back was soon aching, but by dark, I had sliced it all—a hind quarter, forequarter, and what meat I could find on the ribs. I soaked it in brine, and had liver and onions for supper. Then I smoked and watched the new moon.

PICTURESQUE TREES (PROBABLY LIMBAR PINE), NEAR TIMBERLINE IN THE SIERRAS, 1933.

EVERETT AND HIS TWO BURROS IN THE SIERRAS, SUMMER 1933.

In the High Sierras, 1933.

Bill Hughes and Ferguson, above timberline in the Sierras, August 1933.

DEER HUNTERS WHO EMPLOYED EVERETT TO TRANSPORT GEAR AND COOK FOR THEM, NEAR
DEVIL'S POSTPILE, CALIFORNIA, SEPTEMBER 1933.

A QUIET MOMENT BY THE TRIAL THROUGH THE SIERRAS, 1933.

SIERRAS BY EVERETT.

MORE HIJINKS ON A BURRO,
SIERRAS, 1933.

EVERETT AND BURROS IN SEQUOIA NATIONAL PARK, 1933.

LON GARRISON, NATIONAL PARK SERVICE RANGER IN SEQUOIA NATIONAL PARK, WAS A SPECIAL FAVORITE FRIEND OF EVERETT'S.

Dear Family,
Isn't this a
fine view of the Sierra Range?
I am writing this at Wildyrie,
on my way to Devils Post Pile.
All is well. Autumn is upon us,
and the aspen leaves are yellow.
You'll hear from me next in
Yosemite.
Love from Everett

Mr and Mrs. C. G. Ruess
836 N Kingsley Dr.
Hollywood
Calif.

127- MT. WHITNEY, ELEVATION 14501 FT., HIGHEST PEAK IN THE UNITED STATES

EVERETT'S POSTCARD TO HIS PARENTS.

SEPTEMBER 27, WEDNESDAY

Up with the sun. I stretched out my lash rope and hung up the venison, but the brine had not penetrated, for the flies and bees swarmed to it. So I used almost all the rest of my salt and pepper and seared the meat in boiling brine for a few seconds, as Hower had told me. The flies and bees still came so I boiled the last batch in brine, but that did not stop them. I was disheartened and perplexed, for the meat was almost as salty as I could eat. I was hopeless to scare off the flies and bees, so I made breakfast, and enjoyed my oatmeal and toast.

Then I went after the burros. They had run away for some reason. I tracked them 3 miles downstream, and rode Betsy back, whacking her till she bucked. We passed by some splendid stalwart junipers and a sight that appealed to my sense of beauty and mystery, a fallen tree, mostly submerged in the lake, with ghostly mossy branches dimly seen thru the translucent water.

The lake is separated from the river by a narrow slate ridge, with a few hardy trees on its slope. Flame colored aspens were reflected in the water, beside the deeper green of the pines.

The jerky seemed to have dried out considerably. It has been a scorching day. The line glowed redly when the sun shone thru the meat. That which was boiled I had spread on the slicker. It was gray and salt encrusted like that I had from the Flying H ranch. How delicious that was! I will always associate "The Brothers Karamazov" and "Magic Mountain" with that beef jerky. My other jerky was red, like the reindeer jerky I bought in the San Francisco ferry house. That which was obviously gnawed by the bees I put in a separate sack.

I had venison stew for supper, and it was not bad. At dusk when I was taking down the jerky, a bat fluttered overhead, and an owl hooted sepulchrally.

I enjoyed my smoke and peppermints. Betsy brayed occasionally, because I had staked her in the meadow.

SEPTEMBER 28, THURSDAY

A comfortable breakfast of pancakes with prune syrup and coffee. The pack was a little smaller. I made a double loop around each kyak.

There were no signs, and we missed the trail once, crossed the San Joaquin, and started up Shadow Creek canyon. There were some other dubious places, but finally I found an old sign pointing to Thousand Island lake. Then I found two new signs giving distances to points south only. It was midafternoon when I came in sight of the majestic Mt. Rutter and Bonner Park and topped a ridge to Thousand Island lake.

I made camp in the shelter of a wind blown, horizontally growing foxtail pine, above a lagoon.

I read Marco Polo concerning Kin Sai (Hang Chow), the Celestial City. 200 pounds of pepper are sold in the market place every day. Marco is constantly stressing the importance of salt and the enormity of the salt revenue. The Khan spent almost all his colossal revenue to maintain armies. On his hunting and hawking trips he rode with his boon companions in a palace carried on the backs of four elephants.

Only think! Tomorrow I go over the pass into Yosemite Park.

I have not seen anyone since I left Pumice Flats. The deer hunters are discouraged or sated, the school boys have gone back to their studies, and vacation time is over for the populace. But this is not vacation time for me. This is my life.

I watched the moon on the water. An owl circled above me on wings of velvet.

September 29, Friday

The low lying hills bordering the lake, with their lone trees standing out, were piercingly beautiful in the dawn light. I took a picture later when the first rays of light made Bonner Peak glow rosy purple.

I threw away all the deer meat that was not jerked and burnt the sacks. I was not sorry to see the end of it. For a week or more I have been carnivorous, and that is long enough for me.

I found two good rope hobbles in a deserted camp. I am always finding useful things in old camps—here some pickles and jam, there some grasshopper bait and pieces of leather.

We followed a dim trail to Island Pass, then dropped down to Rush Creek and climbed slowly up to Donohue Pass at 11,000. I had to lead the burros over the pass, because the trail was hard to find, and the burros, being tenderfooted, would avoid the rocks and lose their way.

We next descended into Lyell Canyon, and I had an excellent view of Lyell Glacier, glittering defiance to the futile sun. The pools and ponds below it were milky white.

Down and down we went till we reached the head of a broad, level meadow, which extends all the way to the Tuolumne. We camped near Kuna creek, which is almost dry. I read Marco Polo while I munched bread and jam. I noticed that my sketches and sketch paper were getting wrinkled and soiled at the corners. What's the use? I thought at once. All perishes—why struggle?

I tried to catch two huge Loch Leven, but they were so busy playing, they wouldn't even look at the flies or bait.

So I chewed some jerky and raisins, smoked peacefully by the fireside, and finished up the peppermints from Tulare.

A divine musical fragment kept recurring.

September 30, Saturday

Singing gaily, I trotted briskly down the meadow behind the burros, till we reached Ireland creek, which was dry. Up we went to Tuolumne Pass, and down at last to Fletcher Lake. Now I am in the Yosemite that I know, and yet it is still new to me. I stopped for lunch and dried out the jerky somewhat, then read Marco once more, concerning Cipangu.

On again to the Vogelsang camp, now quite deserted, where I found a good piece of rope. We went steeply down a faint path to Booth Lake, then coasted down the canyon of the Merced, between glaciated slopes. We passed a snow marker 12 feet high, and came at last to the side trail to Babcock Lake. I had not seen it in 1930, so I decided to camp there. We forded the Merced and found the lake, very picturesque in its rocky setting. I circled it exploratively, then celebrated Yosemite with delicious lemon pudding and tea.

The sky was overcast and for a while the utter stillness was startling. At even, I looked up to see ethereal rosy clouds against the blue. Then the moon, the silver summer moon, glided through the clouds above the granite hilltop.

October 1, Sunday

Down we went, until beautiful Merced Lake was spread below us, peaceful as the cloudless sky. We passed the deserted camp and took the trail bordering the lake. It led thru graceful, arching groves of slim trunked aspen, and the singing leaves were still green. Then we passed by quiet forest pools, and the green solitudes closed round us.

Later we emerged from the forest and went over bare granite slopes to the Little Yosemite valley. There was a 3 C camp where the old Sierra camp had been. I stopped in a fine little meadow near Lost Lake. There was no water, but I had filled my canteen at the Merced. Thunder had been rumbling and rolling all afternoon, and the sky was dark overhead, but the menace gradually subsided.

I celebrated my arrival with sugared squawbread, most delicious, and finished Marco Polo.

Then I explored my little canyon to the brink of upper Yosemite, searching for bath water. There were only two small puddles. I came back on the other side of the granite ridge, saw a baby king snake, red, yellow, and black, and a flicker in a juniper tree. I circled Lost Lake, which was a treacherous bog, with no water available.

Then moon rise on Half Dome. Tired from 20 miles of hiking, I soon succumbed to slumber.

October 2, Monday

Up before sunrise. I donned my best togs, swung the pack to my shoulder, and started away to see what the valley held for me. The trail was new. Vernal Falls was only a single jet of spray—Yosemite falls were bone dry. All was quiet and deserted. Just for fun, I hailed a clean cut elderly man skimming by in his limousine. He didn't blink. With surprising skill he swung his machine round the sharp turn to the Ahwahne.

I talked with the ranger some while, then washed up in the museum. My self confidence dropped to zero at once. I looked like a ghoul or an ogre. I did my little best to alleviate conditions, then went at once to the barbers, where I enjoyed a shave and haircut for the first time. I was most happy to be rid of the whiskers.

Then I squandered my fortune on various delicacies, and sat under a tree by the river to enjoy myself gustatorily.

The mail from home had been rather disappointing. I do not wish to return to the old sameness for a while. Doris replied too, but that was all. No news from Mrs. Whitnah. I did not know what to write to Pop Myers. Finally I returned to the P.O. just as the mail was leaving and scribbled a hasty note to him.

Then a milk shake at Yosemite Lodge. More lunch and a good talk with the ranger. The postal clerk discovered a batch of my mail which he had misplaced. News from Laurence and home. I figured that there are 15 people owing me letters.

I had a really good talk with the people at Boysen's studio. They admired my prints, but were themselves on the edge of nothing. I left my films there. The girl said to try Ansel Adams studio in Frisco.

More talks with the ranger, and one of them drove me to Happy Isles at dusk. Up and up, sweating copiously. On the moonlit points the canyon was serenely beautiful. At Nevada Falls camp I talked with the trail crew around the fireside. They told me of the bears which have raided their camp every night.

It was a little tricky finding the meadow by dark as I had to go thru some dense forest. I saw the burros on my way.

OCTOBER 3, TUESDAY

Lazy up. I was wakened by the coyotes, howling crazily in broad daylight.

The 3 C packer came in after his horses, and we talked some while. He is a good sort. He thought my venison was sufficiently jerked.

I climbed up to Half Dome, ascending at the last by the aid of the cable, and lunched leisurely on the overhanging edge fronting Tenaya Canyon. Mirror Lake was only a mud puddle, and the valley was dry and yellow. Returning, I filled my canteen and bathed at a spring, and reached camp in time to read and rest. The mosquitoes were exasperating. My thoughts were bleak. At dark I made a fire to cheer myself. Soon the S.F. knot began to untangle, and I began to sing and whoop. I planned how I would rent a little garret on some city hilltop, and have a place all my own. From it I would sally forth to make color studies of tropical fish in the park, to concerts, to library expeditions, and devil may care wanderings in the city, and on the sea front. On what I have, I could do it for a month, at least if careful. I'd visit Dwight and the Jorys and perhaps Uncle Emerson. I wouldn't go to Berkeley till the month was up. I ought to have running water and a place to cook in my garret, but that, and a place to put my bed, is all I'd need. How my heart sang at the anticipation!

OCTOBER 4, WEDNESDAY

The packer came in as I was preparing to leave for Glacier Point. He had seen my burros last night. He took two of my letters which I forgot to mail Monday.

The burros had gone straight down trail, I saw by their tracks. I hoped someone at the trail camp had stopped them, but it turned out they had rattled by at midnight, and were now doubtless in the Happy Isles. I refused to go down for them, and hoped the packer would do a good deed for me. There should be a gate. If the stablemen find them, they will feed them and charge me.

Illilouette falls were beautiful, a white, filmy tracery upon wet granite. At Glacier Point I met Cuesta of Little Yosemite Valley. He is in charge here temporarily. I lunched on the cliff edge, and returned when the mountains were in shadow. I talked to a Mariposa Indian. Near camp, I heard the burro bell, and drove the little beasts into the meadow. They went docilely.

OCTOBER 5, THURSDAY

Early up and away, for a great day. I went down by the old abandoned trail, over the rockslide at the edge of Nevada Falls, and down the Mist Trail at Vernal Falls.

There was no mail. My photographs had been highly successful, and the girl in the studio had done an excellent job of developing and printing, using semi-gloss. We talked for 2 or 3 hours about various important (to us) subjects.

One of the rangers outlined a trip for me that wound up at El Portal. At noon I went over to buy groceries. A 3 C truck gave me a lift. The foreman invited me to lunch, so I dropped my groceries and accepted. There were about twenty boys, a pretty decent bunch, I thought. There was an extra lunch for me.

Then I swarmed piratically thru the stores, filling my pack sack with delicacies. Caviar, Pate de Foie Gras, candy, a tin spoon, a new purse were among the novelties I added.

At the library, I borrowed the Golden Book, and "The Fountain." Again my ranger friend drove me to the Happy Isles at dark. Pop Myers had sent word by the afternoon mail that he was coming, so I was blithe as could be.

Upward I climbed into the rising moon. I lost the trail near camp, but finally arrived, finding things undisturbed.

OCTOBER 6, FRIDAY

Out of the sunny, pale green meadow, into the overarching forest, and up the trail. The cook at Little Yosemite gave me some sugar. We took the Half Dome trail, then the Sunrise trail, following Sunrise Creek to below Cloud's Rest. Then the Forsyth trail. Topping the ridge at last I lunched by a pleasant stream, turning the donkeys loose in the tall grass. I read the Fountain, and my heart leaped when I learned the subject—the contemplative life, the inner stillness which I too am striving to attain, though I am not done with the wild songs of youth.

Then down to a stilly lake and up and over Forsyth's Pass, which I amused myself trying to pronounce. Long I paused at the broad, silver mirror of Tenaya Lake, with the sunlight still shining on a distant canyon, gleaming orange in the water.

I talked with campers till moonrise.

OCTOBER 7, SATURDAY

I tracked the burros for an hour or so, looking up at last to find Betsy innocently regarding me. I drove Granny down in her hobbles.

We followed the Tioga road for three miles, then turned north to May Lake, a large circular lake at the foot of Mt. Hoffman. I had read Muir's description of the view, and I meant to climb the peak. Clouds swept up, however, and I thought I'd wait to see if they cleared. I talked to two girls, then to one of yesterday's campers, an old-timer. His friends were trolling the lake in their canvas boat. Another, a fat state senator from Merced, had climbed the mountain, and came back with ridiculous tales. He laughs too much—no one notices him. His wheezes fairly bubble over.

It began to rain. They left, and I made for camp, building a roaring log fire. The rain stopped, and I read The Fountain. The love complicates it. I suppose a great and soul filling love is perhaps the greatest experience a man may have, but it is such a rarity as to be almost negligible.

Darkness came, and the sky was partly cleared. I built up the fire, and read a chapter or two, then I threw on a night log, and prepared the bed, but the log flared up so brightly that I could not forbear reading by it. I dislike sleep anyway. I could hear the burro bells tingling, and why should I return to nothingness, or tortured dreams, even for a night? So I read on and on, intensely delighting in the descriptions and philosophic discussions. The book is beautifully written, and my admiration for the author is great. Still I do not see why the book was a best seller. I should think few would appreciate the philosophy.

I must recall that the sunset was glorious and ominous. I stood on the lake shore, looking across the wide, glowing water to the rim of firs, with a fiery pallor behind them and a smoky sky above.

Now and then I threw a fresh log on the fire. A spark, unnoticed, burnt a hole in my towel and some other cloths. I sat on the curved root of a tree, with heather growing at its base.

The night sky was glorious with the moon rose silvery. All night long the sky kept changing. Clouds banked up and then blew on. Stars sparkled and were obscured.

OCTOBER 8, SUNDAY

Towards morning I finished the book. It disappointed the first fine promises, but in my heart, I did not expect them fulfilled.

I prepared some caviar and cheese sandwiches, put them in my pack sack with my camera and sketch case, ate a bowl of rice, and began to climb the mountain, up the glaciated slopes. The moon was mostly obscured, but the way was not difficult, but only steep.

I reached the windy cliff ledge just as the first red light gleamed in the east. A smoky grey light spread along the cloud fringes, and a smoldering orange glowed at the tops of the distant peaks. Then black storm clouds swept down dramatically from the north, and enveloped the valleys. One cloud bank detached itself and swept over Mt. Hoffman and me with a flurry of snow. Soon it was gone, and the westerly sky was clear. I looked down on the western brink, at lakes and snowbanks, on the northern cliff, at peaks and storm clouds, on the southern slope, to Yosemite valley and Tenaya Canyon, walled in by Clouds Rest and Half Dome, and on the eastern escarpment, upon May Lake, Tenaya lake, like a bronze shield in a flash of sunlight, and the snowy peaks of Tioga.

I made camera studies and a sketch of twisted trees. Then, after some hours of patrolling the frosty summit, I climbed rapidly down, only hesitating on one difficult ledge.

The burros were close by. Soon we were off for Glen Aulin. We had to follow the Ten Lakes trail for some distance until we were at the foot of Tuolumne Peak. Twice the trail forked and there were no signs. I was uneasy until late in the day when we reached McGee Lake. It was not far to Tuolumne Canyon and Glen Aulin Falls. After reading the Golden Book over my hunter's stew, I had an early smoke, and turned in at dusk, feeling slightly blurred for my seventy hours without sleep.

October 9, Monday

The morning sun peeped from behind a cloud to wake me, then hid again. The skies do not worry me now, for I'll soon be below the snow line. I found two good ropes while donkey wrangling. Soon we were down in the Glen, and how I gloried in it! The stream was wide and quiet, full of deep green pools, and the banks were lined with aspens in October plumage. The wind, like a cry at my heart, plucked at the yellow leaves and flung them swirling across the path. How I felt the beauty and the transience of it! I remembered September in the Kaibab, with sober old Pericles, and the tall aspens raining down gold upon us. Oh the haunting beauty of it!

We passed the waterwheel falls. The highest wheel was now only a foot high.

Then on interminably. The trail climbed the granite ridges back of Muir Gorge.

It was late when I paused for lunch, at the rivers edge. The patie de foie grás (or ruffled goose liver), was more successful than the Cossack brand caviar.

On the burros trundled, as fast as I could make them. Dusk threw cobwebs across the trail before we could reach Pate Valley. Soon the burros were feeling their way through the dense gloom of the silent forest. At last I found camp, a fine site by the river, but there was only dry grass in the meadow.

I ate my cheese macaroni and cocoa by candlelight. At last I climbed into bed, quite happy. Climbed I say, for the bed was about four feet above ground, and well padded with pine needles. There were three such beds here, doubtless built in fear of prowling rattlers.

October 10, Tuesday

I followed the burros back trail to where they had leaped the gate I put up last night. I found them a little further on, and made them repeat the performance.

Near camp was a long, low cliff, with Indian pictographs along it, almost obliterated red zigzags and sun symbols. I dug unsuccessfully for arrow points, among the obsidian flakes in the black soil.

After a plunge in the river, I bent to the Herculean task of washing clothes, finishing in late afternoon. Then I cleaned out the kyaks, and hung my black trousers and old shoes, both worn to a frazzle on one of the trees.

In the Golden Book, I enjoyed Blackwood's description of Fifty Island water, with the pine fringed islands seeming ready to drift away and sail into the sunset sky.

OCTOBER 11, WEDNESDAY

I had packed Grandma for the last time the other day. This time everything went on Betsy, and I sat my old saddle with the buckskin horn once more. Slowly we made the 3,000 ft. ascent to the rim of the canyon. I lunched a little below the top by a little rivulet, where I could look down on the tremulous yellowing green of the aspens. It was as glorious a sea of color as I have ever seen. There was a pale turquoise green and a tender yellow green, all shot with flame color, the whole against a brilliant cobalt sky.

I rode on through the aspen glades to Harden Lake, where I camped in the pines. The burros cropped the short hair grass diligently for several hours after dark.

OCTOBER 12, THURSDAY

I rode down to the Tioga road and along. While I was stopping to gather some blue jay feathers, the fire guard paused with his truck, and offered to carry the load in to Aspen Valley R.S. [Ranger Station], when he came back. He overtook me later and did so. I crossed the middle fork of the Tuolumne and rode Betsy awhile. Then I chased the burros top speed as long as I could, thus we reached Aspen Valley. A little further we reached the ranger station, where I met again Chapman, the fire guard, and Wes Visel, the ranger. I had lunch with them and staked out the burros. They admired my photographs, then I climbed up to Chapman's lookout.

According to his letters, Everett sold his two burros, then hitched a ride to Merced. From there he caught a freight train, that is, rode the rails, to Sacramento and Oakland. By 24 October 1933 he was in San Francisco ready to immerse himself in culture and intelligent conversation. If he kept a journal of his San Francisco experiences, however, it has not been located.

By March 1934 he was back at his parents' home in Los Angeles, preparing for another foray into the red-rock deserts of northern Arizona and southern Utah. It was to be the last journey of his life.

BLOCK PRINT MADE BY EVERETT FROM VIEW IN THE
SIERRAS, 1933.

INDEX

A

"Adventure is for the Adventurous" [Everett quotation], 109
A Dream of John Ball, 71
Aaron [friend], 19
Abbey, Edward [author], 7
Abbott, Wilfred [family friend], writes letter to, 173
Adams, Ansel, 14; Everett told to see, 202
Ager, Raymond, wife Margaret, catch fish, 132
Agnostic [belief], 65
Ahwahne, Yosemite NP, mentioned, 201
Allen, Mr. [camper], gives food to Everett, 166
Alta Meadows: had lunch at, 126; stopped at, 161
Alta Peak, Sequoia NP: plans to visit, 125; reaches crest, 126
Alta Trail, Sequoia NP, road to, 154
Ansel Adams Wilderness Area (CA), 92, 175n
Arabian Nights Tales, 63; reads, 131, 132, 139, 144
Arizona [state], 12, 13, 14, 18, 43; mentioned, 94; trip in 1934 to, 207
As You Like It, 75
Ash Mountain, 95, 155
Aspen Valley, Yosemite NP, arrives, 207
Aster Lake, Sequoia NP, catches fish, 110
Atwood, Sequoia NP, 111
Aztec Lodge (AZ), 21

B

Babcock Lake, Yosemite NP, goes to, 200
Bacchus, Fred, 43
Baker, Mr. & Mrs., 28, 31
Ballad of the Lonely Skyscraper, by Everett Ruess, copy given, 132
Barton Ranch (CA), 164, 166
Bay [horse], aka Jonathan: bought, 44, 65, 66, 69, 71; dies in Canyon de Chelly, 72, 73; mentioned, 77, 79
Bear Creek (CA), passes, 184
Bear Ridge (CA), lion tracks, 184
Bearpaw Meadow, Sequoia NP: stopped at, 154; trail to, 161
Beautiful Valley (AZ), 60, 61
Beauvais, Jeanette [nurse]: gives ride to Everett, 156; dresses his hand, 160
Becker, Jack [boyhood friend], mentioned, 159
Bee stings, encountered, 180
Beethoven, Ludwig von [composer]: melodies of, 154; praises, 162; remembers, 171
Beetle Rock, Sequoia NP, 99; visits, 104; escapes crowds to, 128; lunched on, 129; lays in sun, 156
Behikutso Lake (AZ), 60
Belshazzar, Feast of, 52
Bently [cowboy], 29
Bergera, Gary [author], 13n
Berkeley (CA), plan to visit, 202
Betatakin [Anasazi ruin], referred to, 78
Betsy, aka Blackie [burro]: mentioned, 101, 102, 112, 113, 116, 117, 120, 122–26, 130, 132–36, 140, 142, 144; tries to eat map, 145, 146–49, 153–54, 160–61, 167, 169, 171, 173, 177, 179–81, 184, 187, 191, 198, 204; packed for last time and staked out, 207
Betty [Waldo's girl friend], 92, 95
Bible, discusses validity of, 51
Big Arroyo, Sequoia NP, 134
Big Bird Lake (CA), went to, 164
Big Meadow Creek, Sequoia NP, 21
Big Meadows (CA), mentioned, 173
Bissell, Dwight [ranger naturalist]: helps Everett, 181; mentioned, 182, 183, 184; plans to visit, 202
Black Causeway [burnt tree], Sequoia NP, Everett goes through, 111
Black Kaweah, Sequoia NP, 134, 135; view of, 165
Black Mesa (AZ), mentioned, 186
Black Rock Pass, Sequoia NP, mentioned 136
Blossom family: Charley [cowboy], 93, 94, 95, 96; Dot [daughter], 95; Mrs. [wife], 95; Nora [daughter], 95
Bolong Meadow, Sequoia NP, frog chorus heard, 115
Bonner Park (CA), views, 199
Bonner Peak (CA), views, 199
Booth Lake, Yosemite NP, visits, 200
Boy Scout Camp, Sequoia NP, visits, tells stories, 122
Boysen's Studio, Yosemite NP, visits, 202
Bradley, Lee, testified in Indian Service report, 59
Brahms [composer]: listens to, 158; praises, 162; remembers, 171
Brann, Ashton: talks with, 111, 127; gives beetles to, 128; visits, 129, 160
Brann, Lillian: Everett shows pictures to, 108; sells Everett 13-cent milkshake, 129; mentioned, 156, 157
Breton, Jules [author], 60
Brewer Lake (CA), mentioned 166
Britten [cowboy], 95, 96
Brookline (MA) [Everett's childhood home], 10
Brothers Karamazov, The [book], 25, 27: remembers, 198
Brown [pastor], 51, 52
Bubbs Creek (CA): crosses, 167; mentions, 170
Bullfrog Lake (CA), reaches, 168
Burton, Richard [explorer], mentioned, 182
Bushman, Van [rancher], 41, 42
Bushman's tank, 40, 41, 45
Butterflies, Everett sights, 120, 122
Buzzard House, Mesa Verde NP, 83

C

Cabin Creek (CA), crossed, 119
Cabin Meadow Creek, Sequoia NP, Everett arrives at, 106
Cabin Meadow, Sequoia NP: Everett reaches, 106; headed toward, 115; arrived at, 118
Cahoon Meadow, Sequoia NP, rode up to, 113
California [state], 10, 61, 62, 76
Camp Lewis, 148
Canyon de Chelly (AZ), 12, 13; enters, 63, 63n; traversing, 64–74; horse Jonathan dies, 72–73
Canyon del Muerto, Canyon de Chelly, 63, 68, 71, 72
Carl [Indian trader], 74
Carmel (CA): mentioned, 11; colors compared to, 170